D1713571

WHEN THE POT BOILS

WHEN THE POT BOILS

The Decline and Turnaround of Drexel University

DAVID A. PAUL

STATE UNIVERSITY OF NEW YORK PRESS

Published by
STATE UNIVERSITY OF NEW YORK PRESS, ALBANY

For information, contact State University of New York Press, Albany, NY
www.sunypress.edu

Production, Laurie Searl
Marketing, Anne M. Valentine

Library of Congress Cataloging-in-Publication Data

Paul, David A., 1954–
    When the pot boils : the decline and turnaround of Drexel University / David A. Paul.
        p. cm.
    Includes bibliographical references and index.
    ISBN 978-0-7914-7421-1 (hardcover : alk. paper)
    ISBN 978-0-7914-7422-8 (pbk. : alk. paper)
    1. Drexel University—History. I. Title.
    LD1725.D62P38 2008
    378.748'11   2007034181

10 9 8 7 6 5 4 3 2 1

You know the story, right?

If you place a frog in a pot of boiling water, the frog will try to escape.

However, if you put the frog in a pot of cold water and heat it gradually, the frog will not respond to the gradual change in temperature until it is too late, and ultimately die as the water boils.

Contents

Figures

Foreword

David Paul's brilliant analysis of Drexel University makes clear how important and how difficult are the management and governance of higher education institutions—and by extension, of non-profit organizations more generally. The lesson seems to need regular repeating, for an industry concerned about the transmission of knowledge, higher education often seems obtuse to information and data.

There is a second story in this book, one that can easily be overlooked: Unlike the corporate sector, non-profit institutions have responsibilities to 'do good.' Management and governance are not simply ends to greater profitability, but to the fulfillment of social value. Universities and colleges that suddenly take up corporate management techniques as their new mantra risk betraying the mission of research and teaching that is their soul.

The Drexel story—its near bankruptcy and its resurgence as an institution—sends this essentially dual message. Without constant attention to the market for its offerings, to analysis of its problems and strengths, and to designing and implementing relatively speedy adaptations to changing external circumstances, all institutions—profit and non-profit, whether universities or hospitals—become threats to their own survival. But to become simply an agent of market forces and management raises questions about why have universities at all.

This all seems so obvious that one sometimes wonders why it has to be repeated. Unfortunately, so much of the debate about higher education falls into the trap of either/or, with each side shouting its position at the top of its lungs, like angry adults haranguing the young for failing to act like them. Since the mid-1980s, it has been impossible to escape the constant complaints that institutions of higher education are poorly managed and, as the Drexel story suggests, do not know how to adapt to market forces. When some leaders try to make the adaptation, they are either too weak or the anti-market faculty too strong to change much of anything. On the other side are those trying to maintain the historic mission of higher education, dedicated to the generation and transmission of knowledge, who hold academic freedom as valuable, even sacred, in a world threatened by curbs on the free expression of ideas. They defend the belief that learning should not be for sale as simply an extension of the supermarket shelves. What neither side recognizes sufficiently is that without the two working together, little likelihood exists that universities and colleges can be both fiscally and mission secure.

David Paul's examination reveals this in no uncertain terms. The failure of Drexel's leadership—its board of trustees, administrators, and faculty—to take managerial, governance, and fiscal responsibilities seriously strikes to the very heart of organizational success. The institution itself conspired to self-destruct, in part because almost no one at the University seemed to grasp the complexity of the issues. Simultaneously, that same leadership forgot to ask the simple question, "Why is Drexel here?" and thus had no mission upon which to rely. Without purpose *and* without fulfilling fiduciary responsibilities, the institution failed itself. When it rediscovered its mission and took fiscal management seriously, it recreated itself. This book gives other institutions a chance to learn.

Marvin Lazerson
Professor Emeritus
University of Pennsylvania
and
Distinguished Visiting Professor
Central European University
Budapest, Hungary

Acknowledgments

As I consider the long list of people to whom I am indebted for enabling me to research and write this story, I must begin with my colleagues from Drexel University, whose support of my efforts speaks to both their professionalism and the depth of their commitment to that institution and its very special mission. Taki Papadakis, the architect of the turnaround of Drexel University, was giving of his own time, provided introductions to members of the Board, and created an environment of openness to inquiry and learning about the past. Members of the Board, faculty and staff offered their time, their personal reflections and perspectives on what was a turbulent time. The people with whom I worked in the Office of the Provost were particularly supportive, including Ali Houshmand, Jacques Catudal, and Tony Glascock. Kathleen Cooper, Peg O'Donnell, and Barbara Bryan assisted in transcription and were giving of their time and support. Finally, I want to thank Harvill Eaton, former provost of Drexel and now president of Cumberland University, for his insight and support along the way.

Richard Breslin and William Gaither, former presidents of Drexel, gave generously of their time, memories, and insights. Chuck Pennoni, and George Ross, former board chairs, each discussed their experience at Drexel with openness and candor, as did Jack Johnson, Richard Greenawalt, Paul Ingersoll, and other Board members. Members of the Drexel faculty provided a range of views and a depth of understanding about this institution to which they have committed their professional lives, and I am particularly grateful to Jonathan Awerbuck, Mark Greenberg, Bruce Eisenberg, and Tom Hindelang. Among the staff, Maureen Wade provided historical data and perspective on the events related herein, and Stephen Janick, the University archivist, provided guidance as I wandered through the written record. I am also indebted to former members of the Drexel community, including Richard Schneider, Tom Canavan, Gary Hamme, Don Dickason, and Andy Versilli, who spent time looking back and talking about their years at Drexel.

This book is a product of my dissertation research while completing a doctorate in higher education management at the University of Pennsylvania. I owe a deep debt of gratitude to my committee chair Marvin Lazerson, who pushed me with a simple injunction to "tell a story," to Robert Zemsky and to William Massy, whose probing questions and insights shaped my research. Over my two years at Penn, I worked with a cohort of nineteen colleagues from around the country. The pinnacle of that educational experience was the time I spent with these individuals, whose intellectual energy and friendship I value beyond measure.

Finally, and most importantly, I want to thank my family. My children, Nora, Danny, and Jenna, listened patiently to stories about Drexel as my research unfolded. Most of all, I want to thank my wife, Kathy, who supported by work from beginning to end, including the ultimate act of devotion, actually reading what I had written and providing sage advise to help craft the work as it appears here.

CHAPTER ONE

Introduction

> This process of Creative Destruction is the essential fact about capitalism. It is what capitalism consists in and what every capitalist concern has got to live in . . .
>
> —Joseph Schumpeter, *Capitalism, Socialism and Democracy*

One thing is certain: when Enron Corporation collapsed in 2001, no one doubted that there was a problem. Once the fraud and manipulation that underpinned Enron's arcane business strategies came to light, the evidence of impending failure came swiftly. The company's stock price—the ultimate measure of value in a free market economy— plummeted, and in the wake of that sudden decline the company's bankers and creditors ran for the exits. Lines of credit were closed down, liquidity disappeared, and bankruptcy ensued.

The repercussions of the Enron collapse were widespread. Workers lost their pensions, senior executives went to prison, and Congress enacted the Sarbanes-Oxley Act to tighten management and board accountability. In the corporate marketplace, the metrics of success and failure are known, and the rise of new companies—and the decline and disappearance of others—is the rule rather than the exception. As the buggy whip gave way to the Model T, as Studebaker gave way to Honda, as Royal gave way to IBM, now Microsoft looks to see if Google or some yet unseen threat will be its death knell.

But even as empires rise and fall, and Schumpeter's process of creative destruction rolls onward,[1] the great institutions of higher education have continued, as if immune to the pressures of change. Oxford and Cambridge witnessed the rise and fall of the Empire and continue to reign among the world's great universities, even as the last of England's great industrial companies are being sold off to foreign buyers. America's higher education system remains the enduring jewel in the crown of the world's dominant economy, and great private universities such as Yale, Brown, Duke, Stanford, Carnegie-Mellon, and Vanderbilt have become enduring global brands, long after the men who founded them and the companies they built have faded from view.

Over the past quarter-century, however, competitive pressures have increasingly affected the world of higher education. Beginning in 1975 with the publication of its report *More Than Just Survival*,[2] the Carnegie Foundation warned of the looming impact of demographic changes and declines in student enrollments on the survival of colleges and universities. Eight years later, George Keller opened his book *Academic Strategy* with a daunting statement: "A specter is haunting higher education: the specter of decline and bankruptcy. Experts predict that between 10 percent and 30 percent of America's colleges and universities will close their doors or merge with other institutions by 1995."[3]

Needless to say, 1995 passed and no wave of bankruptcies had taken place. Nonetheless, the nature of the higher education marketplace has changed. The rankings provided by *U.S. News and World Report* have become the most recognized measure of institutional performance and quality, and higher education is increasingly seen by the American public as a private good rather than a public good.[4] However, while few question any longer that higher education is a business, it remains difficult to point to widely accepted metrics of success and failure against which to measure institutional performance. In 2006, the federal Commission on the Future of Higher Education emphasized this state of affairs, as it lamented the lack of data on student learning, institutional effectiveness, or operational productivity.[5]

Against this backdrop, the story of the decline of Drexel University in the 1980s and into the 1990s provides a case study of what the future holds for colleges and universities should they fail to embrace the implications of competitive markets on their world. Unlike the collapse of Enron, which happened with stunning speed, Drexel's decline was drawn out over many years. In the higher education world, market feedback and the related impact on revenues takes years to play out. For trustees, it can be difficult to recognize long-term trends and other signals that herald problems on the horizon, and—as was the case for the trustees of Drexel University—it can be easy to miss the fact that the water temperature around them is rising.

In 1984, Drexel admitted the largest freshman class in its history. Buoyed by the national recognition that it had received two years earlier as the first university in the country to require that all students have a personal computer, the school founded by Anthony Drexel a century earlier was by all measures as strong as it had ever been. In May of that year, long-time president William Walsh Hagerty announced his resignation after leading the institution for twenty-one years.

In the years following Hagerty's departure, the water temperature steadily rose, and within a decade of that high-water mark, the school was teetering. During those years, two presidents led the institution. The first, Hagerty's successor William Gaither, grasped the competitive threats facing the school and crafted a plan to steer the university toward safer waters. But in doing so, Gaither alienated the faculty and academic leadership, and sewed the seeds of his own downfall. His tenure was brief—barely three years—and culminated in a consuming sexual harassment scandal that was the means of his undoing by an alienated and resentful academic community. The second, Richard Breslin, was hired by the board of trustees in large part to ameliorate the stain of the Gaither scandal. Breslin responded to the charge of the board, and created institutions for shared governance and participation. But in the meantime, Gaither's plans for addressing Drexel's weakening competitive position were set aside, and the school's fortunes deteriorated further.

As the Drexel story illustrates, failure in higher educational institutions takes time. They cannot fail in the same way and with the same trajectory as for-profit companies. Unlike in the case of Enron, shareholders cannot exit, stakeholders are bound to a longer-term vision, and the community of alumni and other civic participants who are invested in the survival of the institution work to forestall dissolution.[6] The assets of the institution are difficult to move, employees, faculty, and alumni feel a sense of themselves and their identity bound to the continued existence, and even success, of the institution, and the local community is highly invested in its permanence. In the language of the business world, universities have deep brand equity that enables them to survive through hard times and periods of mismanagement.

Along with these attributes that attenuate the pace of failure, the nature of consumer choice further insulates higher educational institutions from rapid decline. Students enter an institution based on its reputation in the marketplace, among other factors, and intend to continue for four or five years until graduation. This cycle of consumer choice and expenditure has several implications. First, the decision to attend an institution results from the reputation and perception of value that has been built up over a period of years, and while the amount of information available to the student-consumer has increased dramatically with the growth of the Internet, reputation and prestige remain long-lived assets that change slowly. Second, a given freshman class will cycle through an institution over a five or six-year period. As such, declines in freshmen applications and enrollments take years to fully impact an institution, and so it was at Drexel.

Drexel's slide continued for the better part of a decade. By 1995, after years of scandal, layoffs, and a bitter strike, the university's financial reserves had been fully expended, applications had plummeted, SAT scores of incoming students were steadily declining, and the enrolled freshman class was just over half of the size of the class that had entered in Hagerty's last year. Members of the board of trustees feared for the ability of the university to survive, and in informal strategy sessions discussed the possible sale of Drexel to the University of Pennsylvania, its neighbor in West Philadelphia.

Ultimately, the board dismissed Breslin and hired Taki Papadakis as his successor. Papadakis implemented a turnaround plan that mirrored many of the attributes of Gaither's plan from a decade earlier, and that sought to rebuild Drexel's historic brand around technology, cooperative education, and its urban location.

Seven years later, the board announced the acquisition of MCP Hahnemann Medical College, and the creation of the Drexel University College of Medicine. With that acquisition, less than a decade after the nadir of the financial crisis that gripped the university, Drexel's fortunes had reversed. Over the six-year period beginning in 1995, university revenues grew eighty-one percent, externally funded research expenditures grew fivefold, freshman applications tripled, full-time enrollment doubled, and incoming student SAT scores had rebounded to historic levels.[7]

Notwithstanding the attributes that set universities apart from their corporate counterparts, the Drexel experience suggests that there is one prerequisite for a successful higher education turnaround that mirrors the corporate experience. In both worlds, success depends first on the quality of the diagnosis of the problem and development of a plan in response to that diagnosis. In the corporate universe, the linkage between the cause of the decline and the strategy for recovery is taken as gospel. If the problem stems from a market or strategy problem, the turnaround plan must focus on strategy. If the source of the failure was related to internal operational problems, the plan must focus on that. Simply stated, you have to fix what is broken.[8]

This logical construct that leads from the diagnosis of the problem to the strategy for recovery is not an article of faith in the world of higher education. For institutions facing decline, retrenchment and cost-cutting strategies are often the first tack taken in the face of revenue and enrollment downturns and worsening market conditions, for the simple reason that it often appears to be easier to cut the budget than to garner the political support across the institutions necessary to affect fundamental changes in the mission or other essential features of an institution which may have lost salience in the marketplace.[9]

The Drexel story suggests that this conventional wisdom may be misguided. As Taki Papadakis observed upon arriving at Drexel at its nadir, as a high fixed-cost business, a university facing declining enrollment cannot cut its way to solvency, as the result is higher per student costs. As in the corporate world, a decline resulting from shifting markets and failures of strategy must be fixed by addressing the cause of the problem. In Drexel's case, after years of cutting costs, the solution ultimately entailed implementing a market strategy that enabled it to increase both enrollment and price.

The Drexel experience illustrates the risks to higher educational institutions in the competitive marketplace, and the challenges to trustees entrusted with their guidance. Higher educational institutions do not move quickly, as defining institutional attributes such as shared governance and academic tenure mitigate against rapid responses to changes in the competitive landscape, and they do not quickly learn from their competitors' mistakes. The Drexel experience came on the heels of financial crises at New York University in the 1970s and Northeastern University in the 1980s, similar schools that historically served working-class and immigrant populations, and that were buffeted by changes in the competitive landscape—most notably the expansion of lower-cost public college alternatives—that led to shifts in demand and declining enrollments.[10] However, as similar as the crises at NYU and Northeastern may have been, the lessons they might have offered to Drexel trustees went unheeded.

The Drexel story—like those of NYU and Northeastern before it—suggests the fundamental tension that exists as nonprofit universities find themselves in increasingly competitive markets. Unlike for-profit corporations, which are driven to maximize economic opportunity and shareholder value, nonprofit corporations are intended to be mission-driven with the presumption that economic considerations are secondary. In a competitive market, however, universities must compete effectively if they are to survive to serve their mission. In the case of Drexel University, its founding social welfare mission was no longer tenable in the face of lower-cost public alternatives. Caught between the original mission and the immutable realities of the marketplace, the mission was forced to evolve.

The balancing of that tension—between the interpretation of the mission and competitive market forces—is a central challenge for trustees and administrators, and ultimately for faculty if the rhetoric of shared governance is to be born out in practice. The challenge is to chart a course that combines a mission that galvanizes the support of the wide range of constituencies across the community, and a long-term plan that is achievable within the realities of the markets in which the institution competes. Ideally, as was the case for Drexel in its commitment to cooperative education and linking education with work, the mission conveys value to the marketplace and is a source of competitive advantage. Often, however, this is not the case. For schools that have, as former Harvard University president Derek Bok suggests, "lost sight of any clear mission beyond a vague commitment to 'excellence,' "[11] competitive forces may be harsh, and all but the preeminent few may see their competitive position wane and their product increasingly viewed as a commodity.

For trustees and administrators charged with striking that balance and galvanizing the community around a plan, the path forward is difficult. In the case of Drexel, as with NYU and Northeastern, the lack of metrics that might have effectively foreshadowed looming problems undermined the ability of trustees to react sooner and more effectively. However, the larger problem was the lack of recognition by stakeholders across the institution that the university world itself had changed, and perhaps changed forever. A first step, therefore, must entail broadening community understanding that these seemingly eternal institutions have entered a new world, and are now subject to the perennial gale of destructive forces of which Schumpeter warned.

The challenge for higher educational institutions that find themselves in increasingly competitive markets is to develop governance structures that align the interests of the constituencies within the organization. Shared governance, as that term has come to have meaning within the academy, implies a segregation of areas of responsibility between the faculty and the administration. The faculty retains the responsibility for issues of curriculum, program development and termination, and academic policy, while the administration has authority over the nonacademic and business functions necessary to the livelihood of the institution.

The problem with this model of shared governance is that the areas of responsibility are no longer clearly demarcated. Curriculum and budget are increasingly inseparable, yet a faculty committee might control one side and a provost the other. Similarly, in the modern university, academic programs, co-curricular and student life activities, international studies, internships, and advisement are increasingly interwoven and interdependent as elements of undergraduate education. In competitive markets, organizational speed and agility are increasingly important, and a governance structure that gives parties veto power rather than creating inducements to an alignment of interests will serve as a competitive disadvantage over time.

As markets become more competitive, technology evolves, and new modalities of learning become part of the educational landscape, demands for organizational adaptation and learning will require solutions that are more fundamental and less incremental. To the extent that the difficulties faced by any given institution relate to underlying market forces—and that is true in almost all circumstances—then understanding those forces and the linkages between the mission and the market is critical. Ultimately, as has been the case in the corporate world, organizational success in competitive markets will demand, and ultimately reward, new forms of organizational adaptation that go well beyond discreet strategies that impact marginal costs or revenues. Organizational flexibility, learning, and adaptation—bywords of life in the corporate world—are barely nascent characteristics of higher educational institutions, and have long-term implications for organizational culture and collective responsibility for outcomes.

At its most fundamental level, this is a story about the decline and turnaround of an American university. It is in the first instance the story of an institution whose historical mission of service to the urban working class lost salience in an evolving marketplace, the failure of the leadership of the institution to recognize the changes that were occurring, and the turmoil that emerged within the institution in the wake of the events that unfolded. It is in the second instance the story of an organizational turnaround, about the strategies through which the institution found its footing and recovered from a period of severe decline. However, turnarounds are as much an art as a science, and it is not the purpose of this book to provide a "how-to" workbook, or a compendium of strategies that, if diligently applied, will cure the problems of another institution.

The story that unfolds in the following chapters illustrates the difficulty of change. It is a story of decline and turnaround, but perhaps one where the story of decline holds more grist than the turnaround. This is not the norm in the literature. Fewer books focus on the decline than on the rebirth, perhaps because stories of rebirth offer hope and give us heroes. But it is in the decline, and in the struggle, where the human story lies, and where the passions run deep.

CHAPTER TWO

Anthony Drexel's Legacy

Cooperative Education and the Urban Working Class

Drexel University was founded in 1891 by financier Anthony Drexel as the Drexel Institute of Art, Science and Industry. Located in the University City area of West Philadelphia, Drexel University is a research university with sixteen thousand students from one hundred nations. The Drexel University campus covers fifty acres across approximately ten city blocks from Chestnut Street to Race Street and from Thirty-first to Thirty-fourth Streets, bounded by the University of Pennsylvania to the south and west, by the Powelton Village and Mantua neighborhoods to the north, and by Thirtieth Street Station, the railroad yards, and the Schuylkill River to the east.

In contrast to its immediate neighbor, the University of Pennsylvania, the Drexel Institute was created as a school for the urban working class. Drexel University's mission has not changed dramatically since its inception, and members of the Drexel family have been on its board of trustees since the death of its founder two years after it admitted its first class. It remains an institution that values and teaches applied arts and sciences, and that builds both its undergraduate and graduate curricula around work in industry.

Drexel University is one of only three universities in the country with a mandatory cooperative education program as an integrated component of the university curriculum. Drexel's co-op program involves the participation of more than 2,200 employers in business,

government, and educational institutions across the United States and
in fourteen foreign countries. The co-op program requires that students
spend six-month periods working in jobs in industries related to their
chosen field of study. Over the course of a five-year baccalaureate
program, a typical undergraduate student leaves campus for three six-
month co-op assignments.

In 2002, Drexel University merged with the MCPU/Hahnemann
College of Medicine (itself a result of the merger of the Medical College
of Pennsylvania and Hahnemann Medical School), which resulted in the
addition of a College of Medicine, a College of Nursing and Health
Professions, and a School of Public Health. The merger of Drexel University and what is now known as the Drexel University College of
Medicine is not a part of the story of this book. However, the merger
was significant to this story as it represented a symbolic end to the
turnaround process, and the beginning of a new era focused on building
a new future rather than recovering from the events of the past.

HISTORY

The Drexel Main Building at 3141 Chestnut Street is the home of the
University and the Office of the President. The building was designed
at the direction of Anthony Drexel by Philadelphia architect Joseph M.
Wilson in the manner of the great European institutions of the 1800s.[1]
Upon entering the building, a visitor walks into a broad atrium with
double stairways to the upper floor. Between the stairways facing out
over the atrium is the figure of Anthony J. Drexel.

Anthony Drexel was the head of the Drexel & Co. banking firm.
One of the leading businessmen in the country, as well as one of the
richest men of his time, Drexel was a civic leader and philanthropist.
For years preceding the founding of the institute that bears his name,
Drexel was interested in founding an institution of higher education,
but one that would serve needs that were not met by the mainstream
colleges and universities. Influenced by brewer and businessman Mat-
thew Vassar, who had sought his support for the creation of a college
for women, Drexel's early plans involved the creation of a women's
college in the Philadelphia Main Line suburban town of Wayne.[2]

As he was pursuing his plans, his niece and confidant, Katherine
Drexel, was pursuing her more far-reaching plans for creating schools
for Native Americans and African Americans. Influenced by his niece's

aggressive pursuit of her own social and educational vision as well as, perhaps, by the opening of Bryn Mawr College for women in a nearby town, Drexel turned his focus to the idea of creating a school for the immigrants and working class of Philadelphia that would be open to men and women of all faiths and races, and would be "free of any and all cost to its students forever,"[3] as described by Drexel's long-time collaborator George W. Childs in the *Philadelphia Public Ledger* in 1889.

Finally, in 1891, Drexel founded the Drexel Institute of Art, Science and Industry. In contrast to its immediate neighbor, the University of Pennsylvania, and the growing number of universities across the country established to meet the needs of the young nation's middle and upper classes, the Drexel Institute was created as a school for the urban working class along the lines that Childs described two years earlier.

Prior to his death less than two years later, in 1893 Anthony Drexel donated $3 million to his institute, an amount that at the time was comparable to the total assets of the then-150-year old University of Pennsylvania, and twice the assets of the Massachusetts Institute of Technology,[4] a land grant institution created thirty years earlier with funding provided through the provisions of the Morrill Act of 1862.

In 1919, under President Hollis Godfrey, the institute consolidated its eighteen departments into three degree-granting day schools—the School of Engineering, the School of Domestic Science and Arts, and the Secretarial School—and an evening school, and adopted a four-year cooperative education program that went on to become one of its hallmarks.[5] Drexel's cooperative education program was designed from its inception as an integrated part of the educational program, rather than as a means of reducing the cost of tuition or supplementing student income. As the institution evolved over time, the cooperative education program came to dominate the structure and administration of the academic programs.

During the second quarter of the century, the programs of the institute evolved as the demands of the workplace changed. In 1936, during the tenure of President Parke Rexford Kolbe, the name of the institute was changed to the Drexel Institute of Technology. Consistent with the change in name, Kolbe focused on the importance of building the reputation and prestige of the institute through an emphasis on the quality of graduate work and research.[6]

Drexel continued its development as an engineering and technology school through World War II, as it was designated to run the federal government's Engineering Defense Training Program and to run classes for the Army Signal Corps and the Engineering, Science and Management War Training Program. By 1946, enrollment had grown to 5,454 full and part-time students. Growth continued through the 1950s to 7,936 students in 1956 and to 9,200 in 1962—spurred on by the impact of the Federal National Defense Education Act.[7]

By the mid-1960s, the institute was home to the largest private undergraduate engineering college in the nation.[8] Notwithstanding the magnitude of the endowment established by Anthony Drexel before his death, however, seventy years later the institute's endowment hovered below $6 million, just twice the amount of the original endowment and barely 5 percent of the endowment of M.I.T.[9]

MISSION AND MARKETS

From its inception, Drexel University was a market-sensitive institution. Courses of instruction were regularly added and terminated in response to market demand. This adaptive nature was intentional. The mission of the Drexel Institute as envisioned by Anthony Drexel was not to develop a great books curriculum that would ennoble and enlighten, but to provide knowledge and skills that would have immediate and practical value to improve the lives of the students.[10] Usefulness to the students in the workplace and in their lives was the ultimate measure of value. The students would, and should, vote with their feet.

The evolution of the Drexel Institute into the Drexel Institute of Technology and the attendant focus by President Kolbe on research and institutional reputation reflected an awareness of the importance of external validation and the reality of the competition for students, which represented a marked change from the institute's philanthropic roots. The imperative of establishing a market position through research and reputation proved to be important to the survival of the institute through the World War II years when enrollments declined and those revenues were replaced by government contracts. Within a half-century of its founding, the institute had migrated from its mission of offering near-free tuition as an act of beneficence toward the working class to become an institution dependent for its survival on an ability to adapt to the changing demands of the marketplace. The imperative of adaptation was no longer simply a question of meeting student needs, but one of institutional survival.

In this regard, Drexel University, née the Drexel Institute of Art, Science and Industry, was ahead of its time. Its market-driven migration from its position as a near-free institute dedicated to serving the needs of the working class and first-generation students to a research institution offering doctoral research programs mirrors the current migration of community colleges and other skill-based training institutions into comprehensive institutions as they pursue students, revenues, and prestige. President Kolbe's focus on the expansion of Drexel's research presence foreshadowed President Hagerty's pursuit of university status in the 1960s. Both presidents sought recognition, reputation, and prestige for the institution that they led in order to enhance its market competitiveness for students, and ultimately, in the case of Hagerty's drive for university status, for faculty as well. These efforts, and the attendant changes that they entailed within the institution, would loom large in the story of Drexel's decline during the last two decades of the twentieth century.

CHAPTER THREE

The Past as Prologue

Becoming a University 1970–1984

Over its first hundred years, Drexel experienced periods of growth and decline. During flush times, Drexel broadened its focus, expanded into liberal arts, and migrated toward the model of traditional higher educational institutions. When enrollment declined, Drexel would fall back on its traditional strengths as a technical, engineering-oriented school grounded in the workplace and work experiences of its students.

The story of the fiscal crisis of the early 1990s begins with the celebrated creation of Drexel University from the Drexel Institute of Technology in 1970, the changes that were engendered by the assumption of university status, and the last years of the two-decade-long presidency of William Walsh Hagerty. In pursuit of his dream of establishing Drexel among the elite technological institutions in the country, Hagerty took the first steps of building an arts and sciences faculty, and culture, within Drexel. By the end of his presidency, this step had begun to set in motion changes that would become central to the events over the ensuing decade. First, fundamental changes in the academic culture of the institution had begun to take place, and second, the expansion of the faculty increased the pressure on tuition and undermined Drexel's competitive position relative to lower-cost public colleges.

THE HAGERTY PRESIDENCY

In the Main Building of Drexel University is a sepia-toned photograph of two men greeting each other on the tarmac of an airport in 1963, with two women between them. On the left is outgoing president James Creese. On the right, just off the plane from Texas, is William Walsh Hagerty. Between them are Hagerty's wife, Mary McKay Hagerty and their daughter Catherine.

Hagerty came to the Drexel Institute of Technology from the University of Texas, where he was dean of the College of Engineering and director of the Bureau of Engineering Research. He went on to serve as the president of Drexel University for twenty-one years, from 1963 to 1984. Coming on the heels of the presidency of James Creese, who himself had served as president for eighteen years beginning in 1945, Hagerty ran the institute for the latter half of a forty-year period during which only two men stood at the helm of the ship.

Hagerty transformed the face of the Drexel Institute of Technology during those twenty-one years. In 1962, the operating budget was less than $8 million, and only 23 percent of the faculty held doctorates or terminal degrees. Hagerty continued the movement toward graduate education begun under his predecessors. In 1965, the Commonwealth of Pennsylvania granted the Drexel Institute the authority to confer the degree of PhD in Physics, Chemistry, Materials Engineering, Applied Mechanics, and Mathematics. Two years later, this authority was extended to Chemical, Biomedical, and Environmental Engineering.

By the end of the decade the Drexel Institute was offering doctorates in Electrical Engineering, Library Science, Biology, and Mechanical and Civil Engineering and had added a College of Science and a College of Humanities and Social Sciences to its Colleges of Engineering, Home Economics, Library Science, and Business Administration. In 1969, the Faculty Council was created as a representative body to provide a forum for faculty participation in the governance of the institution.[1] In 1970, the Drexel Institute of Technology, pursuant to the acceptance of an application to the Commonwealth of Pennsylvania State Council on Higher Education, became Drexel University. According to the official history of the event commemorating the birth of the university, Hagerty "emphasized that Drexel would not be a university 'in the classic sense,' but rather would be a technological university."[2]

While it was evolving toward research and graduate study, Drexel University remained the institute of A. J. Drexel's imagination. The value proposition was straightforward: the tuition was low, the work was hard, the education was tied closely to work in industry, and when you finished you would have a good job.[3]

Management

The office of the president was on the first floor, in the southeast corner of the Main Building. The adjacent office was the chief financial officer and treasurer. The office of the vice president for academic affairs was housed on a different floor. This arrangement was both highly symbolic and fitting. The culture of the Drexel Institute of Technology was dominated by the administration, and the administration itself was dominated by the president.[4]

The institute as Hagerty found it was a highly tuition dependent institution, much as it remains to this day. As president, he maintained firm control over all of the financial affairs of the institution, including ongoing budget and spending decisions at a departmental level, and paid close attention to enrollment and tuition pricing. Hagerty would establish an annual goal for freshmen enrollment that would provide the funding necessary to support the school. Student demand was always adequate to provide increased revenue, if needed, to support operations, even if it required a relaxing of the admission standards from time to time.

The importance of tuition pricing to the value proposition of the school was particularly important given that Drexel's target student market included working-class and first-generation college students. Hagerty made sure that this was understood by the faculty and began each faculty meeting with a presentation on recruitment and admissions.[5]

William Gaither, the man who would succeed Hagerty as president, noted that the admissions office historically was within the office that ran the cooperative education program, another factor that tied Drexel enrollment to the realities of the marketplace.

> Originally admissions was under co-op. And the reason for that was they didn't want to bring in somebody they couldn't place. Al Soffa, for example, one of the founders of Kulik and Soffa, tried to get into Drexel in about 1939 in Chemical Engineering and they wouldn't admit him because nobody would hire Jewish chemical engineers, or at least the co-op department perceived it that way. So Al studied the situation a little bit and found out that they were hiring Jewish mechanical engineers, so the next year he applied to mechanical engineering, got admitted and went on to become one of the most distinguished and wealthy graduates of Drexel University.[6]

Gaither's observation is a significant one. While from an external perspective, the co-op program is an interesting attribute of Drexel as a higher educational institution, internally it is the dominant driver of life at the institution.[7] The structure of the curriculum, course scheduling, student life, and student and alumni engagement all reflect the impact of co-op and the regular rotation of students in and out of the campus for their six-month placements in industry. The placement of admissions within the office of cooperative education was just one manifestation of the impact of co-op on institutional life.[8]

Becoming a University

While by 1970 Drexel had formally achieved university status, Hagerty was well aware that being designated a *university* was not sufficient to achieve the status and recognition that Hagerty sought. While not a humanist, Hagerty came to understand that his ambitions to build the reputation and stature of Drexel University to the ranks of the premier technology universities demanded that Drexel expand beyond its traditional areas of programmatic strength.[9] Tom Canavan, who went on from the position of Dean of the College for Humanities and Social Sciences to become the first Dean of the College of Arts and Sciences, emphasized Hagerty's recognition that he had to build strength in the humanities and social sciences if Drexel were ever to become the "MIT-on-the-Delaware."[10]

The recognition of the need for strength in the humanities led Hagerty to recruit Martha Montgomery, a scholar from the University of Pennsylvania, to build a strong department of humanities and communications. She was given the charge and the resources to build the faculty in arts and letters that Drexel lacked.

Hagerty's realization that one could not build MIT-on-the-Delaware without building strength in the humanities, and his determination to move in that direction, would have significant long-term ramifications for the institution beyond the nature of the academic program. While Hagerty sought certain attributes of the MITs of the world, at the same time he had no intention of embracing notions of shared governance that would undermine administration authority. However, his move to develop a humanities faculty brought into his institution a core faculty whose adherence to the traditional values of the academy would ultimately begin to erode the engineering culture, which willingly ceded authority to the administration.

Academic tenure was adopted at Drexel in the early 1960s and a representative faculty council created in 1969; however, through his tenure Hagerty, like the presidents that preceded him, wielded near-total control over the day-to-day management of the school. The faculty council that emerged under Hagerty was viewed as a council of elders available to advise Hagerty but that had no formal role in university governance. As a matter of practice, Hagerty largely disregarded the council.

In 1980, Hagerty hired Bernie Sagik from the University of Texas at San Antonio to serve as the Vice President for Academic Affairs of Drexel University. Sagik arrived at an institution that was struggling with its new-found identity as a university. Far from being a community of scholars, Drexel was deeply tied to its own history as an institute focused on the needs of its working-class students and tied more to the business community than its academic brethren. By the time of Sagik's arrival, however, the percentage of faculty with doctorates or terminal degrees had risen to 86 percent from 23 percent seventeen years earlier. With a growing presence of faculty in the traditional arts and sciences, the tenor of the institution was changing, as were the expectations of the faculty for what they viewed as the normal attributes of university life: respect for scholarship, participation in shared governance, and the dominance of academic culture.

The achievement of university status was not universally embraced. Drexel for most of its history had been an undergraduate institution, however, Hagerty saw doctoral production and research as increasingly important to the competitiveness of the institution for faculty and students. Research, while an active part of faculty life, was largely not supported by external funding. Tom Canavan described the "bifurcation" in the faculty during the period:

> Research was flourishing, both funded and unfunded research. In the sciences and in engineering there was a kind of bifurcation in the faculty that I had in humanities and social sciences. The newer faculty who'd been appointed were really people who saw themselves as having a career in both teaching and in scholarship. But the older faculty, those who'd been hired, let's say in the 1960s, saw themselves as being part of a teaching institution as opposed to a research institution. And when they were hired, that's really what it was.[11]

Notwithstanding his authoritarian style, Hagerty would have lunch regularly at the faculty club. He would sit with the faculty who were there, and tell stories. This simple way of connecting, combined with the relative stability of the institution during his tenure, made his style acceptable to faculty who, in later years, would resist accepting similar authoritarian traits in later presidents.[12]

The Board of Trustees

Hagerty's relationship with the board of trustees reflected his total control over the life of the institution. Board meetings were held once a month and were largely social affairs. As one trustee described it later, "The good old boys sort of came in and rubber stamped things and things rode along the way the president was driving them. . . . They came to the board meetings and nodded and went on and went back to their companies."[13] There would be a luncheon followed by a business meeting for an hour or an hour and a half, while the wives of board members might take a tour of the city or go to the museum.

When Hagerty arrived as president, he inherited the Three-Quarter Century Fund Drive, begun in 1963 under long-time president James Creese. This capital campaign would raise $18 million for the institute and would support the continued expansion of campus facilities. While well endowed by its creator, the Drexel Institute of Technology had a meager endowment of just over $6 million by the time of Hagerty's arrival. Hagerty faced some resistance to his fundraising efforts from within the Drexel family itself. Bruce Eisenstein described the aversion of the Drexel family to Hagerty's efforts from a conversation with Antelo Devereaux, a grandson of Anthony Drexel, a member of the Drexel Board, and a polo player of some renown in international play. Devereaux accompanied Eisenstein—then a young member of the faculty—on a walk during a university retreat in the 1960s.

> Hagerty had just presented his plans for a fundraising campaign. Devereaux asked me what I though of Hagerty's presentation. I told him that I though it was great, that it would be good for the institute. Devereaux turned to me and said, "I think it is a horrible idea. Think of it. We are supposed to go to other people begging for money? As if you would go to your neighbor and ask for money so you could buy curtains for your living room. If Hagerty needs money, all he has to do is ask *us*."[14]

However, by all accounts[15]—Devereaux's comment to Eisenstein notwithstanding—the Drexel family had ceased to play a significant role in the financial fortunes of the institute, and neither they nor members of the board in general provided significant financial leadership. One senior university official who recalled the capital campaign and events surrounding the Drexel centennial and the celebration of the elevation to sainthood of Katherine Drexel, lamented the lack of support by the family for the university over the years, and the difficulty that this created for the university:

> The family was not willing to pony up very much at all. They wanted to be engaged and seen, and when we went to Rome for the beatification of Mother Katherine Drexel, all of them showed up. If they had been willing to give us the kind of money that they spent just on going on trips like that it would have helped significantly. . . . The place meant virtually nothing to them. And it's a shame because if you think about four institutions—and all intermarried—Duke, Vanderbilt, Drexel, and Brown. All those families are tied to the Drexel family because they're all married in one way or another to each other. . . . And those places have flourished to a greater degree then we did at Drexel and part of it has to do with the fact that the Drexel family was not so philanthropic as A. J. Drexel or Mother Katherine Drexel was.[16]

In 1975, Hagerty led a Peaks of Progress Campaign that raised a further $40 million for the school. By the time of his departure as president, the endowment was $24 million.

HAGERTY'S LAST YEARS

William Walsh Hagerty served as the president of Drexel University for twenty-one years, during which time the face of the institution and its physical plant changed significantly. Full-time undergraduate enrollment grew from just under six thousand students at the time of his arrival to just over eight thousand in the fall of 1984. The Hagerty presidency spanned a generation. It began during the Kennedy administration and lasted into the presidency of Ronald Reagan, saw the glory days of the space program, the early years and end of the Vietnam war, Détente, and Watergate, and the rise and fall of inflation. Through it all, Hagerty led the Drexel Institute to become a university with few major disruptions or crises. As his supporters among the faculty were known to say in response to those who increasingly sought a more active role in the determination of policies and priorities within the institution, "The man has done an incredible job in terms of managing the institution financially, so why should we mess around, or what could we add in fact to the fiscal direction of the institution?"[17]

Notwithstanding Hagerty's record of accomplishment, his leadership lagged during the end of his tenure, as Tom Hindelang later suggested:

> One of the unfortunate things about Hagerty's presidency, and again he was president for twenty-two or twenty-three years . . . was that he probably was president about five years longer than he should have been . . . the main reason he retired or resigned as president was that his wife convinced him to and he had medical problems that unfortunately probably led to his death within two or three years. It was a very short period and he was clearly in those last four, five years far less effective as president than he had been in his previous eighteen or so years.[18]

During Hagerty's last years in office, several factors emerged as the focus of his administration's attention that would become among the central challenges faced by his successors and the university community.

Building a Residential Institution

Through Hagerty's tenure, Drexel remained largely a commuter school with more than 90 percent of the students from the Philadelphia area and almost as many commuting to school while working to finance their education. Until the construction of the first dormitory in 1967, residential students were assigned to one of the fraternities that were located along the residential streets on the north side of the campus in the area bordering on the Powelton Village neighborhood. The construction of dormitories marked the growth in residential student demand within a traditionally commuter-oriented school. Notwithstanding the growth in the residential population, however, residential life did not for many years permeate the culture of the institution. Student life remained off campus, largely in the fraternities and sororities that remained open at night and on the weekends when the university itself, with the exception of the evening college, was largely closed.

Drexel University is an urban campus. The two neighborhoods to its north, Powelton Village and Mantua, are, respectively, an integrated middle-class neighborhood and a poor neighborhood that is predominantly African American. The relationship between the fraternities and Drexel University was an important relationship, as for many years the university's housing needs were met by the fraternities and sororities, and the university provided loans to support them.

The placement of the fraternities, and ultimately the dormitories, along the north end of the campus placed them between the university and Powelton Village and was a source of ongoing friction with the local residents. Relationships between Drexel and its neighbors came to a head in April 1984. The focus of the complaints was the behavior of the members of the Lambda Chi Alpha fraternity, located on the 3400 block of Powelton Avenue, and the role of the university in regulating fraternity conduct. The episode itself was egregious. The fraternity brothers had a black dog whom they had named "Nigger." When black kids from the neighborhood would walk down the street, they would go outside and call their dog, leading to neighborhood disturbances and ultimately a fistfight between neighborhood youths and members of the fraternity.[19]

At the end of April, Mayor Wilson Goode ordered the fraternity closed as a "threat to the public safety of the city." The Lambda Chi Alpha situation struck at the heart of the dilemma facing the university, though it was not viewed that way at the time. Drexel was a commuter school in terms of the composition of the student body, and also in terms of where the faculty and administration resided. The president of the university traditionally lived in one of the Main Line towns that were the homes to the Philadelphia aristocracy through the years. The faculty also commuted into the university to teach. The Drexel campus was not historically an academic community where students and faculty mingled in the evenings. While the evolution to a university culture was beginning, with the change in the breadth of the faculty and the growing residential student population, the full impact of these changes, and particularly the university's accountability for student conduct, had not yet permeated the institutional culture or organizational structure.

Changes in the Student Market

The market for Drexel's traditional student, the first-generation college student from the urban, working-class neighborhoods, was beginning to shift. Applications in the early years of the 1980s were strong and growing. Freshman applications grew from 4,503 for the class entering in the fall of 1979 to a peak of 5,058 in 1982. However, residential student demand was also growing relative to capacity. While freshman applications were strong, cuts in federal financial aid, and the state of the economy, were having their effect on overall Drexel enrollments. In a board meeting that following December, both Hagerty and his vice president for student affairs, Art Joblin, commented on the unanticipated enrollment declines that had resulted in a deficit of $1 million for the current year, projections of a 25 percent decline in the eighteen-year-old population by the mid-1990s, and the expectation that the northeast section of the country would be disproportionately affected.

Thus, even while applications were climbing, Hagerty and his staff were aware of the deterioration in their traditional market, and they understood that the changes in the market that they were witnessing did not simply indicate a cyclical deterioration. Philadelphia was in the midst of a long-term, withering deterioration in its job base, the middle class was moving to the suburbs, and a third factor was emerging: competition from public-supported institutions for the commuter student. The importance of widening the geographical area for recruiting emerged repeatedly as a theme in board meeting minutes regarding enrollment.[20]

As Figure 1 illustrates, during the early 1980s, the university market position was deteriorating, as notwithstanding rising applications it had to admit more students to achieve its enrollment goals. This also shows the downward trend in average SAT scores that would be reasonably related to rising admit rates and declining yields.[21]

During this period, Hagerty continued his efforts to keep tuition costs under control. At the April 1982 meeting, the proposed increase for the coming fall was recommended to be 9.75 percent, compared to 11–18 percent for twenty-two comparable colleges and universities. The budget was balanced, and in the board minutes particular note is made that maintenance was not being deferred.

At a time when colleges and universities were raising tuition at rates considerably higher than the underlying rate of inflation, Hagerty believed that affordability was critical to Drexel's ability to sustain its enrollment base with its traditional students as the size of the commuter market was declining, as competing public institutions were encroaching on his base, and as shifts in federal financial aid were exacerbating the impact of rising tuition costs. As illustrated in Figure 2,[22] tuition was largely held constant in real terms during the late

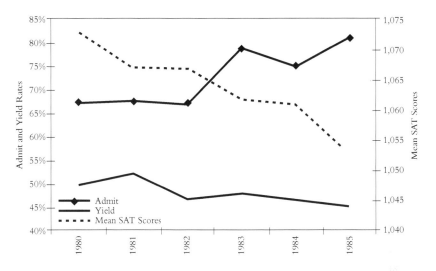

Figure 1. Admissions, Yields, and SAT Scores, 1980–1985

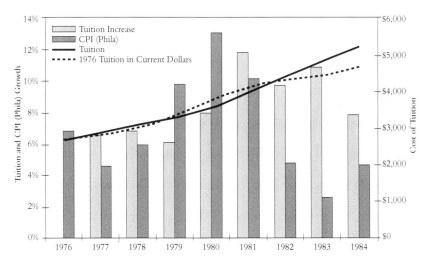

Figure 2. Tuition Growth versus Cost of Living, 1976–1984

1970s and into the 1980s, though increases in tuition costs were just beginning to outstrip the local cost of living growth toward the end of his presidency.

The Microcomputer Initiative

At the October 1982 meeting of the board of trustees, Hagerty announced that Drexel University would be the first university in the country to require that all students have a personal computer. True to the relationship of the board and its president, it was not an item for discussion or debate, it was simply "announced."

The irony of this decision, and the publicity that ensued suggesting that Drexel was a "cutting edge" technological institution, is that internally the university was slow to adopt technology as an administrative tool. Personal computers were not used in the administrative offices, and Richard Schneider, who would join the university administration under President William Gaither in 1985, commented that upon his arrival he was told that he could not order a computer or a Dictaphone as "labor saving devices" were not allowed in the offices under policies that had been in place for many years.[23]

Hagerty was not drawn to the personal computer initiative when it was first proposed to him by Bernie Sagik, as he believed computers to be a passing fad. However, he was convinced by business colleagues outside of Drexel that it would be a source of great publicity for Drexel, and adopted Sagik's idea as his own.[24] This initiative, which began as a pedagogical initiative within engineering, became a public relations boost for the school,[25] and became one of the most important events in establishing the reputation of the Drexel University in the public mind as a technological university.[26]

On April 20, 1983, William Walsh Hagerty announced to the assembled board of trustees his intention to resign as the seventh president of Drexel University, effective August 31, 1994. At that same meeting, the minutes note that the spring graduating class would be the largest class ever "due in part to increased retention of students over their college career." One month later, the board reviewed the needs for $24 million of new bond financing, principally for new dormitory needs. As a side note, at that same meeting, upon the recommendation of Hagerty, board chair Donald Rauth and trustee Lee Everett, all members of the board of directors of Martin Marietta Corporation, the board approved a $5.7 million contract with Martin Marietta Data Systems to develop and implement a new administrative computing system and a student records system to bring computerization to the operations of the university. The project was initiated largely in response to an accreditation review by the Middle States Commission on Higher

Education two years earlier that was critical of the university's administrative computing capability.

In the fall of 1983, spurred on by the publicity surrounding the microcomputer program, Drexel University admitted a freshman class of 1,882 students, the largest class in its history. At its October meeting, the board was informed that undergraduate enrollment could not grow further, due to limits on classroom space and dormitory rooms. Art Joblin reported on "new admissions programs to sustain and stimulate enrollment, including geographic expansion, and area programs in targeted cities." Just weeks earlier, the *Philadelphia Inquirer* ran a story under the headline "Lower Tuition Keeps Enrollment at Community College Growing."[27]

On February 1, 1984, David Wilmerding Jr., the chairman of the finance committee of the board of trustees of Drexel University accompanied university president Hagerty to the monthly finance committee meeting at the Philadelphia Club. These were the moneymen—A. J. Drexel "Drecky" Paul Jr., bankers Philip Seibold and Harold Still, and Sun Company CEO Robert McClements—whose mission, in the eyes of David Wilmerding, was to protect the endowment. Hagerty's purpose was to secure their support for residential life facilities that were urgently needed to support the continuing growth in the residential student body. The committee approved Hagerty's request for funding, but expressed concern for the growing level of debt that was being taken on. Two weeks later, after being admonished again about the urgency of new residential space and with the approval of the finance committee now in hand, on February 15 the board authorized the selection of an architectural team for the project.

Prior to Hagerty's resignation, the board of trustees adopted a resolution upon the Hagerty's recommendation that his successor prepare a ten-year plan for the board's approval within nine months of taking over as president, though Hagerty had felt no such obligation during his tenure as president. In retrospect, the Hagerty years were viewed as a time of strong leadership and few concerns, particularly in light of the story that unfolded. However, the seeds had been planted during his tenure, and the changes that would embroil the institution had already begun, including the sudden and continuing shifts in the student marketplace and a restive faculty that would not accept another authoritarian leader in the mold of William Walsh Hagerty.

CHAPTER FOUR

The Disposable President

William S. Gaither 1984–1987

Hagerty's transformation of the Drexel Institute of Technology into Drexel University canonized Drexel as a graduate and research institution. Hagerty's determination to build the humanities faculty—a necessary step in pursuit of university legitimacy—brought into the Drexel fold a faculty increasingly imbued with the values of the academy. These faculty viewed the university as a community of scholars, as an institution that was defined by the faculty rather than one where, as in the Drexel tradition, the faculty were employees serving under the direction of the administration.

This fundamental conflict in values incubated quietly as Hagerty's tenure wore on and the presence of the newer faculty grew in size and tenure. While William Walsh Hagerty had enjoyed the consent of the governed, the faculty would quickly resist according to his successor the rights and powers that Hagerty had held for the course of his presidency and assert for the first time their proprietary rights over the institution—rights acknowledged in 1970 in the celebration of the birth of a university but held in abeyance as a matter of institutional culture. The board of trustees, for their part slower to awaken to the implications of the end of the Hagety era and little acquainted with the traditions of the academy, would ultimately find itself involved in a power struggle that was rooted in the question of the meaning of the word *university*.

As president, William S. Gaither recognized early on the deterioration that Drexel was facing in its competitive position. The long-term plan that he crafted in response mirrored in many respects the plan that would ultimately be implemented a decade later, but not until enormous damage had been done to the institution. However, he failed to engender the sense of urgency that is a critical step in galvanizing the political support that is critical for implementing change,[1] and his alienation of the faculty led to violent internal turmoil and his ultimate downfall.

THE HIRING OF WILLIAM GAITHER

On May 16, 1984, the board of trustees selected William S. Gaither to succeed William Walsh Hagerty as the president of Drexel University. His term was to take effect on September 1, and his formal inauguration would be held the following April. Gaither was the founder and for fourteen years the dean of the College of Marine Studies of the University of Delaware. An engineer with a PhD in civil engineering from Princeton University, Gaither had previously taught at the University of Florida and worked for Bechtel Corporation

Four years earlier, Gaither competed for the position of Vice President of Academic Affairs of Drexel University, when Hagerty hired Bernie Sagik. At that time, as Gaither recalled, Hagerty told both men that the man he selected would have the inside track to become his successor as president.[2] In the intervening four years, Sagik had developed widespread support among the faculty as an academic leader, and the end of the Hagerty era was viewed by many on the faculty as an opportunity for new, more open leadership. Charles Morscheck Jr., associate professor in the College of Design Arts and an active member of the faculty council, later expressed this sentiment in a *Philadelphia Inquirer Magazine* article written by Mary Walton about the Gaither presidency: "With a new president coming in 'we had very high hopes that we could finally get a president we could talk to,' as well as 'increased governance in the university.' "[3]

The search committee was led by Lee Everett, Chairman and CEO of Philadelphia Electric Company, who would become board chairman in the fall of 1984. The search committee presented the candidates with three central university goals, including (1) raise $100 million, primarily to build endowment, (2) build research to be among the top one hundred public and private universities receiving federal R&D support, and (3) strengthen minority faculty and graduate enrollment.

The board leadership was comprised principally of bankers and businessmen and, historically, under Hagerty's direction had little direct contact with the faculty.[4] The board had been pleased with Hagerty's dominant leadership style and gave little weight to faculty views. Largely detached from day-to-day life in the school, the board could not sense the emergence of a tenured humanities faculty with strong views about the nature of an academic community, the primacy of the faculty role and the importance of shared governance, and the challenge that this presented to the traditional culture of the institution.

The search committee was comprised of trustees, faculty, and students, and met approximately thirty times as they sifted through and evaluated candidates. Sagik emerged as one of the five finalists in the search process, though Peter Bennett, president of the Academy of Natural Sciences became the top choice of the members of the faculty council, and another candidate, Hans Mark, Deputy Administrator of NASA, was the preferred candidate of many in the engineering community. Gaither was among the five and the choice of the board leadership.[5]

As recounted in the University document *The Stewardship of President William S. Gaither*, Gaither presented an aggressive image that would have appealed to corporate leadership on the board in his interview with the board of trustees.

> Let me address my management style. It is aggressive and forward-looking. I am a risk-taker where I am convinced that the concept is sound and that success will contribute significantly to achieving the goals of the University. I attract and motivate first-rate people. My success and the success of the University will be a direct consequence of the successes of our faculty, staff and students. I encourage team spirit and cooperation. This is not to say that controversy will not occur. It will occur from time-to-time when intensely interested and capable people address and come to terms with major issues.[6]

With a split faculty, the board held sway, and Gaither was chosen despite not being the top choice of the committee after the initial voting. In Mary Walton's *Philadelphia Inquirer Magazine* article, John Savchak, professor of accounting and chairman of the faculty council, maintained that there was no real search. "Gaither was pre-picked. When they got it down to five, it was all over."[7]

Reflecting on faculty discontent with the choice and a petition asking that the search be continued, Everett commented in Walton's article "It's nice to please the faculty, but the most important thing is to make sure you have the best man for the job. We thought we did."[8] Ultimately, the Drexel board was a passive board whose role at the time was largely ceremonial, and its business functions were carried out in a perfunctory manner. In hiring Gaither, the board acceded to the preferences of the board leadership, including Everett, Roy Weston, and Sam Hudson. Gaither was on the board of Weston's company. They knew him, and he was their man.[9]

THE GAITHER PRESIDENCY

At the end of May, two weeks after his selection, Gaither arrived at Drexel to meet with William Hagerty and begin to plan the transition in anticipation of assuming the presidency on September 1. There was to be no transition, however. Upon Gaither's arrival, Hagerty met him on his way out of his office and informed him that the following week he was to be operated on for colon cancer, and that Gaither was on his own.[10]

That August, aware of the ongoing dispute with the Powelton Village neighbors and hopeful that their presence could make a difference, Gaither and his wife, Robin, purchased a home in Powelton Village and moved into the neighborhood. They joined the predominantly African American Church of St. Andrew and St. Monica, and became members of the Powelton Village Civic Association.[11]

Gaither arrived at Drexel to find the condition of the institution worse than he had anticipated. The trustees were largely unaware of the unfolding Martin Marietta debacle, and despite Drexel's reputation as a technological institution, the internal operations and office systems had not been computerized, and there was an antipathy to the use of "labor-saving devices."[12] Gaither later recalled the passivity of the board:

> Bill Hagerty really was sicker than I think most people realized. And so some things had begun to slide. . . . The most striking point was the fact that the trustees were really totally in the dark about the Martin Marietta project that they had authorized, without competition of any sort. . . . The main thing was the complacency of the trustees and the faculty at the institution. That struck me as the major issue.[13]

In April of the previous year, Drexel had entered into a contract with Martin Marietta Data Systems to begin the development of a new administrative computing system and a student records system. Martin Marietta was a large defense contractor with specialties in large systems design and systems integration, among other areas, but with little apparent prior experience in higher education. In the weeks prior to assuming the office of president, Gaither found himself embroiled in the project, after economics professor John Savchack suggested during the interview process that there were problems with the data systems contract, and that Savchack thought the project was out of control.[14]

And it was. The project was arguably the largest non-construction project undertaken in the history of the institution. Almost three-quarters of the project budget had been spent and the first phase of the three-phase project had not been completed. Gaither, who had previously worked for Bechtel, understood how in the world of large-scale projects with a company such as Martin Marietta, the project could move ahead in this manner, with the billing progressing even when the project was not.

Upon his arrival in September, Gaither set in motion the termination of the Martin Marietta contract, to the chagrin of the Martin Marietta board members. The contract, drafted by Drexel's attorneys, provided for a maximum of $1 million in compensation in the event of a dispute, and Gaither was advised by university counsel that the university was unlikely to prevail in litigation. Drexel had signed a note for approximately $1 million per year for eight years, and was obligated to Martin Marietta, notwithstanding the cancellation of the project. On May 15, 1985, the board of trustees officially suspended the Martin Marietta contract, after the expenditure of $5.795 million, for which, Rich Schneider would later remark, "we did not receive a single line of code."[15]

One year later, the details of the contract were published in an article by John Daniel Stapleton in the Drexel student newspaper, the *Triangle,* under the headline "$7 million lost to Martin Marietta."

A progress review of the project in September, 1984, revealed that it was 14 months behind schedule, $900,000 over budget, and that 75% of the $5.7 million allocated to the project had been expended. . . . Questions have been raised in this matter concerning the conflict of interests within the Board of Trustees. J. Donald Rauth, former Chairman of Drexel's Board is

Chairman of Martin Marietta's Executive Committee; William
Hagerty, former President of Drexel, was a director of Martin
Marietta. J.L. Everett, former Chairman of Drexel's Board, and
current Vice-Chairman, is a member of the Martin Marietta's
Board of Directors.[16]

Gaither was quoted later on in the story, saying, "It's like making
payments on a car, and then not getting the car." Of particular note in
this story is the suggestion that the project was fourteen months behind
schedule, even though the contract had only been approved sixteen
months before the September 1984 review date.

As Gaither assumed the leadership of the institution, residential
applications continued their strong growth, accompanied by weakness
in commuter applications. The university was at capacity in its dormitories and off-campus, fraternity, and sorority housing alternatives. On
September 1, 1984, the Lambda Chi Alpha fraternity was reopened
following an internal investigation that satisfied the university "that the
unfortunate incident of April 10 was an isolated event." The Philadelphia Human Relations Commission recommended against the reopening, suggesting that it "could pose a threat to the general peace of the
city."[17] Commission chairman Reverend James Allen elaborated in a
letter to the university on August 21 their view that "serious interracial
incidents with area residents . . . could touch off disturbances that would
extend beyond Powelton."[18]

The Powelton Village Civic Association continued its opposition
to the new dormitory project, which led to the rejection in December
of the university's application for city approval of its bond issue for the
project. City council, sensitive to the concerns expressed by the neighborhood, announced that the application was "rejected at this time."[19]
In response to these growing problems with the community, Gaither
and the city set up a university-community council. But of greater
significance, Bill and Robin Gaither eschewed the traditional president's
home on the Main Line and moved into Powelton Village. It was a
decision that shocked the trustees[20] but would build a deep reservoir of
good will toward Gaither in the neighborhood that would be important in the turmoil that was to come.

Over the next six months, the university negotiated changes in
the dormitory design with the neighbors, addressed other issues including student parking and fraternity conduct, and entered into an agreement with the neighborhood regarding the handling of issues of ongoing

concern. In March, the dormitory project was approved by the city, with neighborhood support, enabling the bonds for the project to be issued and the financing to be completed.

The Vision Thing

Bill Gaither came to Drexel University with a clear vision of what he believed it could become. His model was Carnegie Mellon and the dramatic changes that had taken place there under the leadership of President Richard Cyert as it grew from its position as a similar institution to the Drexel Institute to become a premier engineering and technology university. It was, in his mind, a direction that was fully consistent with the path that had been set forth by his predecessor.

> It was a real meat and potatoes university, which was of course good. I was really interested in the business and engineering side of the school, that was its foundation. And they turned out good, solid business people and good, solid engineers. I had planned, as my vision, to put a sharper focus on certain areas and do what Dick Cyert had done out at Carnegie Mellon, which had brought Carnegie Mellon up to a whole new level of respect in the academic world and the research world by focusing in a few very critical and forward looking areas. This, of course, is why it was important that the deans help out with setting that vision.[21]

He set out immediately to fulfill the directive that the trustees had set forth to develop a ten-year plan built around this vision, though he expanded the notion of the ten-year plan into a rolling ten-year plan, to be updated annually, in which the first year of the plan would serve as the operating plan for the coming year. As described in his report to the board on September 19, barely three weeks after his first official day on the job, the planning process would include participation from across the community and encompass three rounds of community review.

As an initial step in the development of the research component of his plan, Gaither invited a consulting team comprising research directors from Georgia Tech and the University of Delaware, and a private sector representative to Drexel in October. The Report of the Research Consulting Team, presented to the Drexel community on November 9, argued for the critical importance of the linkages between undergraduate education and a research enterprise in its opening pages.

During the past quarter century, Drexel University has strength-
ened and consolidated its reputation as a solid regional undergraduate teaching institution. Owing to the university's unique
mandatory co-op program, it is widely perceived as a specialty
technical university particularly well suited to the educational
needs of students from "blue-collar" and middle-class families. . . .

In this role Drexel fills a need that has been neglected by
many other universities and colleges in the United States. We
believe the trustees, faculty and administration should maintain
the school's unique role in undergraduate education while
building, during the next decade, capabilities that are essential
to meet the new and more sophisticated demands of a rapidly
changing and highly competitive educational world.

To accomplish this task, Drexel must make the transition
from a regional undergraduate technical institution to a nationally recognized research university. Only a university with substantial research and graduate programs can provide the kind of
undergraduate education that students expect today. Such schools
draw the best faculty candidates and, largely as a result of their
research programs, have facilities to provide superior undergraduate education. Better faculties and the reputations that go
with them draw better students, at the undergraduate as well
as the graduate level.[22]

Through the commissioning of this report, Gaither was presenting
the first clear statement of his philosophy and direction for the school.
Like Hagerty before him, who recognized that the development of a
strong humanities faculty was critical to the ability of his new university
to make the step away from its regional, institute roots into the universe
of leading institutions of higher education and who also saw the importance of research in that transition, Gaither was looking to the
growth of research universities for a developmental model that would
enable Drexel to build a competitive edge in the "rapidly changing and
highly competitive educational world."

Gaither moved quickly to implement the core recommendations
of the report and build an administrative infrastructure to support growth
in externally funded research. He created an office of research and hired
a colleague from the University of Delaware, Richard Schneider, who
had served on the advisory panel, to serve as his new vice president for
research. Gaither and Schneider developed new policies and created

incentives to support research activity, including providing mechanisms for faculty release time and funding discretionary accounts for research active colleges and departments from a share of university overhead costs recovered from grants.

Gaither also retained a D.C. lobbying firm to assist the university in securing federal funding for its research enterprise—a practice that was not common in the research universe that presented itself to the world as a peer-reviewed, objective distributor of federal funds—and enlisted the support of members of the Philadelphia congressional delegation, most notably Congressman William Gray, a powerful member of the Democratic House leadership and member of the powerful Appropriations Committee. Gaither acknowledged that the method he pursued was unorthodox within the academy, but fully consistent with congressional intent:

> There was of course at the time a great controversy by the haves—the twenty or so universities that got about eighty or ninety percent of the federal research budgets—that peer review was the only thing that would work. We have-nots said, "We understand your reason for doing that because all of the peers are in your schools." MIT, Harvard, Stanford, Princeton, Yale, and so forth, Cornell, because you get ninety percent of the money and want to continue to do so, because you have the peer reviewers. But when you look back at the original legislation for a lot of organizations, including the National Science Foundation, Congress recognized very clearly that the political side of this as an economic development tool was critical to them, and they weren't about to relinquish that right to appropriate money for their own states.[23]

The development of the ten-year plan for the years 1985–1995 took twelve months rather than nine. The process was initiated with an off-site planning conference and included three rounds of community review, but did not engender the degree of collaboration and support among the deans that Gaither envisioned, and in his view the plan emerged as a point of contention with the deans.[24] Tom Canavan, the dean of the College of Humanities and Social Sciences at the time concurred:

> That plan was a pain . . . I mean, he wrote that plan. Don't for one moment think that that plan represents the thinking of a

community, a committee, a group of deans, or anybody else. It was Bill Gaither's plan. And Bill Gaither worked at this day and night for what seemed like years. . . . I don't believe he ever accepted a single idea from me or any of the other deans.[25]

The ten-year plan was presented for consideration by the board of trustees in September 1985. As he addressed the assembled trustees, Gaither argued that Drexel's goal must be to be ranked among the nation's leading universities and colleges by 1995, and Drexel should pursue this goal by improving student quality, becoming one of the nation's one hundred leading research universities, and quadrupling the size of the university endowment.[26]

The plan identified as primary strengths the strong undergraduate teaching tradition, the technological and scientific base, and the co-op program, though it noted that the five-year co-op program could be a competitive disadvantage in the competition for the brightest students looking at more traditional four-year programs. It also suggested that the microcomputer program, while enhancing the university's visibility in the short run, would soon dissipate as a source of competitive advantage if "not developed aggressively."[27]

Gaither recognized that the financial condition of the university that he had inherited was fragile and that Drexel's challenges in the area of enrollment were likely to intensify. The ten-year plan set forth a financial analysis of the period 1980–1984 built around a number of operating and balance sheet ratios that that suggested the weakness of the financial condition of the university compared to industry medians. Gaither and the board had reviewed the financial position of the university at an off-site conference held in January 1985. Gaither felt that the financial ratios were important benchmarks for assessing financial performance, and that at least the bankers on the board, who were familiar with financial ratio analysis, should have understood the implications of what they were seeing. At the same time, Gaither was not concerned that the trustees did not seem to focus on the picture of the university that was implied by the financial evaluation, as he felt that he was walking a fine line between having them involved and not wanting them to feel inclined to meddle in his work.[28] He preferred to save their efforts for areas where he needed help, such as fundraising.

The financial analysis suggested that the university financial position was weak, as represented by its low levels of assets and endowment relative to its level of operating expenditures, and that its operating characteristics made it vulnerable to external events that might adversely affect enrollment or other revenues. The university was highly tuition dependent, direct research expenditures and operations and maintenance expenditures were declining relative to the budget, and it was highly dependent on an annual appropriation from the Commonwealth of Pennsylvania. The plan presented these measures as a basis for assessing organizational effectiveness over time, and specifically focused on the need to raise the level of the university endowment.

The plan presented a goal of increasing undergraduate enrollment modestly back to 7,500, an increase of only 150 students, though it recognized that maintaining enrollment at this level while improving student quality would require substantial effort in the face of an anticipated 25 percent decline in the eighteen-year-old population within the region. The executive summary suggested that "to increase the size and quality of Drexel's applicant pool will require special efforts of national and international dimension." The assessment of the external environment went farther in articulating the rationale for the pursuit of research university status as an issue of competitiveness for students and for broadening the revenue base of the institution. The plan summarized the challenge faced by the Drexel community in the current market environment.

> To achieve its goals in this operating environment, Drexel University must capitalize on its traditional strengths, stemming from its private status, its mandatory co-op program, the success of its graduates, and its long-standing industry contacts. In addition, it must organize so that it can offer a variety of exciting opportunities in education, research, creativity, and entrepreneurship to its students, faculty, staff, industry co-op partners, and alumni.[29]

At the same meeting where the plan was presented, almost as if to underscore the urgency of the challenges facing the university, the enrollment management report indicated that applications for the fall term in 1985 had declined by approximately 10 percent, to the levels prior to the announcement of the microcomputer initiative. Similarly, the entering freshman class had fallen to 1,685 from its peak of 1,872 just two years earlier. Gaither reported that enrollments were 160 below plan, and that the anticipated operating deficit was $1,678,000, higher than the deficit for the prior fiscal year.

Faculty reaction to the plan was negative. As the remarks by both Gaither and Canavan suggest, neither the faculty nor the deans accepted the direction or tone of the plan. The disagreements were both in process and substance. The *Faculty Council Critique of the Long-range Plan* presented a fundamental indictment of the plan:

> The fundamental goals of the Plan do not include the one goal which should be most essential: *to improve the quality of education at Drexel University.* The Plan, as a result of the President's desire for quantification, confounds what is essentially desirable, useful, and of service to students and society, with what is self-promoting and prestigious for the University. It mistakes the yardstick for that which is to be measured. Ultimately, it presents a crass, self-serving university, where means are confused with ends and the highest goal is the status of the University. . . . The Plan gives the impression that the University's priorities are, in order of decreasing importance, prestige, profit, research, education . . .

The faculty council critique continued to attack the "corporate" attitude that it saw in the written document, and its dismissive attitude toward the central role of the faculty:

> The essential achievements and proposal of the Plan tend to establish an administration that runs the University like a corporation. We have seen a dramatic proliferation of Vice-Presidents and other administrative officers, at substantially increased costs, while the hiring of teaching scholars has been restricted or frozen. None of the new Vice-Presidents hired by the President has outstanding credentials in research or teaching but rather strengths in business, finance or administration. . . . The thrust of the plan is to give increasing responsibility to administrators, trustees, outside evaluation groups, consultants, professional lobbyists . . . and to transform the faculty into expendable middle-managers.[30]

Isaac Auerbach, a titan of the computer age and one of the elder statesmen of the College of Engineering, offered a more measured response, and arguably a view that was representative of the engineering community. He questioned the lack of a "sharp focus" in the plan, as well as the intention to reach out to foreign student markets as a component of efforts to broaden the student market. Auerbach also questioned the wisdom of involving the faculty and the academic units in admissions to aid in recruitment, harkening back to the experience of Al Soffa.[31]

Financial Deterioration

With the completion of the plan, the issues with the Powelton Village neighbors resolved, and the Martin Marietta fiasco ended, Gaither's attention turned to the worsening financial picture that was emerging as enrollment continued to decline. Three months later, at the December board meeting, Art Joblin reported to the trustees that they were concerned that applications for the following fall could be off another 25 percent. Anticipating the impact of continued declines in enrollment on the university finances, Gaither informed the trustees that he had created an Enrollment Task Force to undertake a market analysis and return with recommendations as to directions to be pursued, as well as a Financial Management Task Force to recommend immediate budgetary actions to keep the current year deficit below $1 million.

Gaither also announced the creation of a third task force, to be led by Bernie Sagik, on Program Quality and Student Retention. This task force had the most far-reaching challenge, as it reached beyond the financial implications of student persistence into the heart of the academic programs, and touched on areas of responsibility that lay clearly in the faculty domain, including the evaluation and prioritization of academic programs, the guidelines for promotion and tenure, and strategies for addressing student dissatisfaction, including improving teaching and advisement.[32]

In late January 1986, the university announced the elimination of ninety-two nonteaching positions, including the layoffs of twenty-four members of the university support staff. The revised deficit for the current fiscal year was projected to be $3.4 million. $1.2 million of the increased deficit resulted from a decline in anticipated tuition income. The cost of picking up the pieces of the Martin Marietta project also contributed to the growth in the deficit. Other deficit reduction strategies included the reduction in adjunct faculty funding and an attendant 10 percent increase in average class size.

On February 13, the *Philadelphia Inquirer* ran a story under the headline "Drexel May Cut Faculty by 10%." The story cited a memo from Bernie Sagik to the deans and department heads asking for their recommendations on how to achieve the cuts.[33]

Five days later, the administration retracted its threat of faculty cuts, and in a *Philadelphia Inquirer* article on February 19 suggested that it could handle the financial situation through normal attrition.[34] The University Faculty Council (UFC) responded in March with a harsh criticism of the administration, as reported by Joe Saunders in the *Triangle,* which attacked the credibility of administration claims regarding the impact of reduced enrollment and the fallout of the Martin Marietta contract, though the UFC at the same time sought to avoid a war in the press that would rebound negatively against the university.[35]

In April, the Financial Management Task Force presented a budget for the coming fiscal year that pared spending by $6 million, from $102.6 million to $96.3 million. The administration introduced a new word into the Drexel lexicon: "ARF," an acronym for Allocation Reduction Factor, which, in various incarnations, was used as a noun or a verb. In its first ARF, the administration implemented an across-the-board 21 percent cut in the nonfixed costs of each academic unit for the upcoming fiscal year, where fixed costs included primarily salaries, benefits, and direct research project expenditures.

At the same time that the budgets for the following year were reduced, the administration introduced a budget planning and control system that marked a dramatic change in budget management from the Hagerty era. The new budget process provided the academic managers with greater flexibility in the use of funds and included a "carry-forward" provision that allowed 50 percent of the funds saved in one year to be carried forward into a designated account to be used the next year.

Gaither's budget actions, both the cuts and the proposed reform in budget management, were shocks to the system. Historically, the deans and department heads paid no attention to budgets per se, as incremental spending needs in any given year were subject to approval by Hagerty. They had had no previous real responsibilities in the area of budget management, and certainly had little in the way of accountability for the financial results from year to year.

The nominal amount of a departmental budget had little relationship to the actual level of spending in a given year. As a result of this, the implications of the announcement of budget reductions did not have an immediate impact. What department heads had traditionally seen as their "budget" was a small fraction of what they actually spent in a year. A department's spending was not related to that beginning of the year "budget," but to what Hagerty agreed to allow over the course of the year. Therefore, Gaither was introducing two concepts at once: the budget as an allocation of funding that was expected to be sufficient for the year, and the role of the department head or dean as the authority responsible for ongoing prioritization, decision making, and management. In time, the impact and severity of the ARFs sank in, as academic managers realized that it was the total actual amount of the academic unit expenditures that would be affected.

The administration's credibility in the area of finance was weakened by the lack of good financial reporting systems. Members of the faculty council distrusted the financial information that they were given, and sequential changes in the budget structure and form of presentation only exacerbated the situation, as faculty assumed that the administration was deliberately trying to hide information.

As Gaither was addressing a weak financial situation and implementing stringent budget measures for the upcoming fiscal year, the administration was working with the moneymen on the investment committee on measures that might alleviate some of the budget pressures. First, the administration submitted a request for $1.75 million from endowment principal. The request was to fund a number of "one-time" needs, including the cost of computer software development, a marketing campaign, and increased student aid. Second, Gaither requested that the committee forestall a proposed increase in the portion of the endowment invested in equities to 75 percent.

The university did not operate under a spending rule limiting the amount of endowment earnings that could be utilized to fund annual operating costs. The committee had historically invested 40 percent of the portfolio in bonds, and during the high interest rate environment of the late 1970s and early 1980s, when Paul Volker led the Federal Reserve Bank in a policy of tight money and high interest rates, this produced a significant flow of interest earnings that were available for operating needs. The proposal to increase the asset allocation into equities offered a higher potential long-term return to the university, but threatened to reduce the dividends and interest available to fund operations.

The budget management reforms and incentives around research funding mitigated some of the pain of the budget retrenchment, and encouraged and rewarded entrepreneurial behavior within the colleges. From the point of view of the Department of Electrical and Computer Engineering, the ability to develop new programs and keep a large share of the revenues, and the return of overhead funds and salary recovery from research grants to the department, ultimately made up some of the impact of the cuts.[36] However, the impact was quite different for those in the humanities, for whom extramural funding opportunities were limited, and as such the pain of those Gaither's cutbacks were felt differentially across the school. [37]

The irony of the Gaither ten-year plan, the reforms to the budget process, and the budget retrenchment, was that in many respects the opposition and confusion that was engendered was not a result of change, but of transparency. The goals presented in the plan and the authoritarianism that the faculty saw in Gaither's management style did not differ substantially from his predecessor, and the direction of the plan was consistent with the directive articulated during the presidential search by the board. Hagerty, however, controlled information closely, and did not expect or seek consensus in the course on which the university was embarked. Funding cuts, when they occurred, were implemented simply by the withholding of funds or the denial of spending requests. He did not seek the approval of any other dean when he channeled university resources into the creation of a department of humanities. Nor did he allow a debate about his unarguably corporate and directive management style.

What the ten-year plan and the ensuing changes did was to make it clear that the administration—and by their support of the plan, the trustees—were intent on changing the profile of the university in the public eye. The new directions would include building a research infrastructure, rewarding research, and supporting departments in areas of strategic importance. What in the old days would have been done in private and without public discussion was now open for all members of the university to see. And as an institution with limited endowment and no infusion of capital to fund the areas of proposed investment, the funding would be internal and there would be winners and losers in the process. Budget issues, once the sole purview of the president, became a source of ongoing infighting and resentment within the academic departments and served to further undermine the confidence that the faculty had in the administration.

A New Set of Tires

The next shoe to drop in the financial drama that was unfolding was announced in the *Triangle* on April 18, under the banner headline "Board Votes 19% Tuition Increase."[38] The passage of the budget for the upcoming fiscal year included the cuts of $6 million recommended by the Financial Management Task Force, as well as a tuition increase that was nearly twice the increase of other schools in the region cited on the front page of the *Triangle*. The tuition increase definitively ended the practice from the Hagerty era of constraining tuition increases to the rate of growth in the cost of living.

Gaither believed that Hagerty's policy of minimizing price increases was not tenable for a tuition-driven institution with a small endowment, and was at odds with the realities of higher education. The result was the underfunding of many areas at Drexel, including staff that was underpaid—as suggested by annual staff turnover rates of up to 40 percent—and inadequate investment in financial management systems and research support. In addition to decentralizing budget control to provide management with incentives to improve operations, Gaither believed that it was essential to restore overall balance to the financial operations, as he explained years later:

> The other thing I found out [upon assuming the presidency] was that there was a difference in the slope of the line of expenditures and revenues, and expenditures were increasing at a steeper slope than revenues were increasing. So I instituted a nineteen percent tuition increase, which was not large, I likened it to a new set of tires for a kid's car, which of course created some interesting comments by the students.[39]

The response to the tuition increase was immediate and negative, as illustrated by letters to the editor posted in the *Triangle* that laid the problem at the feet of the board and administration.

> Given the financial mess that the University now finds itself in, and the obvious conflict of interest in the awarding of the computer system update to Martin Marietta, the only conclusion that can be drawn is that ex-President Hagerty did not die of cancer, but of guilt. Frank Giraffe[40]

> I wish the Drexel administration would be on the level with students and not glorify what is not. I am most sympathetic with those students who cannot afford the new Drexel increase and must leave. I hope the administration can also understand their grief, perhaps a card would be nice. Louis Buchman[41]

Gaither held a public meeting at the end of April to discuss the tuition increase, but was dismissive of the notion that the increases were dire. When questioned by a student who suggested that "the tuition increases are so grave that I'm telling you right now I will not be enrolled in school next year," Gaither responded by asking, "Well, are you ready to chuck a Drexel education for a new set of tires for your car?" The student walked out after giving his parting comments:

> I would respect your decision if I felt there was going to be a comparable increase in the quality of the education that each of us will be receiving at Drexel. I already work 30 hours a week and have a family to support. I've been doing this for six years. I don't think we are going to get any increase in the quality of education. I think we're going to get a decrease. . . . I have no respect for you.[42]

The confluence of events and issues continued to undermine the already fragile trust that Gaither enjoyed as the leader of the university community. The tuition increase, coupled with cuts in federal financial aid and the unwillingness of the president to assure students that it was a one-time event, undermined morale among the students as well as the faculty.

Rage

Gaither's problems with the faculty were many, and they were not improving. He arrived at Drexel as the choice of a small group on the board who, by all accounts, asserted their will on the board and the rest of the community. He had been rejected four years earlier in the competition for the chief academic officer position, during which the faculty participants had looked askance at his research record. His first declaration of policy through an external consulting report inherently suggested that the key to the future success of the institution rested in the attraction of a new cadre of competitive research faculty, rather than the faculty that were there upon his arrival. He imposed his will on a planning process that in effect took sides in the battle between the humanities and the engineering faculties, and between the faculty who valued teaching and the research-oriented faculty, and failed to use that planning process to galvanize the community around a common vision of the future. He appointed nonacademics to key positions of leadership and authority. He proposed to turn the budget process over to deans and department heads who in the view of the faculty were themselves members of the dark side. And now, by all appearances, he had alienated the core student clientele, pricing the university out of its market and driving the institution into a full-blown financial crisis that appeared to be threatening their economic security. It was not a good start.

Rich Schneider, Gaither's colleague from Delaware, had been concerned from the outset that the Drexel presidency would be a great risk for Gaither. He was at risk of being the classic "disposable president."

> If you have a very long-seated and generally very successful president but certainly a heavy-handed president, the next one is disposable. They usually last about two years, maybe three at the most. What happens is, let's say under a long-seated president, an autocratic one, there's so much pressure built up, it's like a pressure cooker. . . . And when he doesn't solve all of the problems, the ones who loved the old one will say, "Well hell, that wouldn't have happened if Hagerty was still here." The new ones, who were waiting for the old guy to leave, find out that they don't necessarily get what they want from this guy either, say, "He's just as bad as Hagerty." So then you get both groups hating you and then you eventually leave.[43]

Faculty recalling Gaither many years later remain harsh in their criticism of his academic credentials. Most of the criticisms are rooted in their assessment of his research interests. Many believed he was simply crazy, describing his research experiments on ESP, and his ideas about building communities under the ocean to protect the population in the event of a nuclear attack.

These criticisms may have been valid, but they strike a cord as a symptom rather than a cause of faculty disdain. They did not respect him on many levels. Rich Schneider, who knew his research well, offered a different opinion on Gaither's research interests:

> He was very futuristic in his thinking. He had done a lot of stuff with ocean assimilation and the capacity of the world's oceans to absorb what we put in it. . . . He did a project with Princeton and a friend of his, Jahn, looking at phytoplankton. . . . It was kind of like a little weird. We all kind of wondered about this, but the guy that was actually the principal

investigator at Princeton was no slouch engineering scientist, but he was into ESP. There was also some work that was done with energy production through wave mechanics, which actually worked very well, including osmosis. He's a very deep thinker. He is a futurist.[44]

Faculty objections to Gaither's performance as president varied by field. The objection from the College of Engineering was largely economic. Gaither was taking their money and using it elsewhere in the institution, whether investing in the new College of Information Sciences and Technology, or subsidizing the arts and sciences colleges. Drexel was first and foremost an engineering institute and the diversion of funds away from the flagship college was degrading the quality of the facilities, and from the vantage point of the College of Engineering undermining the central mission of the school.[45]

The objections of the academic traditionalists were more fundamental. The hiring of Martha Montgomery and the direction to her to build a humanities faculty had been part of Hagerty's strategy to build the quality and prestige of his new university. Hagerty, who died less than two years after stepping down as president, had not taken great stock of the cultural impact on his institute of broadening the presence of the humanities faculty. Years later, these faculty, whose presence in the tenured ranks was growing, were asserting their values on their university. Their opposition to Gaither was not merely economic, it was ideological. It wasn't about money; it was about the essence of academic freedom and the core values of the institutions.

Jacques Catudal was a philosopher hired by Hagerty. He knew that Hagerty had no interest in his field of study, or in humanities in general. But Catudal also believed that Hagerty would never suggest to a member of the faculty how they should teach their subject, something an administrator should only attempt at their peril. Catudal saw in Gaither a man who did not understand the limits of his own expertise, and who did not respect the rules of the academy that would have suggested that he not impose his notions of content on the faculty.

The resentments of the faculty were evident again as the rolling ten-year plan was revised for the period 1986–1996. Again, the critique submitted by the faculty council focused on the emphasis on research in lieu of undergraduate education, and the threat to faculty hegemony over academic affairs. On October 17, the *Triangle* ran an article by Kenneth Blackney covering the board approval of the revised plan and faculty reaction under the headline "Faculty, Gaither clash over instruction and future," which set forth the faculty council critique of a plan that "places too little emphasis on education, and removed academic control from faculty."[46]

The *Triangle* article continued: "One professor who spoke on the condition of confidentiality said that Gaither wants to 'deemphasize teaching and emphasize research and prestige and profitability.' " Others saw the faculty resentments as rooted in the demands that Gaither was making that the institution grow in the direction that had been, ironically, set in motion by Hagerty.[47]

On October 16, the day the board adopted the revised long-range plan, they also created a Committee on Instruction and Research. The new committee, to be chaired by Gaither's collaborator from Princeton and new board member, Robert Jahn, was to have responsibility for "the quality and content of academic and research programs. . . . The oversight of initiation, review and closure of colleges, departments, majors, areas of instruction and research institutes."[48]

In his address to the board of trustees upon his appointment to the new committee, as reported by the *Triangle* on the following day, Jahn described the purpose of the new committee: "Our task is the recasting of the academic fabric at Drexel."[49] The new committee, in the eyes of some faculty, represented an egregious step by the board into the realm of controlling content and curricular matters that were the sole jurisdiction of the faculty, as was bluntly pointed out in the *Triangle* article:

> AAUP representative William Biddle said such a committee would be an "unconscionable usurpation of faculty duties," and added that "the idea of having outside people come in and make academic policy would indeed give reason for Holy Hell."[50]

That fall, the faculty council convened its Committee on Faculty Governance to pursue changes to the form and process of shared governance at Drexel. The faculty motivations were multiple. The long-range planning process had left the faculty believing that the board and the president were ignoring the traditions of shared governance and forcing their agenda and their values on the academic community. At a more basic level, the continued decline in enrollment and the financial position of the university left faculty council members concerned that the university simply was not being managed effectively, and that, albeit against their own best inclinations, the faculty would need to assert a more active role in management to assure the effective governance of the institution.

In December, Gaither responded to the committee's draft proposal suggesting the creation of a faculty senate with rights and responsibilities in the governance of the institution and proposed broadening the concept from a faculty senate to a university senate. The recommendation was consistent with Gaither's actions as president. He had moved into Powelton Village and joined a predominantly African American church to establish the presence of the university in the community. He had hired the first female and African American vice presidents in the history of the institution. He was committed, in action and in deed, to the values of inclusion, and believed that a university senate should include the representation and voices of the professional and clerical staff, as well as union workers. His stance on the senate, however, was not seen by the faculty committee as an act of inclusion, but rather as one more effort to marginalize the faculty and their contribution, reflective of his disregard and disrespect for faculty values and rights.

Enrollment Management

At the end of 1986, Gaither implemented another change that would prove to be significant. In July of that year, Gaither had retained Lee Stetson, dean of admissions of the University of Pennsylvania, to advise him on the enrollment management problems that Drexel was facing. At the end of the year, based on Stetson's advice and with the concurrent recommendation of the academic deans, Gaither moved Admissions and Financial Aid from under the Vice President of Student Affairs and placed them under the Vice President for Academic Affairs. Gaither appointed Gary Hamme, then head of the cooperative education office, and Dick Mortimer from the faculty to head enrollment management.

The impact of the microcomputer initiative on applications was waning, and applications were continuing to fall. Overall, freshman applications for the fall of 1986 were 20 percent below the level of two years earlier. The bulk of the decline was experienced in the traditional commuter market, while residential enrollments remained strong. This presented a problem for an admissions organization that was not experienced in competing in the national student market and that relied on Drexel's traditional strengths as a local institution to generate an adequate flow of applications and students.

Gaither understood the demographic argument that was generally used by people in the administration to justify the declining enrollments. The number of eighteen-year-olds in the regional market was declining, and the Catholic schools in the city were being particularly hard hit and were seeing a dramatic drop in graduates. Gaither did not believe that that rationale was sufficient, however, and understood that the university was headed on a course that would lead to a continuing decline in student quality as the institution sought to sustain its revenues. Drexel had to reach out and broaden its market.

> As the applicant pool was declining . . . we were maintaining the revenue stream we needed from tuition by taking poorer students, but keeping the numbers up. But I felt we could live with that for a short time while we really put major effort into increasing the applicant pool so we could select higher quality students out of a larger pool. And Mortimer and Hamme made that a reality. . . . In the two years they had responsibility for that, they really changed the slope of the applicant pool curve, so it was a nice steep slope headed up to my goal of ten thousand applicants by 1995, and we were on our way to doing that.[51]

Holy Hell

On October 6–9, an external academic review panel visited the Drexel campus. The panel included the presidents of Bard College and the University of Pittsburgh. In late November they issued their report to the board. In their findings, they noted that "[t]he faculty at Drexel are of high quality," and, "In contrast to the long-range plan, the team does not find the student body inadequate or inappropriate."[52] The weaknesses noted by the panel were more far-reaching and addressed core governance issues:

> The Board of Trustees does not appear to have assumed an adequate dimension of responsibility with respect to the future of Drexel. . . . The committee found a disturbing level of miscommunication and mistrust between the faculty and the administration. . . . It was clear that the process of long-range planning must be reconsidered. . . . The admissions process and staffing were viewed to be weaknesses. . . . Alumni/ae relations to the university are dangerously weak. There is not now a stable and adequate form of faculty governance.[53]

Panel member comments in a *Triangle* article were even more bleak:

> The panel was stopped cold by the "level of disaffection and alienation" between the faculty and administration and concluded that until that changed, "no serious progress towards a long-range plan could be made."[54]

On February 24, 1987, the issue of faculty morale was again brought out into the public debate, as an ad hoc committee appointed by the faculty council published a statement charging that the problems that beset the institution were rooted in faculty disaffection and frustration with the university administration.

As relations between the faculty and the administration deteriorated, an event transpired that would change the future course of the institution. On April 24, Gaither was accused by a female employee of inappropriate sexual contact while the two were at a dinner in Toronto two days earlier. During the dinner, Gaither "put his hand on the knee of a woman during a business dinner and 'squeezed more than once.' "[55] On April 27, the employee withdrew her complaint after Gaither formally apologized to the employee and her spouse, in the presence of the employee's supervisor.

Within days, rumors of the incident had spread across the campus. On May 4, the academic deans met and passed "a resolution of moral outrage" demanding Gaither's immediate removal as president, and suggested that if the board of trustees did not act the deans would resign en masse. At an unofficial board meeting that day, the board created a special committee to investigate Gaither's conduct.

The next day, May 5, the faculty council met and voted unanimously for a resolution that demanded that "the President be immediately relieved of his duties . . . and that he be advised to resign and that steps be taken to legally remove him from office."

The controversy was covered on almost a daily basis by the *Philadelphia Inquirer* and the *Philadelphia Daily News* beginning the day after the faculty council vote. In its coverage on May 7 of the actions by the deans and the faculty council, the *Inquirer* quoted the dean of the College of Science, Francis Dean, who suggested that the motives of the deans were not limited to the sexual harassment incident, but declined to give details. The article went on to quote a professor "who declined to give her name because she was not tenured," who denounced the trustees for having failed to remove Gaither immediately, adding, "I'll need further evidence from the board that they believe in equity for women."[56]

The fight continued to gather momentum in the media. On May 9, the *Philadelphia Daily News* reported Gaither's public threat to fire the deans for their vote demanding his resignation, followed by Dean Davis's retort that "the deans are putting their jobs on the line because they feel so strongly about this" and suggesting the difficulty Gaither would face trying to replace all of the deans at once.[57]

The commentary in the press was fairly blunt in its suggestion that the issue was not as much about the incident itself as about the long-simmering resentment felt by the faculty toward Gaither for, as noted by Huntly Collins in his *Inquirer* article on May 12, "everything from un-warranted budget cuts to his failure to involve them in university decision-making." In that same article, Collins quoted Gaither supporter and marketing professor Mercia Grassi who noted plaintively of Gaither that "he's the most pro-woman and pro-minority president we've ever had."[58]

On May 15, Joe Saunders of the *Triangle* reported on a "speak-out" on the issue attended by four hundred students and faculty.

> A more pervasive sentiment however, was not directed against Gaither personally but to the adverse effects of the publicity surrounding the incident and its repercussions on Drexel's repu-tation. "I think he's dragged Drexel's name through the dirt," a female student said.[59]

Gaither conveyed his own view of the evolving incident in the same article:

> The Board of Trustees has to stand back and look at the insti-tution and say "how can it be managed effectively?" . . . They appreciate the volatility [of a university community], particu-larly of the faculty. . . mercurial is the best way I can describe it, up and down. The perception of this incident by the Board will be that they recognize this as a temporary issue . . . con-tinuity of leadership is the most important thing. . . . It's [the speak-out] the beginning of a trained response [if they remove me] that if you don't like a leader or his programs you can replace that leader immediately [just by making enough noise]. . . . This institution would become unmanageable. . . . I don't think what happened in Toronto is a capital crime.[60]

On May 20, the board of trustees met to review the recommendations of the committee convened to review the incident. While the
six-person committee recommended that Gaither be removed, by a
four to two vote, the board declined to remove him. In the public
statement, the board criticized Gaither and rebuked his opponents.

> The actions by President Gaither in Toronto reflected extremely
> bad judgment and were not in keeping with the standards
> which they expect of the University's chief executive. However,
> his record of contributions for the benefit of people in the
> University and the community at large is well documented.
> This record has led a majority of the Trustees to conclude that
> President Gaither can resolve the strains among the Drexel
> family resulting from this unfortunate incident, and accordingly,
> that he not be asked to resign. . . .
>   The Trustees deplore the imprudent actions taken by some
> members of the Drexel community in an effort to force the
> removal of President Gaither. By prematurely publicizing this
> incident before the Trustees had opportunity to complete their
> own inquiry, those individuals have caused incalculable damage
> to the University.[61]

The swords drawn and the battle engaged, the drama over Gaither's
conduct escalated into a battle between the board and the faculty to
determine the future of the Gaither presidency. Two days after the
board meeting, the *DailyNews'* Joseph Grace and Kit Konolige indicated that their "sources have told the *Daily News* that other allegations
of similar conduct by Gather involving three different women were
made to the trustees and the university's general counsel."[62]
    On May 29, the *Triangle* published a letter from Charles Morschek,
faculty council secretary, setting out the case against Gaither:

> The Faculty did not at first refuse to cooperate with him, even
> though the Board of Trustees forced him upon the University
> in direct contradiction to the due selection process. The Faculty
> did not call for his resignation when he glossed over the $5
> million Martin Marietta rip-off of the University, nor when he
> fired a large fraction of the University, some of which had
> faithfully served Drexel for over 15 years. No one demanded
> his firing when he raised tuition 19% in the face of declining

enrollment . . . nor when he cut back allocable funding by 22%, nor when he paid $5 million for a building that will be torn down to make a parking lot. As for Gaither's long-range plan and being a "visionary," not only the Faculty Council but also a distinguished outside review panel have strongly, in formal documents criticized his vision as being too concerned with prestige, profit and income-producing research and not enough with education. His leadership style is to run the University more as a profit-making corporation than as an institution of higher learning, and his most vigorous actions show him to be more interested in real estate than in educational excellence.

Now, all seven of Drexel's academic Deans, all eighteen Faculty Council representatives, and 86% of the tenured Faculty . . . have formally called for his resignation, for all of the above reasons and because they want it known, for now and the future, that no Drexel Administrator, Professor, or staff member will be found guilty of sexual harassment and keep his job.

The Drexel Deans and Faculty, professional educators, have been striving for 2 1/2 years to attain significant participation in the governance of the University. They have been ignored time and again, by Gaither and the Board of Trustees. If Gaither stays, the only politics at Drexel will be unenlightened despotism.[63]

Gaither appeared undaunted in the face of the onslaught. The next week, on June 2, he chaired a meeting of the university tenured and tenure-track faculty. The meeting was held in the Mandel Theater. Gaither sat at a table on the stage and conducted the meeting as each faculty member walked forward to the stage area and dropped his or her ballot in a box. The result was a 229–18 vote in favor of a resolution of no confidence that concluded: "His ability to lead the University and to represent it to alumni, friends, and the general public has been irreparably damaged."[64]

By any measure, it would appear that by this point in the drama that was a true statement, regardless of one's view of the "merits of the case." Robert Jahn, Gaither's collaborator from Princeton University and member of the board of trustees, saw the conflict with the traditional engineers as related to the underlying academic culture:

There was always a certain tension between those that wanted to make the place more academically elite and those that wanted to continue the more prosaic approach to education that had characterized Drexel in the past. . . . Bill was regarded as an egghead among this one faction who really wanted to maintain the good old boiler engineering image of the place.[65]

In the June 5 *Triangle* account of the meeting, Gaither tried to mollify the situation. "I do regret my actions . . . and I do ask for your forgiveness. . . . I think what we are doing is showing to our students that there are problems in life. We should also teach them forgiveness." To which Andy Verzilli, who had introduced the no-confidence motion, replied, "I think we have to teach our students a number of things, certainly forgiveness is one of those things, but so is responsibility and accountability, and I have seen no accountability or responsibility on the part of the President or the Board. I, as a faculty member, resent it."

The drama continued through the summer. On June 12, the *Daily News'* Joseph Draughen published details of three other incidents where "Gaither made sexual advances, including fondling at least one woman's feet."[66] Later that month, the board affirmed its support for Gaither, while announcing that it would conduct a "broad and thorough review" of Gaither's ability to continue to lead the university, which it would complete by October.[67] Many board members did not believe that the facts of the case warranted Gaither's dismissal and were loath to let the faculty force their hand, as noted by Mary Walton in a *Philadelphia Inquirer Magazine* story published on August 9. "It was the prevailing sentiment of the predominantly male board that 'a hand on the knee' was not sufficient cause to fire the president; moreover, to do so would make it look as if the faculty had the upper hand."[68]

At the same time, faculty, who found themselves immersed in the controversy on a daily basis, expressed resentment toward the board's final say in the matter, as voiced by Roger Corneliussen, an engineering professor on the faculty council:

> This is our life. We're tied up with this place very intimately. If you're a trustee, you come in once a month. Most come in less than that. You have a nice lunch. . . . You don't ever get involved in any serious issues. And you're part of a nice academic atmosphere.[69]

Gaither fought to keep his job. In October he brought in David Brooks Arnold, a mediator with extensive international experience, from the United Nations to mediate his relationship with the faculty. The fall enrollment picture was improving, as the strategies put in place by Gary Hamme and Dick Mortimer had stabilized the situation, and the trajectory of applications was turning positive. Gaither tried to appeal to the board that the managerial problems were in fact behind them, that the ship was turning, and that retaining him was critical to the continued recovery of the institution from its financial difficulties.

The results of the fiscal year that ended on June 30, 1987, were encouraging. Revenue growth had outpaced expenditure growth. The funds that had been appropriated from the endowment were not needed to balance operations. The Suspense Fund, which represented the unrestricted reserve balance, grew from $0.3 million to $1.2 million.

In short, Gaither argued that the institution had weathered the storm. The financial and enrollment crises were abating, and the necessary internal cultural shifts that put greater responsibility on the deans and the faculty for the leadership of academic affairs and the research enterprise were beginning to take hold. The carry-forward provisions that he had introduced to the budget process had resulted in $1.5 million in operating savings, half of which would be returned to the colleges for their reinvestment in the academic program. The changes in research policies had tripled research expenditures over the three-year period, and made indirect cost recovery a substantial revenue stream to the university for the first time.

On October 14, 1987, Gaither published a wide ranging account of the track record of his administration[70] and the goals that his administration was on track to accomplish. In the letter of transmittal, he offered his summation:

> I am proud of the progress made by Drexel University during my first three years of stewardship. I am particularly pleased with progress made during the 1986–87 fiscal year just finished. The Drexel faculty and Board of Trustees, indeed the larger "Drexel Community," is being tested and challenged to face the need for change so that it can continue to grow and prosper as it has in the nearly 100 years since its founding in 1891. The University possesses the necessary attributes of a fine reputation for high-quality education, a dedicated and respected faculty, an involved Board of Trustees, a capable and forward-looking administration, a loyal alumni body, and a city which needs Drexel to become one of the nation's leading universities.[71]

As Bill Gaither reflected on the experience years later, he continued to believe that with a strong board chair such as Lee Everett, he
could have survived as president, but that it was the unwillingness of
Bob McClements to face the media and public pressure that led to his
ultimate departure as president. Rather than look objectively at what he
had accomplished and the direction he was taking the university, Gaither
suggested that McClements chose instead to "just deal the hand again."[72]

George Ross described later how the board ultimately came to
decide not to continue its support of Gaither. The question had become whether he could still lead the university, regardless of how each
of them as individuals might have come to view the facts of the case.

> There were a group of trustees who felt that he had done a
> good job, and what had occurred was not enough to have him
> leave. And there were other trustees, of which I was one, who
> that felt that he could not continue to lead the university. . . . We
> actually brought in three or four retired presidents . . . to inter-
> view the students, faculty, trustees, staff, to get a sense of what
> was happening. They reported to the board that this president
> could not lead this university at this time. He [Gaither] sat, he
> was a member of the board, and he refused to recuse himself,
> and the board was still split. . . . He brought someone in, who
> had been with the UN to be his liaison with the faculty. And
> after this person had had the job a couple of days, he said, "Bill,
> you have to resign."[73]

At the end of the day, Gaither's strongest supporters were the
neighborhood leaders in Powelton Village and Mantua, the neighborhoods in which he and his wife Robin lived, attended church, and were
involved in the community. They came to his defense at the beginning
of the crisis and stood by him. When it was all over, he would continue
to live in the neighborhood for many years.

On October 20, William Gaither chose not to stand for reap-
pointment to the position of president of Drexel University. He was not
fired by the board of trustees.

The Beginning of the Unraveling

> I sort of saw the ending of it. The board of trustees at that
> point pretty much defended him. There were editorials in the

newspaper. Claude Lewis wrote this . . . incredibly compelling argument in favor of Gaither. But the faculty was really against Gaither and I'm not sure exactly why. I mean, I don't think it had very much to do with him fondling people's feet, which I think he should have been removed for, but there was a general dislike of him, maybe because he wasn't Hagerty, a guy I never met, I don't know. So, that really was the beginning of the unraveling.[74]

David Brooks Arnold, the former UN official brought in by Gaither to try to mediate his conflict with the faculty, recognized the roots of the Gaither drama in the determination by President Hagerty to transform the Drexel Institute of Technology into Drexel University, and in the impact of the decision to develop a humanities faculty that would bring with them their own view of what it means to be a modern university.

In an op-ed piece published in the *Philadelphia Inquirer* on 10/21/87, the day after Gaither stepped down, Arnold presented his views of the situation at Drexel, which would turn out to be prophetic:

> No one should anticipate that Gaither's departure is going to end the problems that beset Drexel. . . . I have found that Philadelphians, including most at the university, think that the crisis has arisen from the personality and management style of this president. With the guidance of outside advisors during my mission, I have concluded otherwise.
>
> I believe strongly that the widely recognized rupture at Drexel University has been caused not by the persona or professional actions of its president, but by an identity crisis within the Drexel community. . . . What I see there is an institute of technology that decided in 1970 to become a university, that has found neither the market nor the resources since to complete such a transition. . . .
>
> It may be that, in retrospect, Gaither did not turn out to be the kind of president the school really needed. However, with a lack of clarity existent then and evident still as to what Drexel can and should be, the school's board of trustees got the president it was looking for. And, the trustees of Drexel University, if they stay on the course on which I perceive they are currently set, are not going to do any better with, or by, their next choice.[75]

Arnold, who had served the UN in the Congo and was no stranger to internecine conflict, did not mince words in his suggestion that responsibility for the crisis went far beyond the conduct of William Gaither, and that the parties to the conflict at Drexel had lost the moral high ground:

> The Drexel University deans and faculty may think that they have been dishonored by their president. Not so. I believe that they have been bruised by the conflict between their humanities and social science professors, whose standard for Drexel is the University of Pennsylvania, and their science and technology professors, whose standard for Drexel is Massachusetts Institute of Technology.
>
> It was the humanities and social science professors who stonewalled what they took to be my mission on campus, supposing—and publicly stating—that no purpose could be served by my presence. That stance provided me with the first signal that the Drexel brouhaha concerns far more than whether Gaither stays or goes. The second indication came from the surprise, and then the dismay, of those members of the board who heard me say that the crisis at Drexel will not be resolved—indeed it will be compounded—by Gaither's decision to step down as president.
>
> Unfortunately, the players in the Drexel affair give no indication that they understand why they have assumed the roles they have, or that they recognize the wider U.S. higher education repertory from which they have chosen their drama. Without such comprehension, the crisis at Drexel will continue, and what is now merely rent asunder will eventually be destroyed. Drexel University shall find that by shedding its institute-of-technology—and in not acknowledging the implications of this decision—it has gained nothing and lost all.[76]

Three days later, writing on the same page, newly installed interim president Harold M. Myers disputed Arnold's assertion:

> [Arnold suggests that] the recent controversies surrounding Drexel University's leadership are merely a symptom of an internal identity crisis within the Drexel community. I disagree. I see a strong continuity in the mission of the university.[77]

Notable in Myers's response, in which he asserted the consistent vision and value of the Drexel education, was his use of the word *merely*. Arnold by no means suggested that the internal identity crisis—the tension between the vision of an academic community resident in the aspirations of the humanities and social sciences faculty and manifest in the universe of the liberal arts colleges and universities, and the research-based, technological view of the science and engineering faculty that saw their standard in MIT and its brethren—was a small matter. It was, in fact, central to his assessment that the crisis facing the institution could continue to spiral out of control and threaten even greater damage to the institution.

Harold Myers's effort to downplay Arnold's commentary could be seen as the attempt of an incoming interim president to downplay the crisis, take it off the pages of the newspapers, and let everyone settle down and go back to work. Harold Myers was a long-time member of the Drexel community who cared deeply about the people and the intensity of the conflict that had erupted, and longed to put the genie back in the bottle and return to the halcyon Hagerty days. Myers's comments, however, were also reflective of a deeper problem, also alluded to by Arnold. The trustees of the university were caught in the middle of a maelstrom involving factors that were at once beyond their comprehension—faculty aspirations and politics; those beyond their control—shifting markets for higher education, a declining local economy and shifting demographics; and those that they would prefer not to touch with a ten-foot pole—claims of sexual harassment against the chief executive of an institution of which they served as voluntary trustees. The deeper problem was that the trustees, who had only a few years earlier viewed their role as being primarily social and ceremonial, were slow in waking up to the fact that they were the fiduciaries for an institution that was under assault by forces from without and within, and largely forces about which they had little direct experience or understanding.

CHAPTER FIVE

Taking Stock

On October 21, the day after Gaither's departure was announced, John Savchak, chairman of the faculty council, commented in the morning *Inquirer*:

> "It's a shame that the idea seems to permeate the community that the faculty took out after him because of some trivial accusation of sexual harassment," he said. "It was more his lack of management ability."[1]

The Gaither episode left the board fractured and chastened. Two members had resigned in the wake of the early vote by the board to override the 4–2 vote of its special committee recommending that Gaither be removed. Many members held strongly to the conviction that the charges were overblown and that the board's authority had been deliberately undermined by the faculty—both notions supported by Savchak's comments.

Board chairman Bob McClements reached out to the leadership of the faculty to begin to build bridges where historically none had previously existed. He invited the faculty to meet with him at his offices at Sun Oil, and they in turn invited him to a faculty meeting.

Harold Myers had assumed the leadership of Drexel University with a personality that soothed the institution at a moment of total exhaustion. He was not a partisan in the battle that had ensued, but rather was dedicated to the university itself. He served as the acting president for eight months and left an enduring legacy of affection with the faculty and staff, if only, perhaps, for the respite that attended his incumbency.

UNHEALED WOUNDS

The story of President Gaither's leaving took on a life of its own, a mythology that was in many ways as important as the events themselves. Faculty, recalling the denouement many years later, continue to reflect the irony of Savchak's comment at the time. Gaither is at first blush excoriated for his sexual misconduct, and then quickly the comments devolve to a litany of his failings as president. The ambiguity of the grounds for faculty "taking out after him" remain. Like many aspects of the Drexel story, the perspectives of the participants do not appear to have softened with time.

For his own part, reflecting on the events that led to his departure as president, William Gaither suggested that with stronger board leadership he could have survived the ordeal and continued to lead the institution. If the more aggressive and dominant Lee Everett had been the board chair rather than Bob McClements, Gaither posits, the board would have held firm.[2] The enrollment struggles of the mid-1980s had been overcome, a solid plan was in place, and the university was on track to grow and prosper. By the year 2000, Gaither later suggested in a private correspondence with a prominent member of the board of trustees, Drexel University would have earned its rightful place as one of the premier technology universities in the land.[3]

Gaither's view may be correct in one sense. As both David Brooks Arnold and John Savchak concluded at the time, the charges brought against Gaither were the symptom, not the problem, and the board could have put that fact forward and demanded that any decision on Gaither's tenure be based on his ability to lead the institution, not the sexual harassment charges that became the issue of record. However, Arnold and Savchak shared a similar conclusion, if for different reasons, that at the end of the day, Gaither no longer enjoyed the "consent of the governed," and in that sense Gaither's view is not convincing.

In examining the historical record, one must accept Savchak at his word: the sexual harassment charge, withdrawn three days after it was filed, would not have felled a leader with popular support. It was instead the means to remove him, or as another member of the faculty commented, "He handed the faculty a pick ax, and they used it." However, if the notion permeates the historical record that Gaither was brought down on charges of sexual misconduct, it is because those are the charges that were leveled in the public dispute, regardless of the underlying motivations in the minds of his antagonists. When Gaither's name is mentioned, even years later, in the *Philadelphia Inquirer*, it is followed by a stock phrase "who resigned over allegations of sexual harassment against Drexel employees." Once the episode had passed no one involved, save Gaither and perhaps a few close associates, had the inclination or the energy to ask that the public record accurately reflect the events as they transpired, and even fewer were interested in listening.

For Drexel's board of trustees, Gaither's removal was a more complicated story, and one that finally demanded their awakening as a real board. The recollection of the Gaither events comes across with less clarity from board members today than from other participants, perhaps reflective of their collective disengagement at the time. That failure of memory may also reflect the recognition that at the historical moment when a board's wisdom was called forth to address serious rifts in the institution, the board was found wanting. Notwithstanding the cogent assessment of the problem set forth at the time by Arnold, one is left with the questions of whether the board at the time understood the nature of the underlying conflict that had beset the institution, and whether through its failure to understand the problem it faced found the wrong solution, and prolonged and deepened the problems facing the institution.

THE DREXEL EDUCATION AND THE STUDENT MARKET

> You want to see something special, you go to a Drexel graduation. The whole family comes out. It's really an event. It's a wonderful thing. In my case, my father went to three colleges and universities, all in the evening, and never received a degree. So I am the first person, even though his father came here in 1880, I am the first person in my family to receive a college degree.[4]

By the late 1980s, the market for Drexel students was beginning to shift. There were several factors at play simultaneously. First, the Philadelphia economy was in the midst of a long period of decline as employment and population migrated out of the city. This economic and demographic shift undercut the traditional urban, commuter student base that had historically been Drexel's core market.

66   WHEN THE POT BOILS

Second, the number of high school graduates was declining in-state and nationally, as illustrated in Figure 3,[5] reducing the overall pool of potential candidates for which higher educational institutions were competing.

Finally, the dramatic rise in college participation rates nationally—which did serve to offset the impact of the declining absolute numbers of high school graduates—was accompanied by a rise in the public funding of a multitiered higher education industry, from the flagship state schools to the community colleges, that comprised a new market of competitive, low-cost educational options for incoming and returning college students.

At the same time, the cost of tuition at Drexel was rising in real terms, with annual increases now substantially above the rate of inflation. In addition, for prospective students, Drexel University offered a five-year baccalaureate degree, in contrast to the normal four-year programs offered by competitors. The traditional argument that co-op earnings enabled students to pay for part of their education was offset by the growing cost, and the additional fifth year.

Bruce Eisenstein, who had observed the shift in the University and the student body since the early 1960s, described the changes as Drexel increasingly competed in the broader student market and students began to demand more than the traditional, barebones Drexel experience:

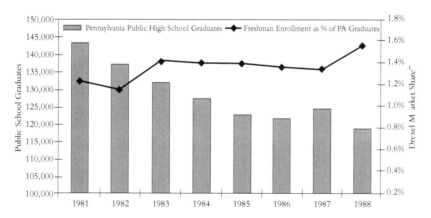

Figure 3. Drexel Fall Freshman Enrollment as Percentage of Pennsylvania Public School Graduates, 1981–1988

Somewhere around the 1980s, we started seeing the children of the baby boomers starting to come to college. And those kids were expecting more from a college education. In fact, what they were expecting was what they call a college experience, not just the education, not the training, not the jobs. It was the whole package. And the whole package consisted of a lot of student-oriented features: leisure time, a much more relaxed atmosphere on the campus, not the intensity that a place like Drexel had traditionally had. And I guess most importantly it was the residential experience. . . . So, on the one hand, we had a decline in the number of students coming to school; and we had a change in the student attitudes towards the kind of educational experience that they wanted.[6]

From the perspective of the board members, who were presented with enrollment data at every meeting, enrollment was a cyclical matter at Drexel, following the trends in the local and national economy. During its history, Drexel enrollment had experienced peaks and valleys, and the volatility during Gaither's administration was no exception. The financial pressures experienced under Gaither differed from earlier years, though, in ways that were not immediately apparent to the board. The university operating structure was evolving as it migrated from its traditional position as a predominantly commuter institute to a residential comprehensive university. The increasing ranks of permanent faculty and the growing debt service related to the financing of dormitories and dining facilities added to the rigidity of the operating budget and increased the operating leverage of the university. This operating leverage placed the university at greater risk in the event of a downturn in enrollments, and increased the urgency of adding additional students at the margin to meet revenue goals, as had been the customary practice since the Hagerty days. However, from the data presented to the board during the period, the dip in freshman enrollments that was experienced in 1986 and 1987, and that led to significant financial pressures, was corrected in 1988, and overall enrollment appeared to be back on track.

Notwithstanding this perspective, Drexel's profile was changing. The residential population, less than 20 percent of the undergraduate student body and housed primarily in the fraternities and sororities the beginning of the decade, was approaching 30 percent by the end of the

decade. The enrollment pressure that was being felt was in the declining
commuter applications. The tuition pricing policy followed by Hagerty
of keeping increases in tuition in line with the growth in inflation had
also shifted under Gaither, and, as Figure 4 illustrates,[7] Drexel University tuition had begun to grow in real terms and outstrip the growth
in the cost of living.

The most conventional analysis of the impact of the combined
shifts in the student market and the university pricing policy was beginning to become evident in the admit and yield rates. These data
were periodically presented to the board members during the period,
but as of 1988 there was no board committee that focused on the
importance of the data or other evidence that the emerging trends
were a matter of discussion or concern. As illustrated in Figure 5,[8] the
admit rate rose sharply in 1983, even in the face of the rising numbers
of applications resulting from the microcomputer program publicity, as
the university expanded its freshman enrollment to meet funding needs.
In the face of rising need for tuition revenue and subsiding applications,
admit rates continued to rise dramatically as the real cost of tuition was
increasing, from the 67 percent rate in 1982 to more than 89 percent
in 1989, while yields remained in the 45–48 percent range, and average
SAT scores declined slightly during the period.

The market pressures were affecting Drexel in a range of ways
beyond the financial dimension. The most obvious pressure was the

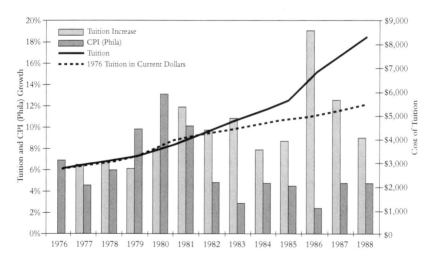

Figure 4. Tuition Growth versus Cost of Living, 1976–1988

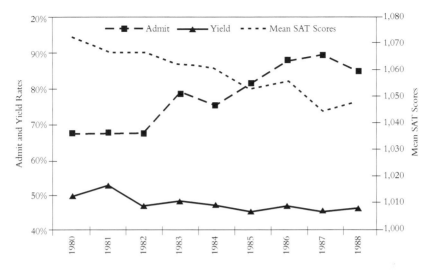

Figure 5. Admissions, Yields, and SAT Scores, 1980–1988

demand for residential facilities, the cost of building dormitories and creating a student life infrastructure. The shift to residential life also had the attendant impact on community relations and the political overlay that was manifest in the Lambda Chi Alpha episode. The more subtle change, though clearly the most significant, was the evolution to university status—an event that was ultimately driven by the combined competitive demands of the faculty, research, and student markets—the attendant development of a humanities faculty, and the unintended and underappreciated cultural and organizational consequences that ensued.

The pricing issue that first became a subject of public debate at the time of the 19 percent price increase reflected the tension between the historical mission of Anthony Drexel's institute and the market realities of running a university. Drexel University, like New York University before it,[9] was slow to realize the inherent conflict of being a private university with a quasi-public mission. Simply stated, the mission-market tension at Drexel was manifest in its efforts to remain a university for the working class while relying on tuition to fund its continued growth and development. The market requirements that it upgrade its facilities and build and retain a quality faculty created significant upward pressures on tuition. This tuition growth, at the same time, made Drexel more vulnerable to competition from the growing public competitors. As Figure 6 illustrates,[10] tuition cost growth was outstripping the growth in per capita income within the city, increasing

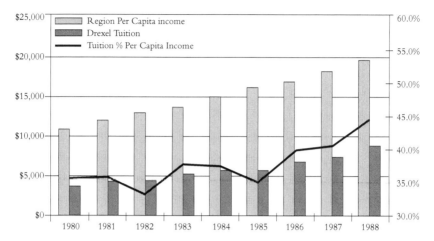

Figure 6. Drexel Undergraduate Tuition versus Regional Income Per Capita

from less than 35 percent of per capita income to 45 percent in just three years, and affecting affordability for the long-time core student market.

The financial crisis that had briefly emerged during Gaither's presidency had subsided. In March 1988, applications were up by 17 percent, auguring the second year of rising enrollments, rising SAT scores, and a declining admit rate under the leadership of the new team running enrollment management. The changes instituted by the new team were not built on new strategic insights, but rather on a simple strategy of emphasizing co-op and the Philadelphia location. Figure 7 illustrates the dip and rebound in applications and acceptances.[11]

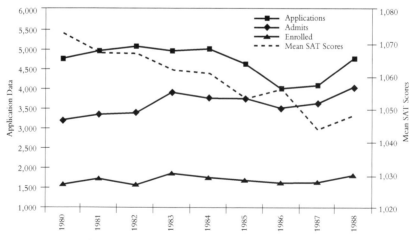

Figure 7. Applications, Admits, and Freshman Enrollment, 1980–1988

FINANCIAL CONDITION
AND THE SEARCH FOR A NEW PRESIDENT

Through the 1980s the board of trustees did not have a finance committee charged with general oversight of the financial condition of the institution. Financial matters were brought to the investment committee or a separate committee that was consulted on matters of salaries and tuition. Gaither did incorporate a presentation of financial ratios within the annual presentation of the ten-year plan to the board of trustees, though the weakness portrayed in the cross-industry comparison did not elicit great concern even among the bankers on the board who were familiar with such analysis. A 1988 financial workshop did result in a set of recommendations to the board, including a prohibition on the further issuance of debt "within the foreseeable future," that further capital expansion projects be contingent on being "fully funded either through gifts or grants," that future programmatic expansion be "carefully examined" in terms of budget impact, and that the university develop a long-range financial plan as a component of a long-range plan.[12]

In December 1987, as a first step in the new presidential search, a consulting team from the Presidential Search Consultation Service (PSCS) of the Association of Governing Boards of Universities and Colleges visited the Drexel campus, and prepared and presented a report to the trustees. The PSCS report would serve to provide the framework for the search that was about to begin, including the needs of the institution, the candidate profile, the search process, and other recommendations. The confidential report focused on issues of governance, board development, and relationships across and participation of constituencies in the institution.

The report to the board, presenting the criteria for the selection of a new president, did not refer to the financial difficulties that had recently beset the institution, the financial condition as suggested in the ratio analysis provided in the ten-year plan, or the enrollment downturn and market challenges that were facing the institution. In the range of desired qualifications for a candidate that is presented in the report, PSCS failed to suggest that a demonstrated understanding of these issues would be warranted. At the time of the initiation of the search for the next president of Drexel University, the issues of the financial condition of the institution and enrollment were simply not of material concern.

The Search

The board leadership was determined to conduct a search that was inclusive of groups across the community, while preserving the ability of the board to control the process. A number of board members felt that their authority had been usurped by the faculty during the Gaither episode, and they were determined not to have their selection of a new president undermined.

The search process that was to be implemented reflected the recommendations from the PSCS report. Bob McClements, the outgoing board chair from Sun Oil, led a nine-member search committee, including trustees and faculty, and a larger, thirty-member advisory committee chaired by Drexel alumnus and board member George Ross. The combined group would define the ideal candidate, and the search committee would be charged to find the person that most closely met that description. The search committee would report back regularly on its progress to the advisory committee, providing details on the progress but without giving names of candidates.

Harold Still, chairman and CEO of Meridian Bancorp, had replaced Bob McClements as board chair in December. The prototypical small-town, patrician banker, Still was a sincere man who was liked and respected across the community. He had agreed to assume the post reluctantly. Still had served on the board for twenty years, but was neither a member of the Drexel family nor a Drexel graduate.

On January 21, 1988, Still met with the combined search committee to give them their charge and did not mince words about the importance of their undertaking for the institution. The search was "the most critical in the long and illustrious history of the university. Drexel has been through a traumatic period, one which stained those basic values of faith and trust, values which are crucial to the life of every human organization." The search was about the fundamental question of "what Drexel should strive to be over the next decade."[13]

At that meeting, the needs of the university were discussed as reflected in the PSCS report submitted one month earlier. The goals of the search reflected issues of governance, organizational development, and the creation of a capital campaign, but omitted any mention of the financial and enrollment matters that had beset the institution. The committee similarly adopted the qualifications statement from the PSCS report almost verbatim, with emphasis on openness, collegiality, and respect across a range of issues including student and minority concerns, shared governance, development, and planning.

Robert Kirkwood, the director of the Middle States Commission, contacted Richard Breslin, then president of the University of Charleston, a small, liberal arts college in West Virginia, to ask if he could submit Breslin's name as a candidate. Breslin had served as the president at Charleston for four years, during which time he had helped to stabilize a struggling, small liberal arts college. Kirkwood believed that Breslin could be effective in board development and addressing the key issues of trust between the faculty and the administration:

> I knew Bill Hagerty, and I knew Bill had a tendency to play things pretty close to the vest. And I thought it was time for Drexel to open up and give the faculty a greater sense of their importance and a greater sense of their involvement in the development of the university. I felt that Breslin's experience at Charleston and particularly at Villanova, in working with the faculty and giving the faculty a sense of their importance and a sense of their involvement in the ongoing development of the institution, would be very useful at Drexel.
>
> And I had the feeling too that he could work with a board in a way which perhaps Hagerty hadn't. Hagerty hadn't achieved a great deal at Drexel. I don't mean to diminish his contributions to Drexel, but I think because of his closeness, his feeling of running a kind of one-man show, isn't quite what Drexel needed. And I had the feeling that Breslin might open things up and might bring people more directly in the development of the university.[14]

Breslin had an unusual profile for the presidency of Drexel. A former Augustinian priest, Breslin's background was as president of a small, liberal arts college, and before that as the dean of the College of Arts and Sciences at nearby Villanova University. In contrast, as suggested by one member of the faculty council leadership at the time,[15] the traditional profile for a candidate for the Drexel presidency would have been an engineer or a businessperson. Nonetheless, by the middle of May, Breslin had emerged as one of four finalists in what had been an exhaustive process. Breslin submitted sixty-five references, and the search committee contacted and interviewed each of them. In addition, a small group of faculty and trustees flew to Charleston where Breslin served as president and interviewed people across the institution. The feedback that they received was uniformly positive.

While the faculty on the search committee were excited about the Breslin candidacy, the search committee recommendation elicited mixed reviews when it was presented to the community. Faculty questioned his qualifications on three counts, first that he was neither an engineer nor a businessperson, second that his experience was at smaller institutions, and finally that he was a priest.

The board, on the other hand, felt that they had their man. They were looking for a president who would salve the wounds of the Gaither presidency. As a priest, Breslin brought a clean image to Drexel, as well as a commitment to working to build a faculty senate, both central issues of concern to the board. The board, trustee George Ross recalled upon reflection, was optimistic about the selection and the future:

> I, like others, were impressed. He had an uncanny way—a very bright man—an uncanny way of remembering everyone's name. So he would come into a room and there were ten people and introduced once he would remember everyone's name. . . . And he was very charming. We had a lot of hope.[16]

CHAPTER SIX

Redemption

The Presidency of Richard Breslin 1988–1992

The board, awakened from the quiescence of the Hagerty years, selected a president to counter the stain of sexual scandal and heal the rift with the faculty. Neither of these would prove, however, to be the matters of greatest urgency for the institution. The challenges that the new president would face would not be ones of image, process, or shared values, but of charting a path for the institution to survive as its traditional market was moving away and the very mission of the institution seemed to lack salience in the competitive higher education environment in which it increasingly sought to compete.

As the Breslin administration struggled with a weakening enrollment picture, it moved the university into direct competition with traditional four-year undergraduate institutions and worsened an already fragile market position. Whether this strategy reflected a lack of understanding of Drexel's traditional market or a determination to migrate away from the university's urban, co-op brand toward the higher educational mainstream would remain unclear and a subject of debate. However, as the situation deteriorated, the perception that the new president did not share the educational values of the institution that he was leading became an underlying source of tension for faculty and trustees alike.

The board's fundamental failure was one of diagnosis: the problems that they thought they were solving were not the real problems that the university faced, and the skills of the president they hired were not attuned to those real problems. Plan after plan and strategy after strategy would be put forward, but none, ironically, sought to build on the plan that had begun to work under Gaither, and none worked. Then, even as the university was reeling, it was hit with a strike by the Teamsters that destroyed whatever was left of the credibility of the leadership and led many across the community to fear for the institution's survival.

THE APPOINTMENT OF RICK BRESLIN

On June 29, 1988, the board of trustees named Richard Breslin to be the tenth president of Drexel University, with a term to commence the following September 1. The same day, the National Science Foundation selected Drexel University to be the lead institution for the development of a new engineering curriculum, as the head of a consortium that would include the University of Pennsylvania, Purdue, Illinois, and others. The NSF received proposals from 190 engineering colleges, and Drexel was awarded a $2.1 million grant.

The fiscal year ending the next day would, in the later words of the chief financial officer, show "substantial improvement in financial position." Enrollment management performance for the coming fall was positive, with enrollment up 17 percent over the prior year, a decline in the admit rate, and an entering class of 1,848 freshman, just thirty-four students below the record class of 1983. Overall, there was reason for optimism.

Upon his appointment as president, Breslin met with three members of the board to agree upon an agenda for his administration. The goals discussed at that meeting, which comprised the measures against which his performance would be evaluated, focused on relationships with the faculty, the development of a new strategic plan, and outreach to the alumni in preparation for a centennial capital campaign.

Upon his arrival, Breslin found an institution that faced real challenges, both organizational and financial, that needed to be addressed if the university was to reach its potential. While he was hired by the board in large part because of the board's determination to counter the problem of Gaither's conduct, Breslin sought to migrate the institution from its engineering roots toward the mainstream of the higher education community. While Breslin saw his role as one of uplifting the faculty, the faculty had a different perspective on the problems facing the institution. From their vantage point, the problem that faced Drexel was not the faculty, but the administration itself.

Overhauling Governance

Based upon the agenda set forth by the board and his own assessment of the institution, Breslin immediately set to work to address the issue of shared governance and the creation of a faculty senate, to develop a new strategic plan, and to lay the foundation for the Centennial Campaign fundraising drive, set to occur in conjunction with the one hundredth anniversary of the institute in 1991. Fundamental to all of these was the larger issue of board development and the board's role in the institution.

Breslin's assessment of the board was that it was disengaged and lacking in financial commitment to the institution. He saw board development as a major challenge, and critical to the ability to implement a successful capital campaign. In his first board report, dated September 21, 1988, less than one month after the beginning of his administration, Breslin informed the board that he had engaged Dr. Richard Chait, a national expert in board development, to lead a board retreat focused on "the Board's understanding of its role" and to serve as board mentor. In this report, he also stressed the importance of board leadership and engagement in fundraising.

> It is my honest judgment that the Board needs to give serious attention to the role it will play in not only assisting the University, but also in making it possible for the potential of Drexel to be realized. It is my preliminary judgment that Drexel verges on the brink of greatness. We have an excellent faculty, a strong student body, and a national reputation. Our co-op education program is the most comprehensive co-op plan in the country. Our faculty's publication record has increased significantly and research dollars for Drexel are at an all time high.
>
> Concomitantly, we are confronted with major opportunities and challenges which, at times, can be met without new funding. In other instances, it will be the availability of external financial resources that will make the difference between mediocrity and greatness. It is very clear that our University community will look to the University's chief development officer, its president and most especially to the STEWARDS of the University to allow Drexel to fully flower.[1]

In addition to the direct work with the board, Breslin viewed the creation of a faculty senate, one of the central goals established by the

board, as an important step in improving the governance of the institution, and as a key commitment that he had made to the faculty. He
engaged Barbara Taylor, a co-author with Richard Chait and affiliated
with the Association of Governing Boards, to serve as his advisor in the
creation of the new charter that would "at one and the same time,
recognize the policy-setting role of Trustees, the leadership role of the
president, and the participatory role of the faculty."[2] Breslin also reor-
ganized the offices in the Main Building to reflect his intention to
elevate the status of the faculty in the institution. The office of the
financial vice president, traditionally located adjacent to the office of
the president on the first floor, was moved up to the second floor, and
the office of the university vice president for academic affairs and
provost was moved to the space adjacent to his office.

In December, Breslin informed the board that he had reached
substantial agreement with the faculty on the principal terms of a charter
for the creation of a faculty senate. The proposed document would
concede to the faculty primary control over curricular matters and
membership on key nonfinancial board committees. In his December
report, Breslin quoted Barbara Taylor giving her views on the link between effective governance and board-faculty collaboration, in which she
effectively labeled the problems with the Drexel board as it had evolved.

> Effective boards tend to view themselves as part of the univer-
> sity community while ineffective boards appear to see them-
> selves more as outsiders and supervisors. Effective boards seek
> faculty input even if the process is painful, while, in contrast,
> ineffective boards tend to isolate themselves and often see faculty
> as adversaries to be outwitted and outmaneuvered. Faculty-
> trustee contact appears to benefit both parties, demystifying for
> each the role of the other and helping to break down stereo-
> types and correct misinformation that gets in the way of shared
> decision making.[3]

Taylor came to her work for Drexel from the perspective of
having worked with a cross section of universities and colleges. However, as a private school outside the liberal arts tradition, Drexel's board
was historically detached from the community that it was empowered
to govern, and the norms and traditions of higher educational governance were not reflected in the Drexel experience. The existence of an
increasingly assertive faculty that embraced the shared governance tra-

ditions of the liberal arts institution and fully expected to have those traditions respected at Drexel represented a direct challenge to the culture of governance at Drexel. While many members of the board recognized the legitimacy of faculty demands for a greater role in the governance of the institution, others believed that the faculty had usurped board authority in their attack on William Gaither and were overstepping their proper role in the institution.

The faculty shared this sense of antagonism between themselves and the board, and the perspective that the creation of a faculty senate would not end the harsh divide that existed. One long-time member of the faculty noted the readiness of the faculty to go after the new president when the time came in the same manner that they had in "taking out" Gaither:

> That's one of the places that he [Breslin] and the trustees may have had a misunderstanding. Take a code word that says, "Improve the relations between the administration and the faculty." And the president takes that to mean, "Establish a university senate that will mediate and improve relations," whereas the Trustees meant, "Kick the hell out of the faculty and kick them in the ass." I don't know if that's true, but it struck me at the time. But in any case the people who were most active in the faculty senate were inevitably those who had been most involved with taking out Gaither. So that as soon as Breslin began to be perceived as acting like Gaither, the knives were already sharpened and they came right out of the bureau drawer.[4]

Breslin pushed ahead with the negotiations with the faculty. On December 21, the chair of the faculty council presented a favorable report on the proposed charter, which emphasized the new areas of faculty participation in the governance of the institution, and closed with an affirmative statement of the ultimate authority of the board:

> It was recognized throughout the development and discussion of this Charter that the trustees retain the ultimate responsibility for the operation of the University and nothing contained in the Charter is construed to be a waiver of their authority.[5]

Breslin presented the completed document to the trustees for their consideration and ultimate approval. In Breslin's mind, the document that was delivered to the trustees marked a fundamental change in the institution, and he had made good on his commitments. Within one year of his arrival he had delivered on one of the central goals that he had been hired to achieve.

The trustees gave their approval in principle on March 15, with final details to be completed. Covering the story the next day, Huntly Collins of the *Inquirer* quoted Harold Still declaring the new charter "a major step forward. For the first time in several years, we have faculty, the board and the administration all working together as a team." Jackie Mancall, the chair of the faculty council declared, "This is a new era for Drexel," and the faculty leaders credited Breslin with providing the leadership to enable the agreement to be successfully negotiated.[6]

The irony of the collective sense of enthusiasm at the time of the adoption of the senate charter was that it reflected more a sense of relief than a coming together on a statement of shared values. While the notion of a misunderstanding over the meanings of words may be overstated and cynical, it nonetheless holds a degree of truth. The faculty notions of shared governance derived from the principle that the faculty was the core of the institution, and that the senate charter was an articulation of that principle and the powers that flowed from it. The board, newly engaged in the life of the institution and comprising largely corporate leaders with little grounding in the history of the academy, saw the faculty as an important constituency of the institution, but certainly not one with rights or moral standing equal to or greater than the administration or the board itself.

The violations of the charter that would become a regular occurrence in the years ahead would create a festering sore that would vitiate the teamwork that Still saw emerging upon its original passage. Those violations stemmed from a fundamental misunderstanding over what was being celebrated that day. For the faculty, it was the true birth of Drexel as a university, while for the newly engaged board it was a means to placate the faculty so that the institution could move onto the business at hand.

Strategic Planning

Strategic planning was one of the key priorities articulated by the board in its conversations with Breslin, along with governance and fundraising, and Breslin understood that effective strategic planning would build on the efforts that he was making in improving board participation and faculty shared governance. Breslin engaged the community early on in the evaluation of the university mission statement and the development of a strategic plan that would represent a true, community-wide statement of goals, values, and direction.

The board engaged in a two-day retreat on strategic issues in February 1989 that galvanized board understanding of the importance of the mission statement and greater direct board participation if they were to carry out their stewardship role in overseeing the academic and financial well-being of the university. Several key issues emerged from the retreat. The board determined that an endowment fund of $250 to 350 million was appropriate to the size of the institution and mission, in contrast with the current level of approximately $70 million. The continued level of tuition dependency was disturbing. Admissions remained a problem, as well as the growing level of deferred maintenance. The timeline for the development of the strategic plan was to have a draft plan completed for consideration by the board at its December meeting.

Management Changes

As Breslin looked across the senior cadre of management, he had determined to bring new, professional leadership into key areas, including academic affairs, development, government relations, and enrollment management. In the cases of board development, governance, and enrollment management, he engaged national industry advisors to assist him in analyzing the issues facing the institution, and to assist in identifying candidates for the positions.

As Breslin sought to reorganize enrollment management and admissions, he appointed a national consultant, Ron Ingersoll of Ingersoll Williams, to assess the situation. In his October 1988 board report—the same month that freshman enrollment neared its all-time high—Breslin lauded Ingersoll as "among the very best people in the field of admissions."

On January 10, Ingersoll Williams offered their preliminary conclusions that the university's financial aid budget was insufficient to enable the university to achieve its targets for student quantity or quality.[7] By any reasonable comparison, financial aid had historically been underfunded at Drexel. The enrollment study undertaken by Ingersoll Williams suggested that Drexel University was spending $0.08 per tuition dollar on financial aid, in contrast with a range of $0.14–0.22 at competing schools. Problems with retention to graduation had generally been linked to the underfunding of financial aid, and the reduced amounts of aid available to upperclass students. The application of co-op earnings to offset financial aid eligibility after a student's freshman year was one of the dominant aspects of the "Drexel Shaft."

By the following May, Breslin implemented an overhaul of the enrollment management area, including the appointment of a dean reporting to the president, a substantial increase in budget support, and the integration of admissions, financial aid, retention, and institutional research "to improve our marketing posture and meet the challenges of a more competitive marketplace."[8]

Gary Hamme, who had come over from the co-op office to run admissions, was not allowed to apply for the position. Breslin's determination to remove Hamme was reflective of his preference for external advice and expertise over internal staff.[9] Officially, Hamme recalled later, he was judged to be not qualified for the position, as his two years in admissions at Drexel were his only experience in enrollment management.[10] From his own vantage point, he and Dick Mortimer had successfully reversed the decline in applications and enrollments, and delivered the second largest class in the school's history that fall. In Hamme's view, Breslin was determined to move away from co-op and the attributes that had made Drexel successful in the past. Hamme was crushed by the experience.[11]

Vincent Stach, who served as treasurer at the time, and had worked in the administration since the waning days of the Hagerty administration, was puzzled by Breslin's determination to remove Hamme and Mortimer, in light of their dramatic success in spurring applications and enrollment:

> During this very brief period, like a year or two, applications skyrocketed. Actually applications hit an all-time high up until that point. . . . Gary Hamme was the type of guy that, if you gave him a challenge, he would find ways to solve the challenge, ways to do it, and that's how he and Mortimer approached this enrollment issue and they did quite well. And it's hard to say what would have happened after that, except that Gaither ended up being forced to resign and then Breslin came in. And . . . I was never quite clear on this even though I asked some of those people directly, I still never got a straight answer, but those two guys were moved out of that position and enrollment suffered.[12]

Financial Problems Emerge

During the first six months of his administration, Breslin had completed the creation of a faculty senate, engaged the board in the early stage work of board development necessary for the centennial capital campaign, initiated the development of a new strategic plan by engaging the trustees and faculty in the development of a mission statement, and taken steps to implement administrative reorganization in key areas. In a short period of time, Breslin had moved forward in the key priority areas laid out by the board of trustees. Ironically, however, it was the areas that had been viewed as less critical during the presidential search that would loom as the most significant challenges to the institution.

Over the course of the winter months and into the spring of 1989, the admissions prospects for the coming fall were weak, as applications were down 20 percent from the prior year. As a tuition-dependent institution, the prospect of a decline in enrollments had immediate budgetary consequences. In response to the difficult budget process that emerged, Breslin created the Priorities Review Committee (PRC) as a joint faculty/administration committee to weigh budget priorities and provide for broad-based input on budgetary matters from across the school. The creation of advisory committees emerged early on in Breslin's administration as a strategy for engaging broad constituencies in addressing issues facing the institution.

At a winter board retreat, financial matters were beginning to assume a more prominent role, and the "need for longer-range budget planning, and long-range goals to be developed and implemented."[13] Tuition dependency, admissions, and deferred maintenance were among the areas deemed critical. In his report to the finance committee of the board in March, Breslin suggested that tuition increases, which had totaled 39 percent over the previous three years, needed to be reduced, while financial aid needed to be increased. He recognized that holding down tuition and increasing the commitment to financial aid would force other hard choices on the expenditure side.

Breslin's recommendation to the finance committee of a 7.95 percent tuition increase for the coming year, only modestly above the 5 percent inflation rate at the time, was rejected by the finance committee two weeks later in favor of an 8.5 percent increase, with the increase dedicated to funding deferred maintenance. Board members at the time noted that this small adjustment upward was "a small price to pay" in order to "make a small down payment" on addressing the

looming problem of deferred maintenance.[14] Of course, this noble statement was easy to make when the small price was extracted from the
students' pockets rather than their own.

At that same meeting, the finance committee charged the administration to (1) establish a two-year program of cost controls and
specifically address both academic and administrative program cost
growth, (2) develop a three-year plan to improve the financial condition of the university with a special focus on development and enrollment management, (3) keep tuition increases to a minimum to minimize
the impact on recruitment and retention, and (4) assess the overall
workforce and develop a staffing plan that was consistent with the
current and projected enrollment trends of the university.[15]

The urgency of the resolution was echoed by the admonition of
the investment committee report at the meeting that "cautioned against
any further withdrawals from endowment, for any reason" in response
to a board action in December that authorized borrowing up to $6
million from the endowment.[16]

In April, the board approved a budget for the 1989–90 fiscal year
based on a 1,770-student freshman class plus 230 transfers for a total of
two thousand new students. The budget required a contribution of
$1.25 million from reserves. In his May 1989 board report, Breslin set
aside earlier urgent calls for the construction of a new residential dormitory, noting that the project was no longer economically viable. At
the end of the same report, Breslin made the opening argument for a
fundamental change in the direction of the university toward a smaller,
leaner but higher quality institution. Faced with declining enrollments,
Breslin suggested planning for a downsizing of the university, as he
argued that the university "cannot be all things to all people" and
suggested a new "philosophy of selective excellence."[17]

By June 1989, the executive committee of the board determined to
implement a contingency plan cutting $2.5 million from the budget for
the fiscal year that would start at the end of that month, believing that
the goal of two thousand incoming students would not be achieved. By
the end of the summer, the confirmed freshman class would be 1,510—
338 students below the prior fall—and 1,696 new students overall.

SETTING FORTH THE BRESLIN AGENDA

On September 19, 1989, Richard Breslin delivered his first State of
the University speech. One year into his presidency, he presented his

vision for the university in a way that blended the mission of the school and the perspective that he brought to the institution from his ecclesiastic background.

> As a University with a well-deserved reputation for techno-
> logical expertise, Drexel will play a critically important role in
> our society though the 1990s and into the 21st century. That
> role is to teach the moral and ethical application of technology,
> to equip our students with the knowledge and wisdom to help
> meet the pressing needs of our society. I am convinced that
> Drexel will play a special role in higher education, namely, to
> be a leader in the critically important task of providing a moral
> context to the pursuit and dissemination of knowledge.
>   As is the case with all great universities, we need to reflect
> on the ethical principles undergirding our academic disciplines,
> and to embrace a philosophy of ethics across the curriculum.
> Surely, if we teach well and research well, but do not prepare
> our students for the real world in which they will live and
> work, we will have failed them. It is my view that we must
> communicate ethical principles not just in theory but also in
> practice. . . . In a word, if we have to compromise our prin-
> ciples, our positions as teachers, researchers, staff, and adminis-
> trators become unworthy of their inherent dignity.[18]

At the same time that he articulated a vision for the direction of the university, Breslin described the harsh realities that would challenge the institution at least in the short term. He noted specifically the demographic changes and the projected decline in the number of eighteen-year-olds. In addition, he suggested that the rate of attrition was too high, and laid the blame on the pattern of tuition increases over the previous years and the lack of financial aid. And he suggested that the impact of the school's recent turmoil could not be understated. Faced with the reality of the financial situation, from the budgeted level of two thousand students to a revised target of 1,750, Breslin suggested that a downsizing of the university was a possible consequence.

> Consequently, we need to cut costs, enhance revenues, and plan
> well for our future. While we have barely begun to study the
> implications of the term "downsize," we need to approach our
> situation very practically and realistically, never losing sight of

our founder's vision and our distinct niche in higher education. As we are tuition-driven, we cannot continue to expand in personnel and programs. For the long-term good of the University, we must assess the total number of personnel and programs the University can afford. It is my professional judgment that across-the-board cuts mediocritize an institution and should never be a strategy undertaken by the University.[19]

Finally, having opened his remarks by praising the progress toward shared governance that had been realized in the creation of the faculty senate, he indicated that in the spirit of shared governance, he would look to the newly created Priorities Review Committee to assess the ways in which budget reductions could best be realized.[20]

Changing Business as Usual

In September 1989, a *Policy Perspectives* article, published by the Institute for Research in Higher Education at the University of Pennsylvania and funded by the Pew Charitable Trusts, opened with the following statement:

It happened again last spring. Only after the president's recommendation of another 8.5 percent increase in tuition had been formally adopted did this trustee emeritus give voice to his frustration: "How long," he asked, "before the day of reckoning? For how many more years will tuition have to increase faster than inflation? Is it not possible to achieve savings—ever? What special privilege allows the college to abandon good business practices?"[21]

President Breslin included a copy of the article in his distribution to the board members, and at the October board meeting articulated the philosophy set forth in the report, specifically that Drexel needed to cap tuition rate increases in the 5 percent range to stay competitive, rather than continuing with higher increases.[22]

In early October, CFO Freddie Gallot reported to the finance committee on the results of the fiscal year ended June 30, 1989. Gallot noted that the results for the year had been favorable, in large measure due to the budget cuts earlier in the year, though he noted that deferred maintenance needs had grown to more than $30 million. The Suspense Fund, which represented the general reserves, had grown from $2.7 million to $4.1 million, a trend that he wanted to see continue.

Gallot's presentation noted the inclusion of a $2.5 million contingency line item for the current year, and the early stages of budget planning for the next fiscal year that would include a continued hiring freeze and the implementation of an expenditure control system to keep department heads from overspending their budgets. Tuition increases would be capped at 5 percent as part of the implementation of a new tuition philosophy, in which Gallot concurred. "This in our judgment is extremely critical considering the increases assessed over the past five years and the fact that we are quickly pricing ourselves out of the market."[23]

At the October board meeting, the impact of the decline in freshman enrollment for the fall of 1989 was a matter of serious concern. In addition to having three hundred fewer students, there were empty dorm beds. The financial analysis stressed the long-term impact of the decline, as the loss of students in the incoming class would continue to have a negative impact on the university's financial position as that class passed through the institution over the subsequent five years. The lost students represented $2.8 million in lost tuition revenue plus $125,000 in lost dorm fees.

At the January meeting of the finance committee, Breslin noted that over the prior five years, tuition had increased by an average of 11.6 percent in comparison with a Consumer Price Index increase of 4 percent, while during the same period fall undergraduate enrollment fell from 7,434 to 6,612. Breslin's perspective on the enrollment problems that Drexel was facing focused on two conclusions: first, that the market decline was manifest in the smaller number of graduating eighteen-year-olds in the region, and second, that through its large tuition increases Drexel was pricing itself out of the market. In economic terms, the institution faced declining demand and price inelasticity. Breslin recommended that the board limit the tuition increase to 6 percent, and downsize and reallocate resources accordingly.

The conclusions that the administration had reached about the nature of the student market left Drexel with little room to maneuver. Enrollment was likely to decline as the number of graduating high school students declined, and demand was highly inelastic, so that further tuition increases would in turn further reduce the number of enrolled students. The *Policy Perspectives* report had become an article of faith: the problem was one of market forces not of marketing effectiveness.

On February 7, 1990, Breslin was quoted by Huntly Collins in a *Philadelphia Inquirer* article extolling the virtues of the new-found perspective on tuition setting:

Breslin said the way the tuition increase was arrived at was as important as the figure itself. Instead of adding up expenses and then setting its tuition to help cover them, school officials set the tuition and then pared their expenditures to fit budget constraints, he said. "This procedure, used so successfully in the corporate world, will ensure maximum efficiency in the university operations," Breslin said.

The procedure was recently recommended for all colleges and universities by a national panel of leading educators assembled by the Philadelphia-based Pew Charitable Trusts. Drexel is one of the first schools in the Philadelphia area to actually adopt such a plan.[24]

Taking a more cynical view, Tony Glascock, professor of anthropology, saw Breslin's behavior in a different light. The tuition policy was not a sign of conviction or a keen sense of the market, but rather an infatuation with the latest proclamation of opinion leaders in the industry, mirroring Breslin's affection for well-known, highly paid consultants.[25]

Implementing Shared Governance

The creation of the faculty senate was a significant accomplishment during the early period of the Breslin presidency in the eyes of the faculty and Breslin alike. Tom Canavan saw the strengths that Breslin brought to the institution in his commitment to shared governance:

> His style was very open. . . . It was Rick's idea to try to establish a meaningful faculty senate that would have a real role in governance within the institution. . . . Rick, unlike his predecessors, was able to take criticism, disagreement easily, really easily. One of his favorite statements is, "There's no such thing as a stupid question." But he also was able to entertain objections all the time and never held it against anybody, so far as I could ever determine, that a person disagreed with him.[26]

One senior member of the faculty who was active in faculty governance over the years held a more sardonic view of Breslin's efforts, suggesting that while he worked diligently to negotiate the senate charter with the faculty, "he violated it also every time it was convenient for him, like they all do."[27]

The primary area of dispute early on came in early 1990 when Breslin decided to combine the College of Humanities and Social Sciences and the College of Science to create a College of Arts and Sciences. It was a natural move for Breslin to pursue, as he himself was a humanist from an arts and sciences tradition, and had seen the value of creating a combined college of arts and sciences from the beginning of his tenure. However, his determination to move ahead became a point of friction with the newly created senate. He asked for senate approval, but when they failed to act in a timely manner, he simply merged the colleges.

The College of Arts and Sciences at Drexel University, seen early on by William Hagerty as important element of a great technological university, finally came into being at Drexel University on July 1, 1990. Its final emergence, however, was not as the lynchpin of Hagerty's plan to create a great technological university, but rather the product of a humanist-president in pursuit of his own liberal arts vision, who in the process superceded the governance process that had been his own creation.

But as a general matter, the faculty had demanded shared governance, and they got it. They served on board committees, and they participated in the budget process through the priorities review committee. The university was now faced with escalating financial pressures, as Breslin had clearly articulated in his speech. Undergraduate enrollment, the primary source of revenue, was stagnant at best—a situation generally viewed as due to demographic factors beyond anyone's control—and the days of large tuition increases were over. Faced with fiscal constraints, the board was increasingly unwilling to allow draws on the endowment to shield the operating budget from the realities of the marketplace. The bottom line was cost control. Drexel, like most schools, continually added courses and programs and rarely eliminated them and, in the eyes of the administration, continued to offer too many courses that had small numbers of students in them.

On May 10, 1990, Breslin sent a memo to the steering committee of the faculty senate creating the Blue Ribbon Commission on the Quality and Scope of Academic Life, setting forth the market challenges facing the school and the new committee:

> There are a number of external factors which have the potential to affect, profoundly, Drexel's future. Higher education is facing a shrinking demographic pool at the traditional full-time

undergraduate level. For the northeast, in fact, the steepest drop
in the slope has only just begun. Moreover, there are significant
signs that, in these smaller graduating high school classes, fewer
students may opt for a technological education. A further com-
plication which seems to be emerging is a difficult choice between public and private education being visited upon families
by virtue of economic considerations. The affordability of a college
education has forced cost into the forefront of family decisions
regarding the selection of a college. Thus, Drexel now competes
for students with many public colleges and universities which
were formerly not significant alternatives for our applicants.[28]

The commission would comprise the vice president of academic
affairs, the deans of the colleges of Arts and Sciences, Business, and
Engineering, two trustees and six members of the faculty. The commission was charged with the hard and unforgiving work of determining
the priorities toward the downsizing of the institution. It would review
enrollment trends, determine which academic programs and support
services should be emphasized, maintained, curtailed, or eliminated, and
ultimately recommend to the president which instructional and research programs and support services should receive increased funding;
current funding; decreased funding; or, no funding at all.[29] The commission would begin on June 30, 1990, and present preliminary results
on January 31, 1991, and final recommendations on April 30, 1991.

Ethics Day

Consistent with the vision that he had proclaimed in his first State of
the University speech, Breslin announced that the university convocation scheduled for October 17, 1989 would be celebrated as "Ethics
Day." It was designed as a day of workshops and speakers illustrating the
ethical dimension of all facets of the Drexel curriculum and life. Ethics
Day became viewed by some as emblematic of problems that were
emerging between the president and the faculty.

As articulated in his speech a few weeks earlier, Breslin saw the
integration of the humanities with engineering and the sciences as an
opportunity for growth in all of the dimensions of the university, and
saw the power of integrating ethics into the core curriculum and
culture of a technology university as an important role in society. The
National Science Foundation project for which Drexel had been named

the lead institution was exactly about the integration of humanities into the engineering sciences.

Others were less forgiving in their interpretation of Breslin's vision and his motives. At its most basic level, the unease engendered by Ethics Day was in the position that it suggested about the president of the institution relative to the faculty. Jacques Catudal, himself a philosopher and ethicist—who on Ethics Day chaired a panel on "Ethics in the Academy"—took great offense at Breslin's having declared himself at the outset of his tenure to be the "ethical president" and saw it as a profound—and profoundly disturbing—misinterpretation of the events surrounding his appointment as president:

> When he proclaimed himself the ethical president, I thought, "This can't be." . . . How could they have hired two such deluded people in a row. That he was the ethical president who would save us from our original sin . . . there was always the assumption that we were lost children.[30]

A senior member of the faculty council reacted acerbically, recalling the day, some ten years later. "It was like we had sinned and this was to be our absolution. Whatever Gaither did, Gaither did. We didn't deserve that."[31]

Ethics Day became a metaphor for the growing sense of discomfort between Breslin and certain groups within the faculty, particularly those who saw his vision as shifting the focus of the institution away from its traditional strengths. Some saw the source of the discomfort as located in Breslin's identity as a humanist rather than an engineer, and the belief that he was seeking to downplay the role of engineering in the university. For others, Breslin's vision for Drexel was simply inconsistent with Drexel's history and core mission.

WATER TORTURE

In March 1990, the board adopted a budget for the coming school year. Tom Wieckowski, dean of enrollment management, indicated that applications for the fall were generally positive, and the budget was once again predicated on a total of two thousand new students, including 1,750 freshman and 250 transfers. The board also approved funding $1.25 million of the current year operating deficit from the unrestricted endowment, and in contravention of its resolution in June 1988 and the vocal concerns expressed earlier by the CFO Freddie Gallot, authorized the issuance of $25 million in new bonds, including $2.0 million to fund deferred maintenance costs, which were estimated to exceed $30 million. The board also approved a tuition increase of 5.95 percent.[32]

Over the ensuing months, a number of issues arose that continued to undermine further the projected financial position of the university. These included internal actions that served to constrain resources, as well as external political and market forces. Taken together, these issues compounded one upon the other to exacerbate the problems facing the institution, and to undermine the confidence of the community and credibility of its leadership.

Implementing an Endowment Spending Rule

In May 1990, the investment committee and finance committee held two special meetings to move forward with the creation of a spending rule to limit future expenditures of the endowment on operations. The meeting was called "to consider the prospect of installing a Spending Rule to protect and insulate the University Endowments against inflation and invasion for operating or other administration purposes."[33]

The dilemma was twofold. First, the university was dependent on the endowment funds to supplement tuition revenue that was not meeting the operating needs of the institution because of enrollment declines and the suggested restraint on tuition increases. Second, the university badly needed to build up its long-term endowment, and the current practice of investing heavily in bonds to produce current income had limited the overall investment return and the growth in principal value.

The investment committee members were of the view that the board was using the endowment inappropriately, and sought a constraint on borrowing endowment funds for operating purposes. The determination of the investment committee to protect the endowment reflected their sense of fiduciary responsibility to the institution over the long term, and the administration's lack of credibility around current year budget discussions due to the historical unpredictability of enrollment and undergraduate tuition revenue.

At a second meeting, the administration "restated their need for a dependable stream of revenue and assistance from the endowment fund in order to balance the budget in this transitional period. The changes and programs currently being initiated need time to take effect.

If the endowment money is not available, drastic spending cuts must be undertaken immediately."[34]

The moneymen would have their way, but provided a modicum of latitude. The committees agreed to a phase-in of a spending rule over a three-year period. Upon a motion by A. J. Drexel Paul, the committees agreed to install a spending rule, to rescind the $1.25 million loan previously approved by the board, and to provide a minimum level of operating budget support for the 1990–91 and 1991–92 fiscal years.[35]

Enrollment Declines Continue

Meeting on June 18, 1990, the finance committee suggested that the strategic plan in process should be modified to reflect an average class of 1,500 freshmen. This recommendation, and the awareness of the spending cuts that it would compel, elicited a response from Tom Hindelang, professor of finance and the president of the faculty senate. Hindelang, a long-time observer of the operations of the institution, indicated that the faculty believed that more emphasis should be placed on increasing revenue rather than continuing with program cuts. In response, David Wilmerding, long-time member of the board and the investment committee chair, expressed concern as to whether the faculty understood the severity of the university's financial situation. Hindelang noted his "appreciation for the improvements which had been made in incorporating faculty in the building of the budget and the establishment of the priorities."[36] But the frustration on the part of both parties was evident.

Two days later, at the June 20, 1990, executive committee meeting, the administration recommended a $2 million cut in the budget as a result of a projected shortfall of 188 students below the fall freshman admissions target of two thousand, as well as an anticipated cutback in state aid of $385,000. The finance committee indicated that it had reviewed all of the proposed cuts, while the investment committee "reiterated concerns about withdrawals from endowment, due to the essentiality of growth in endowment to the future of the University."[37] As reflected in the minutes of the meeting, Breslin announced with fanfare the formation of a new committee to help address the situation, "The very important Blue Ribbon Commission on the Quality and Scope of Academic Life at Drexel University,"[38] to be chaired by provost Denny Brown.[39] At the same meeting, the committee approved the rescission of the $1.25 million loan to the operating budget and the adoption of the spending rule.

At the September 26 board meeting, the board addressed the issue of continued faculty growth and a majority of the board stressed the need for the budget committees that had been created "to confront the realities of the situation facing the University and to deal with those realities in a positive and responsible way."[40]

In December, the board continued to grapple with budget matters as the priorities review committee under Richard Schneider was preparing recommendations for $6 million in further budget cuts. The blue ribbon commission was facing greater difficulty as it sought to tackle the issues of program elimination, and its work was likely to be delayed, as the president informed the Board.

> As the charge to the University Advisory Committee transcends the enhancement, maintenance, or elimination of programs, [Provost] Brown will report to you that some additional time will be needed before the Advisory Committee can complete the charge given to it. I believe that we will find that the University Advisory Committee's work will produce an even more focused university and there will be economies effected by the work being done by the Provost and this Committee.[41]

Finally, at the December meeting, Dean Wieckowski indicated that applications were running 20 percent below the prior year.

Two months later, in February 1991, the financial presentation to the finance committee indicated that performance was 12 percent over budget, with tuition revenue estimated to be $1.8 million ahead of projections. Fall freshman enrollment of 1,596 turned out to be 154 below the originally budgeted number, but thirty-four higher than the revised estimate later in the enrollment cycle and 5 percent higher than the previous class. For the coming fall of 1991, however, Wieckowski indicated that applications were down 41 percent from the prior year. The only factor different from the prior year was a computer problem that led to a two-week delay in responding to 1,200 inquiries.

At the same meeting, a newly formed board committee on enrollment management commented that one cause for alarm was a change in the perception of the university in a number of traditional feeder schools where "previous lowering of the academic standards required to be accepted have hurt the university's image in our targeted high schools where we are now considered a "safety school" of last resort."[42]

Vincent Stach described a budgeting process that could never achieve balance, as the continual downward revisions in enrollment projections led to new rounds of cuts:

> As soon as the budget is presented, you would go back and work on contingency cuts. We always had a couple million bucks, a million, two million bucks, in a contingency, until the enrollment was known in the fall, and we found out we blew right through the contingency, and we had to do some other things. . . . It would be like cutting to the bone. Everything had already been cut, and we would cut some more. . . . Everything you could think of was probably done from a cost-cutting, expense-saving standpoint, with minimal focus on revenue generation.[43]

On March 6, 1991, Tom Wieckowski described the rationale for deciding to eliminate application deadlines—a step that arguably worsened both the appeal of the university and the ability to predict enrollment—in an article in the *Chronicle of Higher Education* entitled "Applications Down at Private Campuses and Up at Public Colleges":

> Private colleges are really in trouble. This generation of parents is just not willing to sacrifice $20,000. At the end of the decade, many colleges will be out of business if they can't show students they have a special niche. . . . Students are applying late because they know nobody will turn them down. We won't be putting any great dependency on deadlines, because we will be better off institutionally if we can get those additional students.[44]

Two weeks later, Huntly Collins, writing in the *Philadelphia Inquirer,* noted that other schools in the city were experiencing application declines, with the University of Pennsylvania down 8 percent, Temple down 24 percent, and Drexel down 29 percent:

> Thomas Wieckowski, dean of enrollment management at Drexel, said the university had been especially hard-hit by the decline in 18-year-olds. At some of Drexel's feeder high schools in the area, there had been a 20 percent drop in the number of

graduating seniors this spring alone, he said. In addition, Drexel has been tarnished by what Wieckowski called "Philadelphia-bashing" here and elsewhere in the country. 'We have been finding that high school counselors are telling students that Philadelphia had a 'problem' and they don't recommend it for college," he said.[45]

On March 28, 1991, Collins, again writing in the *Inquirer,* covered the next act in the drama under the story, "Drexel eliminates 94 jobs to slow growth of tuition":

> Richard W. Schneider, senior vice president, said more cuts may be needed if the General Assembly approves a $3.5 million reduction in Drexel's state funding. The cut, recommended by Governor Casey, amounts to about 60 percent of Drexel's state appropriation. No faculty jobs would be cut.[46]

Loss of State Appropriations

In Pennsylvania, for many years, private higher educational institutions received funding from the state on an annual basis. For Drexel University, the funding level had approximated $4.5 million annually, and had grown to $5.8 million in the fiscal year ending June 30, 1990. Governor Robert Casey, facing fiscal difficulties in the state, had determined to eliminate funding for private schools in the state budget, and in the budget for the fiscal year beginning July 1, 1991, had proposed a 60 percent cut, or a $3.5 million cut in what Drexel had budgeted for the year.

At the February 1991 finance committee meeting—a committee on which the faculty were not represented—President Breslin indicated that the prospect of state funding was looking worse, and while Drexel was discussing a collective lobbying strategy with the nearby University of Pennsylvania, he suggested that the trustees may want to begin to consider courses of action that included ending the university's status as a state-aided institution. The loss of state aid would have a permanent impact on the financial profile of the institution, as it represented 8.5 percent of net tuition revenue.

Trustee Ervin Bickley responded to the prospect of a combined impact of a state aid cut and continued enrollment declines by suggesting that "if additional funds had to be cut from the budget . . . the faculty would have to participate in the reductions." Richard Schneider had completed a presentation of the $6 million in cuts in noninstructional areas, including a reduction-in-force of eighty people, and it was the view of Bickley and chairman Ross "that the non-academic budgets could not withstand any further reductions." Ross indicated "that it was difficult to cut back on instructional programs, however faculty growth had gotten out of sync with the student population."[47] The finance committee went on to discuss the question of how faculty tenure might constrain their options, and the singular importance of student recruitment and retention efforts.

On June 6, writing in the *Inquirer*, Collins covered the story in greater detail in an article entitled "Drexel University Head Plans Austerity Moves":

Drexel University President Richard D. Breslin told faculty members yesterday that the school would have to pare down some of its academic offerings and other programs to head off a deficit in 1992–3. The recommended cuts, which follow two other rounds of budget reductions over the past year, include merging some academic programs, eliminating jobs, closing some facilities, ending some graduate programs and curtailing tenure, which virtually guarantees lifetime employment for faculty. . . .

The latest budget problems, Breslin said, stem from Gov. Casey's proposal to cut $3.5 million from the private school's state appropriation of $5.8 million, and from an expected 17 percent reduction in the size of the freshman class this fall. Breslin said the drop in freshman enrollment, which will cause a sharp decline in tuition revenue, is due to a drop in the number of 18-year-olds in the population and to dwindling student interest nationwide in science and engineering, two of Drexel's strengths. . . .

Faculty reaction to the latest moves at Drexel was mixed. Thomas J. Hindelang, president of Drexel's faculty senate, said faculty members wanted the school to increase its revenues before paring its budget any more. "There is a very strong opinion on the part of the faculty that we really have to look at the revenue side of the picture," he said. "To date, no major initiatives have been undertaken by Drexel to pursue several outstanding ideas for enhancing revenue. . . ." David Noble, a history professor, questioned the need for cuts when the administration was spending thousands of dollars to renovate the president's office on the school's West Philadelphia campus. Breslin said the approximately $400,000 in renovations were being paid with "gifts" from outside the university, not the school's operating budget.[48]

Decline of the Evening College

Whatever the difficulties that Drexel University faced during the late 1980s and early 1990s as the demographics of the traditional student market declined, the college at Drexel University that faced the greatest enrollment decline was the old evening college, renamed the University College by President Gaither. The evening college was an important part of the history of Drexel and many of the most prominent and dedicated alumni of the institution went through the evening college.

The problem that the university faced was a familiar one faced by schools with evening divisions. The daytime colleges had long wanted control of the evening college, and, faced with budgetary pressure, Breslin agreed in the interest of management efficiency. No sooner was the administrative structure of the evening school dissolved and ceded to the day colleges, than the esprit de corps of the unit and enrollments plummeted. The daytime colleges, as it turned out, neither cared about nor knew how to run an evening division.[49] Years later, Gary Hamme could recite the evening college enrollment numbers, illustrated by the middle, declining line in Figure 8,[50] from memory:

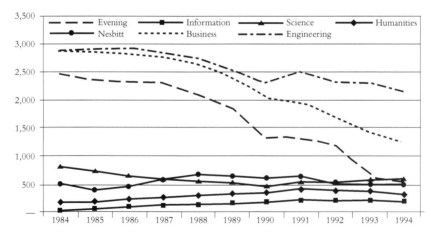

Figure 8. Enrollments by College, 1984–1994

They started making changes to how [the evening college] was being administered and how it was being run. And they lost their edge, lost it completely. . . . Breslin comes in in June of 1988. And in September of 1988, enrollment in the evening school is twenty-two hundred. By January of 1989 it's seventeen hundred. A year later it's fifteen hundred. By 1992 it's twelve hundred.[51]

During this period of decline in the enrollment in the evening college, dramatic growth was taking place at Philadelphia Community College, the low-cost, public competitor to the evening college. Figure 9[52] illustrates enrollments at Drexel University, the evening college, and Philadelphia Community College during the period 1987–1994.

Strategic Planning in a Period of Revenue Uncertainty

At the December 1990 and March 1991 board meetings, the trustees had discussed and been asked to approve a strategic long-range plan, entitled "Pathways to the Future," that envisioned a modest downsizing of the undergraduate student body from the 7,339 full-time equivalent enrollment during the 1990–91 fiscal year to a projected level of 7,054

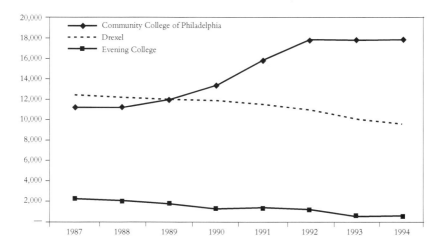

Figure 9. Drexel Evening College and Community College Enrollments, 1987–1994

in the 1993–94 fiscal year. The continuing rapid enrollment decline
and, worse still, the unpredictability of the enrollment levels left board
members without confidence that there was a predictable enrollment
base that could be counted on for planning purposes.

Breslin addressed this uncertainty in his March 1991 board report
that reflected the suggestion by Rich Schneider at the February finance
committee meeting that all other activities be suspended while management focused on enrollment.

> The University community, including Trustees, had given great
> consideration to the University's Strategic Plan. Since our
> December Board meeting, however, the University has en-
> countered two new major issues: (1) there has been a remark-
> able decline in the number of applications to the University;
> and, (2) the Governor's proposed budget cuts 60 percent from
> the University's State-aided appropriation. While we have put
> in place any number of interventionist strategies to deal with
> the applications issue (and these seem to be meeting with
> success), and while we have put in place a series of strategies
> to attempt to restore the proposed cut in our State aid, the
> University's Senior Management Team is coming to the con-
> clusion that, while the planning process and the constituative
> [sic] parts of the Plan are fine, we need to rethink our strategic
> efforts for the next three years and, perhaps, reorder priorities,
> making admissions and retention our primary focus.[53]

Two months later, following the reduction-in-force in March, there
was no sense that the steps being taken to balance the budget were
enabling the institution to reach a point of equilibrium. Breslin suggested
to the board during its May meeting his view of "critical matters that
require bold and definitive action now. If we do not take appropriate
steps to plan for our own future, we will have abandoned our stewardship
responsibility for the long term good of Drexel University."

Breslin proposed a set of "guiding principles" to be considered
over the summer months as a business plan was prepared for action by
the board in September 1991 "demonstrating the manner in which the
University will balance its 1992-93 budget." He suggested that "no new
programmatic decisions have been made to deal with our financial
constraints. What has been set forth is the irreducible fact that action

must be taken to bring expenditures into line with our revenues. We must live within our means." The guiding principles included:

- A "business as usual" syndrome must be changed to a commitment to continuous improvement. Accountability and incentives, leading to efficiencies, will be the hallmarks of our mode of operation.

- Each and every aspect of the university will be examined for cost reductions, but cuts will *not* be made across the board as this will lead to a mediocritization of the university.

- Our short-term solutions must have long-term salutary effects. We are designing our university to emerge from financial constraints in a stronger position both financially and academically.

- After careful analysis to see if it will work at Drexel, the "each tub on its own bottom" model deserves serious consideration as an operating principle.

- Breslin set forth action steps that included "curtailing tenure," consolidation, further personnel reductions, an early retirement program, elimination of some programs, and the introduction of four-year, non-co-op majors.[54]

On September 18, 1991, Breslin published the promised business plan, entitled "Into the Second Century: an Action Plan for Drexel University." The plan was built around revenue assumptions that included a Fall 1992 freshman class of 1,325, growing to 1,450 and 1,520 over the subsequent two years. The suggestion in the March board letter that the interventionist strategies were succeeding in dealing with the applications issue had not proven out. Applications for admission for Fall 1991 declined 28 percent from the prior year, and freshman enrollment for the fall of 1991 was 1,207, a decline of 389 from the prior year. Combined with 326 transfers, the incoming class totaled 1,533, a 16 percent drop from the prior year. By the September 1991 board meeting, however, this was hailed as a success, as it was two hundred students above the budgeted levels.

Undergraduate enrollment in Fall 1991 totaled 6,967. This meant that in less than a year enrollment had already declined to below the level set as the enrollment floor in the five-year strategic planning document that had been considered by the board the previous December. One trustee would later comment on his experience serving as a trustee during this time period, and his realization that each board or committee meeting might well bring a new surprise that would further complicate the financial picture and the prospects for recovery:

> We went through such a financial crisis, during those Breslin years, that almost every board meeting we had a million dollar surprise on the negative side. We actually borrowed from the endowment for operating funds. . . . Admissions always went down, it seemed like we were always surprised. The computer broke one year and didn't get the responses out to the prospects in time, and every time we had a board meeting it was another surprise that just seemed to pop out of the woodwork. . . . And that's really why even though Breslin was good with the institution's faculty and senate, and sort of helped from an ethics and morals standpoint quite a bit in the image, the financial and business leadership wasn't there.[55]

This observation highlighted the emerging tension within the institution as Breslin's inability to craft a successful response to the worsening enrollment and fiscal situation came at a point when the board was growing stronger and more confident, and beginning to embrace its responsibility for the leadership of the institution. Ironically, as Breslin succeeded in bringing stronger voices onto the board, that same board would lose patience with the inability of the administration to stem the continuing decline.

Declines in Student Quality

In December 1991, Breslin informed the board of a national search for a permanent dean of enrollment management. Ron Ingersoll, who first arrived at Drexel as a consultant evaluating Drexel's efforts in that area, was serving as the acting dean and was an applicant for the permanent position. In the December board report, Breslin was once again optimistic about the coming fall enrollment.

> You will note in Provost Brown's report that our enrollment figures are positive for our new term as well as for 1992–93. . . . As you would hope and expect, we are continuing to

raise fundamental questions concerning the quality base of our inbound students as we recognize the necessity of improving the qualitative standards for admission to Drexel.

In these interesting but uncertain days, I do not know anyone heading a major corporation who is having necessarily the time of his/her life. The economy is not good, and we find this reflected in the financial lives of our students who are having grave difficulty in meeting their financial obligations to the University.

The demographic trends for full-time undergraduates continue to be problematical, and we know that this pattern will continue through 1995. However, we have developed an enrollment management plan that should enable the University to attract the number of students needed to meet our budgetary goals; and there are, as well, proactive plans in place to attract nontraditional and transfer students to the University.[56]

Breslin's comments allude to several additional factors that were emerging as the enrollment problems continued. The first was the perceived decline in the quality of the students, and the second was increasing student financial difficulties affording and paying tuition.

Tony Glascock, professor of anthropology, described his view of the enrollment dynamic that developed during the period of enrollment decline. At first, faculty in his department became aware that students' needs were changing and that they had to offer an increasing number of remedial courses. As the enrollment situation worsened, the university effectively migrated toward an open enrollment process that admitted students with poorer academic preparation as long as they had the ability to pay. This, in his view, had the effect of driving out the high-performing students. Finally, the university, seeking bodies to fill the seats, admitted students who were poorly prepared and had a low ability to pay. These students had to work longer hours outside of school as the financial aid declined in later years and they were increasingly likely to leave school prior to graduation.[57] The dynamic described by Glascock is illustrated in Figure 10[58] which presents the upward trend in the admit rate, peaking at 91 percent in 1990, and SAT scores hitting their lowest point two years later.

In the engineering school, declining student quality placed demands on the faculty to teach remedial courses in precollege mathematics and undermined the school's ability to implement the innovative,

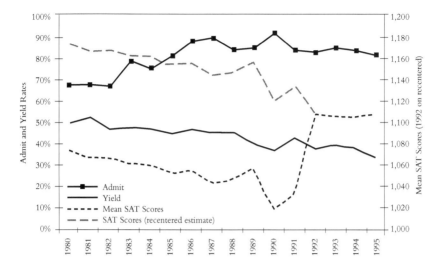

Figure 10. Admissions, Yields, and SAT Scores, 1980–1995

NSF-funded 4E engineering curriculum. As Bruce Eisenstein recalled, this left the faculty fighting a two-front war, against Breslin's determination to downgrade engineering at the university, and the inability to implement Drexel's signature engineering curriculum due to declining student quality.[59]

THINGS FALL APART

At the December board meeting in 1990, the board of trustees gave Rick Breslin a new contract for a five-year term, and by all evidence the board was pleased with Breslin's performance as president.

One year later, 1992 loomed as a critical year for the university. The freshman class of 1991 was 1,207, down more than one-third from the fall of 1988 when Breslin arrived. Breslin had made good progress on the key goals established by the board upon his arrival. The faculty senate had been created, the strategic planning process was moving forward in a collaborative manner, annual giving had risen almost 50 percent, and in October 1991 the university had celebrated its centennial amid great fanfare and in a "celebratory atmosphere," in which, a *Philadelphia Inquirer* editorial noted, "not much was said about Drexel's recent difficulties in maintaining enrollment."[60]

However, even if institutional finances were not foremost among the priorities of the board upon Breslin's hiring as president, the ability to maintain enrollment, a competitive market position and a stable revenue base are an implied core objective for any president or institutional CEO. As Figure 11 illustrates,[61] by 1992, the institution was realizing an absolute decline in net tuition revenue (NTR) and net tuition revenue was falling below the growth in the consumer price index at a time when operating costs for higher educational institutions were widely recognized as growing at a substantially higher rate. Simply stated, annual tuition increases were failing to generate meaningful revenue growth.

During 1992, events at the institution escalated. When the trustee quoted above reflected that "every time we had a board meeting it was another surprise that just seemed to pop out of the woodwork," he observed that one of the things that made governance during the period difficult was that there were positive signs of hope that would precede each negative surprise.[62] In 1992, the negatives gained the upper hand and the sense of hope dissipated.

Ten years later, with the events receding into myth and faded memory, some participants looked back in wonder at the turmoil, some still felt the pain of the events as an unsalved wound, while others questioned whether a crisis really existed at all. When asked about the latter group, comprising faculty who look back and ask if the crisis

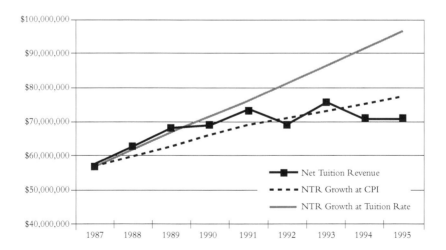

Figure 11. Net Tuition Revenue Growth, 1987–1995

truly existed or whether it was largely fabricated in order to extract
concessions from the faculty, Gary Hamme, who lived through it all,
was incredulous:

> Well, I don't know where the hell they were. . . . We were
> damn near eating our young. That sounds like a typical naïve
> comment from faculty because they were getting paid, and
> they were still teaching and maybe doing their consulting. I
> mean, all they've got to do is look at the budgets.[63]

Enrollment Management Puzzle

Enrollment management remained an unsolved problem as enrollment
continued to decline and net tuition revenue growth turned negative.
Some on the faculty had been critical of the continued tuition increases
and viewed the declining enrollment as a simple consequence of the
inelasticity of demand for education. Andy Verzilli, professor of economics, who had served on the search committees for Gaither and
Breslin, was a vocal opponent of both the downsizing of the institution
and the tuition increases. Verzilli was a Drexel graduate from an immigrant family and was devoted to the institution. As he saw it, downsizing
would only destroy the institution that Anthony Drexel had built and
which had lifted so many like himself into the American mainstream.
As an economist, he saw the tuition increases as the worst strategy in
the face of inelastic demand.[64]

However, the upturn in applications and enrollment the late 1980s,
and again in later years, suggested that price elasticity was not the
dominant factor that affected the level of applications and enrollment.
Rather, the issue was one of understanding the market for a Drexel
education and the unique nature of the market for co-op education.
That was the argument that Tom Hindelang made to the board and
which was echoed by other leaders of the faculty senate at the time.
Their arguments questioned both the competency of the enrollment
management team and the overall failure to focus on revenue enhance-
ment, and the vision for the institution that Breslin sought to create,
which was derisively referred to among the engineering faculty as
"Villanova-on-the-Schuylkill."

Breslin understood that the enrollment situation was critical to
the institution, and continued to search for permanent leadership in
that position. In early 1992, following a national search for a new dean

of enrollment management, Rick Breslin hired Don Dickason from Peterson's Guides of Princeton, who brought experience in admissions from Penn State and Cornell.

When reflecting on the cause of the financial decline, Dickason saw the direct cause in the demographic trends affecting the northeast and mirrored in Drexel's target regional market, as well as the aspirations to national stature of the Gaither administration, and the subsequent reduced attention to the feeder schools in the local market:

> We found that Gaither had decided that it was better to become a national university than a regional one. And so, for instance, he stopped sending people to Cherry Hill West and Cherry Hill East. . . . We were getting thirty-eight to forty people a year from Cherry Hill West, and that number dropped to five, six, seven, eight people. So what we had to do is go back and reverse any number of things that a previous administration had started.[65]

Dickason arrived with a vision of Drexel as a technical university, but similar to others at which he had worked over a thirty-year career, and aware of the expectations that he would quickly solve the puzzle of declining admissions. What he found, and what he believed was also central to the difficulties that Breslin had, was that the nature of co-op education had a profound impact both on the operation of the institution and how it was perceived and could be effectively marketed. He also saw the difficulty that he and others, particularly Breslin, had in coming into Drexel and understanding its unique nature as a co-op institution. It became apparent to him that Breslin's vision of changing Drexel into a Villanova-type school clashed with the core working-class values of Drexel and co-op, and was a nearly impossible sale in the market for liberal arts students.[66]

Dickason and enrollment management struggled through 1992. The action plan adopted by the Board in the Fall of 1991 projected a Fall 1992 freshman class of 1,325. In April 1992, Dickason and provost Brown suggested that the projected Fall enrollment was likely to be closer to 1,250. By late May, the anticipated number reflected in the budget for the year to begin in July had dropped to 1,100.

On September 8, 1992, Breslin wrote a letter to the trustees expressing his own uncertainty as to how to deal with a situation that continued to unravel:

I cannot ignore the fact that, despite our sound financial position, significantly improved fund raising, etcetera, the University continues to have a major problem, i.e. attracting a sufficient
number of undergraduates. Extraordinary efforts and the expenditure of serious dollars have not arrested the downward
spiral in the University's undergraduate population.

In all candor, we do not understand fully the reason(s) we
are falling short of projected goals.[67]

Fall enrollment by the time of the October census was 1,050.

Collaboration and Credibility

Through the creation of the faculty senate, Rick Breslin had acquired
a great deal of credibility with the faculty regarding his commitment
to their interests. As the budget situation deteriorated, Breslin counted
on the priorities review committee and faculty participation to develop a community consensus on how to deal with what were in fact
very difficult choices, though until 1991, the budget cuts focused on
administrative cost reduction and academic department operating
budgets. Part of the budget cuts in 1991 finally hit the faculty in their
pocketbook, as raises were eliminated for faculty and staff alike.
Tom Canavan commented on the morale impact of the continual
budget struggles:

> It was a very complex time. I mean, the faculty morale was very,
> very poor. Staff morale was probably even worse. At least the
> faculty had the satisfaction of classroom instruction itself and
> maybe some level of success in their research programs. But the
> staff was faced with little or no salary increments. There was
> huge staff turnover. There were two or three reductions-in-force,
> with deans having to make decisions on which people would
> literally not be around in the future. There was a great, great deal
> of negativity. . . . It was a really wrenching time.[68]

Tom Hindelang noted the problem of credibility that emerged in
the administration's dealing with the faculty around budget matters, as
the form of budget presentation continued to change from year to year.
Hindelang reflected on the issue of credibility that this created:

Jonathan [Awerbuch] and I found with every meeting that the financial guys would come in with new formats in terms of the ways that they looked at the budget and reconciling what they had given us the previous time to this time. So they kept changing everything they could to try to keep everybody as much in the dark as possible in terms of what was really going on with the operating budget of the university.[69]

The faculty continued to participate in the strategic planning process through 1991, though parts of the faculty, notably the engineers, believed that the direction that Breslin wanted to take the institution was away from its roots as a co-op school and technical institution and toward a traditional four-year undergraduate program, and that his plan was in conflict with the core values of the university.[70]

The planning process was a marked contrast to Gaither, but unearthed ideological fault lines within the institution, largely between the science and technology faculty and the humanists, as had emerged earlier. Breslin held a strategic planning conference off-site to work on the mission of the institution, which became a significant event in the alienation of the engineering faculty that participated. Tom Canavan described the event:

> We went off to one of the houses, a Temple [University] house in Chestnut Hill, for a two- or three-day retreat. . . . It became more like a sixties group analysis session conducted by a bad analyst than a professional discussion of mission conducted by a facilitator. I mean, people were literally dissolved in tears. People became argumentative, accusatory. It was terrible. The whole thing dissolved. And it wasn't Rick's fault. It was actually, I think, the fault of the facilitator. There were two facilitators there. And one of the facilitators was actually a member of the board of trustees. But nevertheless, a mission statement did emerge.[71]

Bruce Eisenstein, who also participated, described the meeting:

> It was a strategic planning meeting. The nominal goal was to come up with a mission statement for the university, and also to provide some sense of direction, strategic plan for the university. And at one point, one person who was there, and I just

frankly don't remember who she was, but one person who was there made the following statement. She said that engineering has very few women either as students or as professors, and that indicates a prejudiced and biased attitude on the part of engineers against women. And it's the kind of thing that we should not tolerate at Drexel. And as a result, we ought to, I don't know if she used the words "eliminate engineering," but clearly the thrust was that engineering should not be part of the mission statement or the future of the university. And Breslin agreed with that. He said . . . he said that the lack of women in engineering is a disgrace, and it's something that engineers should be embarrassed about. And I, and some others that were there, had tried to say something. I realized that everything I said at that point was hopelessly defensive. It sounded hollow. . . . When I got out of that meeting I sat in my car for a half an hour crying. I just realized that this was going to be the end of the university, that we were . . . in a death spiral. . . . The comment stung me two ways . . . three ways maybe. One of them was that it was untrue. The second thing is that, in fact, they were being the hypocrites. And the third thing is it's not the way you run a university.[72]

In May 1992, the continued financial pressure engendered the initiation of another planning effort around institutional downsizing. While it had been successfully fought in prior years, the fiscal year to begin that July loomed as the year in which the governor of Pennsylvania would finally succeed in cutting the funding to private institutions. As a result, Drexel faced a cut of almost $3 million in its expected level of state aid, along with the continued decline in incoming freshman. Breslin commented on the coming year's budget in his May 11 letter to the trustees and the need to push back the timing of a new strategic plan that might address the continuing deterioration:

It is important to note that there is substantial disagreement in some quarters of the University with the Administration's approach to the 1992–93 budget. The Faculty Senate, for example, believes the cut should not occur in one year, but over two or three years to accommodate salary increases which are not envisioned for 1992–93. Candidly, my concern stems from observing other institutions of higher learning which have not confronted fiscal problems adequately and eventually found themselves in financial disequilibrium. This we cannot allow to happen at Drexel. . . .

Our goals must be two-fold: preserve the academic integrity of the University and maintain its financial stability. To suggest that these are not directly interrelated would be foolish, but the relationship is indeed delicate. . . .

While we had anticipated presenting the next planning document to the Board this month, I believe it will be more efficacious to use the next four or five months finalizing a document that demonstrates not only the major initiatives to be undertaken by the University but also the manner in which they will be funded. It is axiomatic that it is incumbent upon the Administration and Board to plan well and wisely for the University's future . . .[73]

The faculty disagreements with the administration extended beyond parochial conflicts over vision and mission to faculty lack of confidence in the administration's competence in the execution of its responsibilities, particularly with respect to enrollment management. Confronted with a new proposal for a strategic planning process, and one that was now to be geared to the downsizing, or "right sizing" of the institution, the faculty reacted negatively, and publicly. On June 24, the faculty senate passed a resolution harshly critical of the past two years of planning efforts and the statement by the president "that the planning process envisioned over the next six months must result in recommendations to close academic programs and that tenure track, and even tenured faculty, might be released from the University as a result." The resolution stated, among other things:

Faculty Senate believes that decisions to close academic programs (which have taken decades to design and staff with faculty having national and international reputations) are viewed as much more extreme than warranted and will result in irreparable damage to the University. . . .

Premature closing of academic programs will accelerate the downward spiral of Drexel's status, image, and reputation, as a major academic institution in the region. . . .

Constitutionally, the Faculty Senate cannot participate in a process which violates the very basic principles of its own Charter. . . .

Faculty Senate has made at least eight recommendations in writing to the Administration concerning ways to significantly reduce cost and increase revenues to the University and to date none of these has been implemented. . . .

The process used to date by the President in establishing the planning committees has not been one of consultation with Faculty Senate or true shared governance but rather one in which the charge, structure, timetable, and faculty selected for the committees has been practically dictated by the President.[74]

The resolution further stated that the faculty senate would not participate, nor nominate members to participate in the proposed process, and that "the President, the Board, and the faculty who will serve on Strategic Planning Committees should understand that neither the process nor the resulting outcomes will constitute consultation with the faculty."[75]

The resolution of the faculty senate reflected the deterioration of Breslin's credibility across the institution. Jacques Catudal recalled a meeting with Breslin while a member of the junior faculty:

I walked into his office. I was being considered for tenure. I think it was ninety-one or ninety-two. He wanted to interview all of us. Gave you a sense he was really being hands-on. And I walked into his office, and there was absolutely no furniture. With the exception of two wooden horses and a board on top of them. And I said to him, "This is your furniture?" And he said, "My needs are very little." And I think it was two weeks later the furniture came in, and the Sub-Zero refrigerator and the this and the that. What was that about? He wasn't joking when he said that to me. He was dead serious.[76]

Catudal's story highlighted what emerged over the course of 1992 as a critical issue in Breslin's credibility as a leader, that is the perception that he was, as Tom Canavan suggested, "acquisitive,"[77] and demanded sacrifice from others in the name of austerity that he did not impose on himself. Vincent Stach mirrored Catudal's comments with a story that illustrated how Breslin's personal use of university funds emerged as a significant impediment to maintaining the respect of the broad university community:

He had a Lexus. And at the time, Lexuses had one airbag. And when he found out they had dual airbags coming out, he wanted one with dual airbags. But obviously this was during times when cuts were taking place and things like that. So, he worked it out with [CFO] Freddie [Gallot] that they would turn one in off of lease and get the other one, but this was supposed to be kept confidential. So the only people who knew about it were Freddie, Breslin. Freddie told me, you know, in confidence. And then the person who had the [lease payment] coupon book down in the controller's office. I don't even think the controller knew about this thing. So all of a sudden I get a call from the payroll superintendent, who worked for me, she says, "What's this about Breslin getting a new car?" And I said, "How did you know about this?" And she goes, "Well, his Lexus has temporary tags on it." People were thriving on that kind of information. The Lexus was identical, you wouldn't really know it except for the double airbags. He had goofy things like that that people like myself knew, and you lost respect for someone who had that type of mindset . . ."[78]

Vincent Stach reflected the irony of the faculty disenchantment with Breslin as he recalled a conversation at the faculty club with a member of the business faculty who was complaining about Breslin, and who, Stach reminded him, had a few years earlier complained incessantly about Gaither:

He said, "You know, Vince," he said, "as crazy and as loony as Gaither was, we knew that he had Drexel's best interest out there. It was Drexel that he was interested in. But Breslin, the only thing he's interested in is himself." And that's the big difference there. I think that probably sums it up. He was more self-oriented, more directed toward his own well-being, as opposed to the success of the university.[79]

The Strike

On September 14, fifty maintenance workers in Teamsters Local 115 went on strike against the university. The Teamsters, whose contract with the university had expired on June 30, had been working without a contract and were seeking a wage increase similar to one recently agreed to between the university and the electricians. The estimated cost of the proposed wage increase was $30,000.

President Breslin took the position in negotiations that because of a wage freeze that had been imposed across the institution as part of the budget situation, the university would not consider a wage increase for the maintenance workers. The union position was that they had been negotiating in good faith toward an agreement that paralleled other contracts that were in place, and that Breslin's decision constituted bad faith.

During the period leading up to the strike, efforts were made to come to a resolution that would give the union what it wanted without violating the no-raise policy of the university. The Teamsters were willing to hide the raises as overtime or bonuses, but they insisted on getting paid.[80]

The strike that ensued was a shattering experience for the institution. It was, in the words of Bob Kirkwood, Drexel trustee and executive director of the Middle States Association, "probably one of the worst experiences any institution had with any union and as a result, Breslin's family was even in jeopardy at times."[81] When talks broke down, the Teamsters set up picket lines, which other union employees, including the custodial workers, groundskeepers, construction workers, some postal employees, as well as parents and students from working-class and union families refused to cross. The Teamsters surrounded the Main Building with sound trucks that blared a single song, "We Will Rock You," as Tom Canavan recalled later:

> The strike was something that you simply could not ignore. Imagine having trucks on Thirty-second Street, on Chestnut Street, on Market Street blaring the same tune from morning 'til night "We Will Rock You," by Queen. No other thing was played for months. And nearly every day the sheriff was asked by the college, by the university, to come to campus and to check the decibel level to see if it exceeded the allowable noise level in the city of Philadelphia. And even though fines were levied, et cetera, there was still "We Will Rock You" for every minute of your working day. And that went on, I would say, for three or four months. . . .
>
> And the strike had elements in it that were kind of repugnant in terms of, you know, what could happen in an

institution of higher education. We were as faculty or administrators really cursed out violently on the street as we would
go from our office building, let's say, to the Main building to
attend a meeting. Occasionally, people would literally follow
us and shout at us. It was an extremely unpleasant situation.
And I think there was also the suspicion that somehow the
administration could have been able to arrive at some level of
compromise or accommodation. It should not have been
allowed to go on for as long as it did and in the way that
it did.[82]

Canavan went on to describe his personal concern, as Kirkwood
had, for Breslin's safety.

And there was a lot of fear. I mean, I remember one night
leaving the Main building after a meeting, and I walked across
the quad with Rick Breslin. And there were Teamsters around,
strikers around. And he had, for whatever reason, parked his car
somewhere up on Thirty-third Street. And I actually felt that
I had to walk with him just so that he would be safe. And what
I'm trying to convey is that I think it was this sense that, in fact,
people who were closely allied to the administration, in this
case specifically the president himself, might not be safe on the
campus because of the level of anger that simply existed.[83]

One long-time trustee who spent a career in industry, recalled the
strike as one of the worst labor actions that he could remember:

If you have ever lived through a strike in an industrial plant,
and I did in a refinery, I actually was on strike duty as a
management employee driving a truck. And the Teamsters put
down a bed of nails and actually shot at some of our drivers
and cabs driving the oil trucks while the refinery was on strike.
Except for that strike that I actually served on, I don't remember one worse than the one here.[84]

The strike became personalized as the Teamsters secured and made
public a copy of Breslin's contract, which suggested that the president
was not sharing in the austerity expected of the union workers and
staff, as Tony Glascock recalled:

I walk in one day. In my mailbox there was an envelope. I open
up the envelope, it says you cannot copy the enclosed and you
have to put it back in your box an hour after you pick it
up. . . . It was Breslin's contract. This president said we all had
to sacrifice. And I read the contract. It had everything in it. It
talked about the remodeling of his house, the private school
tuition, the electric bills. It had every f—— penny this university spent on Breslin. And it was absolutely criminal. I read it,
I looked at it, I put it back in my box. When I went to lunch,
it was no longer there. I don't know where it came from. I
don't know how they got it. But I'll tell you, that's why the
Teamsters were angry. He was talking about sacrifice and everything else, and Breslin was just sucking this place dry.[85]

While for the union the issue was one of the availability of funds
for a $30,000 contract, for the faculty the broader question was the
honesty and integrity with which the administration was dealing with
the fiscal crisis. During or just prior to the strike, Breslin had $600,000
of improvements done on his office, as Jacques Catudal alluded to
earlier. This and other expenditures exacerbated the sense of Breslin's
inappropriate expenditure of funds, as Bruce Eisenstein recalled:

The second thing the Teamsters did was they managed to get
a hold of not only Breslin's contract, but it turns out, of all
things, they were the ones, they and the carpenter's union
were doing the renovations to his office. And they found out
that he had . . . and they circulated the spec sheet on the
bathroom, the private bathroom he had put in with a two
thousand dollar toilet and a five thousand dollar shower. And
the word started going out that he had specified that all the
wood in the office had to be cherry. . . . It was the kind of
excesses that started reminding people of Marie Antoinette. It
was really beyond anything that you'd see at an academic
institution. . . . Now lost in all this was that for three out of
five years in a row there were no raises at Drexel, and all
salaries fell horribly behind our peer institutions. We went
way, way down. . . . It was really a terrible situation. So, we
had . . . we had a death spiral going on at the time. We were
losing students; the loss of students caused us to cut budgets;
the budgets that were cut caused the institution to look awful

and to behave in bad ways, that is, by reducing staff in the student-oriented offices we couldn't do student services. The students became uncomfortable. The reputation of the place was sagging because we were taking in, desperately taking in any student that applied. And the result was that we lost more students, particularly the good students. And frankly, none of us could see the end of that spiral.[86]

George Ross, the board chair at the time, saw the strike as an event that came close to destroying what hope the university had of pulling itself out of the downturn:

It was a terrible period. Because it came at a time when we were down. . . . The strike was a killer, because we were down. The strike could have put us out. They had a tractor-trailer on campus, right by the side of the Main Building, on Thirty-second Street. The biggest tractor-trailer you have ever seen. It must have had, if it had one speaker it had thirty speakers. And they played loud music all day and all over the place. . . . We had to pay, I can't swear to these numbers, this is what sticks in my mind, we needed six sheriffs on duty all the time. A thousand dollars a day per sheriff. I could be wrong. Those are the numbers that stick in my mind. It went on and on. . . . And I didn't know what to do. I really felt that if it continued we were doomed. We were so weak it could deliver the fatal blow. So David Cohen had just negotiated with the municipal work-ers of Philadelphia, and I got him to bring the parties into a hotel room and make a deal.[87]

The strike lasted ninety-three days, though if you ask people who were there, they tend to recall it as six to nine months. The settlement that was reached was similar to the terms that were offered before the strike.[88] The Teamsters were paid but through "overtime," as a face-saving mechanism to enable the university to stick by its no-raise policy. The settlement, originally estimated at $30–50,000, was dwarfed by the costs, both out-of-pocket and in lost revenue, that the strike cost the institution.

The greatest cost, however, was probably to the credibility of the president himself, whose perks and compensation became a subject of scorn and ridicule, and cost him the respect that is so critical to the ability to lead an institution. Bob Kirkwood, long-time executive director of the Middle States Association and Breslin era trustee, recalled:

> The strike took Breslin away from some of the things he was most concerned about and got him involved in a situation that was a no-win situation. Some of the faculty were very sympathetic to the union and I think in some ways Breslin wasn't as sensitive as he needed to be. And Breslin himself, unfortunately, had lost some of the ideals of his priestly existence. For example, he wanted Judy to be paid as the wife of the president and I think a lot of people just resented that idea regardless of how much time or effort the president's wife devoted, it was not seen as a paid position but Breslin was very adamant about it. And I think that alienated a number of board members and I'm not sure many of the faculty were aware of that, but I'm sure that any faculty who were aware, were offended by it. One of the things that the union played very hard on was the fact here was Breslin riding around in a very expensive car when the university was having financial difficulty. Why didn't he just drive a Ford instead of a Lexus and I think, again, that had a negative impact on the thinking of a lot of people. And I think, justifiably, because it did show a lack of sensitivity on Breslin's part at a time when the university was experiencing a difficult financial time.[89]

Andy Verzilli, who had been among Breslin's strongest supporters, finally resigned from his tenure at the university in disgust and embarrassment over Breslin's leadership.[90]

The End of a Bad Year

On December 9, 1992, in the midst of the continuing strike, the board of trustees adopted what Rick Breslin called a "watershed" document, the Strategic Plan for 1993–1996, "Building a Bridge to our Future." The plan, as reported by Sal Paolantonio the next day in the *Philadelphia Inquirer*, called for "dramatic downsizing, including the loss of 70 of Drexel's 450 full-time faculty positions by September 1995, the elimination of two departments and the phasing out of three majors."[91]

Breslin had hoped to migrate from the five-year bachelor of science degree to a more conventional four-year baccalaureate program.

However, the plan did not go that far. Among other things, a financial analysis of proposed changes in the tuition structure of undergraduate degree programs, provided by Coopers and Lybrand, demonstrated the likely revenue loss of migrating to a four-year program, for the simple reason that every student admitted would stay for a shorter time. The strategic plan did, however, deemphasize cooperative education by suggesting that the university develop "variations on those programs, including four-year co-operative education and non-co-operative education programs . . . to make possible the student's achievement of the baccalaureate degree in three or four years and the achievement of baccalaureate and master's degrees in four or five years."[92]

Breslin was quoted by Paolantonio in the *Inquirer* as suggesting that the plan constituted "the cutting edge in curriculum reform in the entire country."[93] The faculty senate was less enthusiastic, reflecting the long-simmering dispute between the faculty and the board about leadership of the institution, as Paolantonio's article noted:

> "Where is the philosophy that guides this plan?" Jack Kay, the chairman of the faculty senate, asked the board in a strongly worded address. "If this plan describes a bridge, where does the bridge lead?" Kay said that faculty members had heard that they "need to get on board and get their oars in the water" in support of Breslin's plan. "I think what you should be concerned about is whether they're looking for their life jackets rather than whether they are rowing."[94]

Gary Hamme, who had overseen enrollment management the last time it had experienced an upward trajectory, noted that the underlying issue was the failure to execute a strategy to curtail the decline in enrollment, and that everything else fed on and contributed to a continuing cycle of decline:

> They [enrollments] didn't stop declining. So, all you had to do was look year-to-year-to-year, it was going down. Well, then you're going into budget cuts. The windows weren't being washed. I mean, all the symbols that were happening at that point are of an institution that's in trouble. You had the strike. The quality of the kids was going down. So, you know, you kind of had all that stuff that was . . . they were all symbols of you're in trouble.[95]

THE TRAJECTORY OF DECLINE:
DREXEL UNIVERSITY AND THE ARGENTI CURVE

In his work on corporate collapse,[96] John Argenti suggested that management problems lead to two classic errors of omission and three of commission. The two acts of omission include (1) the neglect of accounting information systems, including budgeting, cash flow, and cost analysis, and (2) failure to respond to environmental changes, including competitive, political, social, economic, and technology factors. The three acts of commission are (1) the tendency to overreach through overexpanding beyond the ability to internally finance, (2) launching new initiatives that may overtax available resources, and (3) overleveraging in a manner that increases risk exposure to normal business cycles and hazards. As these problems develop, and become evident through performance ratios, he suggested that creative accounting would be utilized to avoid recognizing the problem. Nonfinancial measures of decline also signal impending failure, including declining employee morale and reputation with customers.

Argenti's observation, and in particular his *Type 3* pattern of decline, illustrated in Figure 12 in a simplified form, resonates with the story of decline at Drexel University. Along area 1, the company has been in good-to-excellent shape, though with some management defects, perhaps one-person rule, lack of management depth, or a passive board. There are likely defects in the accounting information system, and the board does not pay close attention to the budgetary figures, cash flow forecasts, or product costing. Changes are likely occurring in the competitive arena, but those threats are being dismissed. This description describes the end of the Hagerty era in every detail, including the passivity of the board, the weakness in the information systems, and one-person rule. At the end of the Hagerty era, the microcomputer initiative provided an upturn in applications and enrollments that served to mask the underlying changes that were taking place in the marketplace.

The inflection point that occurs into area 2, in Argenti's paradigm, may result from a normal business event, external pressure constraints on the business, or a failed project, that combine to cause a significant setback to the company. In the case of Drexel University, Figure 13[97] illustrates the patterns of freshman applications, acceptances, and enrollments that provide the most direct indicators of market feedback to the institution, as well as providing and predicting the future trend in revenues as the freshman class works its way through the institution

Type 3 trajectory

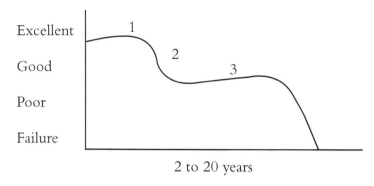

Figure 12. Type 3 Trajectory of Decline

over a five to six year period. While there are other reasonable measures, such as annual giving, graduate enrollment, and research funding, Drexel's strong dependency on undergraduate tuition make this a more reasonable benchmark for tracking decline.

Along the downward trajectory in area 2, a number of things happen. Financial performance begins to deteriorate, morale falls, and other nonfinancial symptoms appear. In the Drexel experience, the Gaither presidency coincided with the decline in applications and enrollments following the microcomputer "bounce" when the shift in market demand away from the commuter student emerged as a material challenge

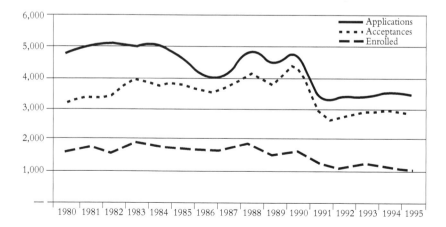

Figure 13. Drexel University: Pattern of Decline

for the institution. In addition, the failure of the Martin Marietta project imposed a significant financial burden on the institution, as well as exacerbating the morale problem that emerged as the unique challenge facing the institution following its long period of one-man rule.

Near the next inflection point into the plateau of area 3, management has begun creative accounting and financial engineering to try to deflect problems. Financial performance levels out, but at a lower level. The general health of the company is poor, and its cash flow just covers its fixed costs. To improve at this point, the company must sell assets or otherwise shed fixed costs, and all of the options mean shrinking the size of the business and finding a new operating equilibrium. In the Drexel experience, the cost-cutting efforts begun by Gaither were followed by the success of the Hamme/Mortimer team in enrollment management that produced the uptick in applications and enrollment that actually materialized after the end of the Gaither presidency. This upturn occurred despite the continuation of the downturn in the commuter student market, and the deteriorating demographics that were beginning to affect college enrollments regionally. The significance of this upturn, and the implication that effective strategy implementation outweighed changing market demographics, is an important piece of the Drexel story, and reemerges as an important aspect of the turnaround that ultimately transpires.

The final downturn in the Argenti model is similar to the inflection point from area 1 to area 2, a combination of poor decisions and external events, but at this point the company lacks the resiliency to survive. In the Drexel story, the second downturn is as much a function of board error as management error. The lack of communication within the organization led the board to incorrectly diagnose the problems of the Gaither presidency. Both David Brooks Arnold and John Savchak concluded at the time that the overriding issues within the institution were related to the evolution of the faculty and the willingness, or lack of willingness, to support William Gaither as president in large part due to his autocratic leadership style and unwillingness to accommodate the newly assertive faculty. The board diagnosed the issue as one related to sexual harassment and appointed a president who they believed could address the symbolic issues of ethics, rather than focusing on the broader demands of leading Drexel University as a technological, co-op university.

The subsequent inflection and downturn reflected the problems that Breslin faced as he was forced to address the issues of management and leadership that emerged, but that were not the issues that he

understood to be of greatest concern to the board. He believed to the
end that he had been hired to be a moral leader, to be the lead
fundraiser, and to build institutions of shared governance. The actual
challenges that he faced were those that Gaither faced before him: how
to migrate the culture of the institution to that of a modern university,
and to build toward a vision of Drexel University as an urban, technological, co-op institution during a period when the contours of the
student marketplace were rapidly shifting.

The flexibility that Drexel had to withstand mistakes in enrollment management was limited. Drexel's operating structure, like most
universities, is highly leveraged. University fixed costs include a large
tenured and tenure-track faculty whose employment is not discretionary during the ups and downs of the business cycle, as well as debt
related to facilities. Universities have a contract with students that effectively makes short-term programmatic shifts very difficult and mitigates against cost cutting beyond the margin within the instructional
side of the institution. This was evidenced during the decline at Drexel
by successive reductions in force that did not touch the faculty ranks.

At the same time, the immunity of the faculty from employment
cuts led the board to discount the importance of faculty perspectives
on strategies to improve the performance of the institution. Board
members, who were largely from the corporate world, were quick to
discount as self-serving the faculty concerns or suggestions. This reflected
an assumption that because the faculty were not subject to employment
cuts that they lacked a sense of alignment with the institution in its
financial struggles. One senior member of the Drexel faculty, long
active in faculty affairs, suggested that this view reflected a misunderstanding of the motivation of the faculty, who in his view are uniquely
interested in the plight of the institution:

> I don't think that faculty care much about the salaries. Yes, we
> do think about salaries if we compare ourselves to other insti-
> tutions, because it is a matter of dignity and self-respect. . . . Our
> career, uniquely to any other employee in any other working
> place, of the faculty at a university, is to build the institution,
> because the reputation of the institution is our reputation. No
> other place is like this. No other worker feels this.[98]

At the end of the day, the ultimate failure of the Breslin administration
was in the area of blocking and tackling, in execution rather than vision
and mission. For all of the disagreements that emerged about Breslin's

vision for the institution, the broad consensus of those interviewed for
this story was that if the enrollment problems had not gotten out of
hand, all of the other disagreements would have been moot. Many of
those interviewed offered the same conclusion offered by Vincent Stach:

> I would just say this. . . . Had he not moved Hamme and
> Mortimer. He might still be president right now.[99]

CHAPTER SEVEN

Hitting Bottom

The End of the Breslin Presidency 1993–1995

For all of the turmoil that Drexel University endured at the end of the Gaither years, few could have predicted that Drexel's market and financial position would erode so quickly in the years following Gaither's departure. At the end of Gaither's tenure, the enrollment struggles of the mid-1980s had been overcome, research dollars were growing, and the institution's financial position was stable. While the president may have resigned amid controversy and conflict, the state of the institution appeared sound.

The world, however, looked quite different five years later. Freshman enrollment had continued to slide, and the declining incoming class size led to a steady erosion in overall enrollment as each class worked its way through the school. An institution that had paid attention to pricing, while enjoying a market niche that provided for a degree of price elasticity and traditionally high enrollment yields, was beginning to experience net price deflation. Staff morale was at a low point as reductions in force and cuts in operating budgets left the institution understaffed and undermaintained.

While Rick Breslin would continue to serve as the president of Drexel University until the fall of 1994, by the first light of 1993 the damage of the strike and the failure to stanch the bleeding had severely undermined confidence in the Breslin presidency within the community and the board. The irony is that in reflecting back on his presidency, Rick Breslin, like Gaither before him, faulted the board leadership for precipitous action when they asked him to relinquish the presidency. In Breslin's view, the hard work had been done to address the difficulties that beset the institution. A new strategic plan was in place, and the new leadership in enrollment management had stabilized incoming enrollment in the face of the daunting demographics that had sapped the financial strength of the institution.

Breslin abjured any suggestion that the university was in or approaching a situation of financial exigency either during or by the end of his tenure. He viewed the situation as one of a cyclical market enrollment problem compounded by the lack of effective financial management leadership. The bottom line was that every year the board gave him positive reviews and provided substantial merit pay increases. Even with the benefit of hindsight and time to reflect on the past, the determination of the board leadership to remove him was inconsistent and unexplained. Like Gaither before him, Breslin seemed unable to grasp the depth of the problems afflicting the institution, the uncertainty and sense of helplessness experienced by the individual trustees, and his own ultimate responsibility as president for identifying and solving the problems that the university faced.

For their part, the board had little confidence in the ability of the administration to pull the institution out of its downward spiral, but nonetheless remained reluctant to step in and change leaders a second time. The continued decline in institutional finances would ultimately force their hand, though for each trustee the catalyst would be different. For some of the older institutional moneymen, continued requests to draw down on the endowment to fund operations were the sign that it was time to make a change. For the deeply loyal Drexel alumni, the notion of the University of Pennsylvania lurking in the wings to take over the school that had lifted them up along with generations before them spurred a response. Finally, for Drexel heir Paul Ingersoll, it was the prospect of selling the magnificent art collection that touched a nerve.

A SCARY TIME

During the twenty months from the beginning of 1993 to the September day in 1994 when George Ross, acting as board chair, asked Breslin to step aside as president, the board and the administration continued to grapple with the financial crisis that had beset the institution. By New Years Day 1993, the Teamsters strike was resolved and the new strategic plan was in place, and Drexel University returned to business as usual, with usual being a state of crisis management as the onslaught of negative events continued.

After several years of threats, Governor Robert Casey made good on his plan to significantly reduce the state funding to the university. The board fought back, producing at its March Board meeting an economic impact report that demonstrated that the university generated $440 million of total economic activity within the state, supported more than eight thousand jobs, and attracted between $490 and $620 million of funds from out of state. At the end of the day, the university lost half of its $5.6 million appropriation from the prior year, but nonetheless received an amount that was $2 million more than budgeted.

At that meeting, Dr. Alceste Pappas, a consultant hired to provide a financial analysis of the strategic plan approved the prior December, suggested that the university needed to cut its operating budget a further $4.3 million over the next three years, and raise an additional $100 million in endowment to compensate for the prospective continued loss of state aid. The endowment fund at the time was $87 million.[1]

In his memorandum of May 12 to the board in advance of the May 1993 board meeting when the budget for the fiscal year to begin July 1 was to be approved, and at a point that marked the fifth anniversary of his service as president, Breslin provided a positive view of the growth of the university under his watch, though tempered by the continuing problem of enrollment declines:

> In many ways, from a qualitative perspective, these have been growth years for the University while, at the same time, we have suffered at the hands of the economy and demography. From a qualitative perspective, we have seen a remarkable metamorphosis in our Board of Trustees. We now enjoy a very strong, engaged Board of Trustees, whose members are functioning as Stewards of the University. We have promoted and tenured a remarkable array of talented individuals, who represent the future of the University. We have attracted a better quality inbound freshman class each year for the last five years, and this improvement augers well for the qualitative reputation of the institution. In *The U.S. News and World Report* coverage of the nation's best universities, Drexel ranks in the top ten percent of all colleges and universities, and we have moved from the fourth quartile to the third in these rankings. . . .

Undergraduate enrollment remains a daunting problem. We have reason to believe that the decline in the undergraduate student body will be arrested this September as the inbound freshman class is projected to be as large as last year's class.[2]

The budget transmittal letter was submitted to the board from Roger Hardy of the Pappas Consulting Group, albeit on Drexel letterhead, and took on the tone of a letter from a member of the staff, rather than from an external advisor:

Achieving further base reduction after the recent downsizing activity at Drexel will require extraordinary commitment and determination. This process must not damage the critical core of our teaching, student life and research mission. To be successful, the reallocation must be accomplished in a spirit of unity, with focused and well-communicated objectives. Bringing our expenditures into line with realistic revenue expectations while building our capacity to generate those revenues can and will be done.

The budget provided for a reduction of $9 million in expenditures from the current year actual expenditures of $120 million and an $8 million decline in revenues.[3]

Breslin's report of May 12 commented on the budget process and highlighted the seriousness of the financial condition:

The budgeting process the University has followed this year has been the most exacting undertaken in recent memory. We have our arms around our revenue projections. . . . As the University's financial condition is fragile, one recognizes that the budget does not contain monies necessary to implement the Plan fully, nor does it provide funding for projects I deem necessary. . . .

I believe it is essential that the Trustees understand the seriousness of this issue, as our fiduciary responsibility clearly transcends the financial. Our collective quest obviously includes all that we can do to improve Drexel qualitatively, and I do not believe the proposed budget addresses this issue adequately. Nonetheless, we have to be realistic and the budget, as presented, is realistic in view of the University's current fiscal circumstances.[4]

The admonition offered by Breslin regarding the trustee under-standing of the situation was not a rhetorical one. The more active trustees certainly understood the depth of the challenges facing the institution, however for other trustees that understanding was never apparent. Years later, George Ross suggested that the "seriousness of the issue" was clear:

> We went from eighteen hundred incoming freshman to under a thousand, and when you're a school that is very tuition driven—the size of the endowment at that time was probably about sixty million dollars—you're in trouble. And we were eating into the endowment, the unrestricted endowment, which was probably about eighteen million dollars. I remember one trustee, I can't remember his name, from somewhere in New England, very good guy, he said, "We're not to the bones, we're to the marrow of the bones at this institution." It was a scary time.[5]

In contrast, Drexel family member and emeritus trustee Paul Ingersoll reflected the view of trustees less involved with the daily life of the institution. "I don't have any particular recollection that the place was really in hot water. I think that we were aware that it was running a deficit, but not the end of the world, and that there were problems with the enrollment."[6]

For his own part, one long-time trustee and alumnus saw the greater problem not in the absolute condition of the institution, but the inability of the administration to successfully project enrollment and revenues from one period to the next. He was unable to embrace any particular notion of downsizing because of the inability to establish with any credibility what "size" might be achievable. Each time a plan was put in place, the enrollment numbers quickly declined to below the anticipated level. After watching that cycle repeat itself several times, he realized he had no idea at what level enrollment would bottom out, and lost his remaining faith in the credibility and management capacity of the administration.[7]

Enrollment

The crux of the matter was enrollment. During 1993, the questions surrounding enrollment management and the market for Drexel began to focus on the most basic aspects of the university, specifically the

mandatory co-op program and the quarter system. Breslin and others
advocated adopting degree programs that would make Drexel more
similar to the liberal arts institutions that predominated in the competitive marketplace, notwithstanding Don Dickason's view that as a co-op
school Drexel was unlikely to be able to compete in that market.

The facts on the table were not pleasant. As Figure 14 illustrates,[8]
the commuter student market was declining precipitously, accounting
for almost all of the enrollment decline as the residential student popu-
late declined only slightly.

At the same time, as illustrated earlier in Figure 10,[9] admission
rates remained near 90 percent of those applying, up from historical
levels near 70 percent, as the institution fought to sustain enrollment
and tuition revenues in the face of a reduced pool of applicants. The
percentage of those admitted who accepted, the yield rate, remained
relatively steady during the period. However, SAT scores, the only
available measure of incoming student quality during the period, were
continuing to trend downward.

The principal demographic argument that was made to justify the
continuing decline in applications and enrollment was that the aggregate number of high school graduates had dropped during the 1990s.
This argument had particular salience for Drexel University when one
looked at the number of graduates from the parochial school system in
Philadelphia during the period, a historically significant source of enrollment for Drexel University. Figure 15[10] illustrates the declining trend
in parochial school graduates and the decline in the incoming freshman
class in the fall of the same year at Drexel.

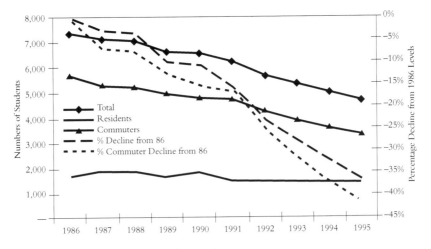

Figure 14. Student Mix and Trends

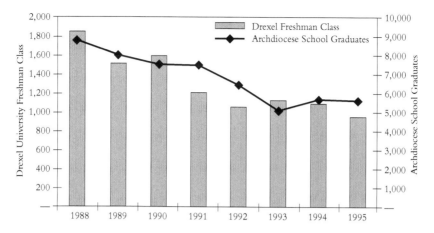

Figure 15. Drexel Freshman Enrollment and Philadelphia Archdiocese School Graduates

The aggregated data for Pennsylvania, however, suggests that the demographic explanation alone is not sufficient. Figure 16[11] presents the number of high school graduates in the Commonwealth of Pennsylvania and Drexel University's "market share," calculated as the size of the freshman class in the fall of the graduating year as a percent of total graduates in the commonwealth. This graph illustrates both a rise in the "effectiveness" of enrollment relative to the market during the late 1980s, and a decline in market share beginning with the fall freshman class of 1991.

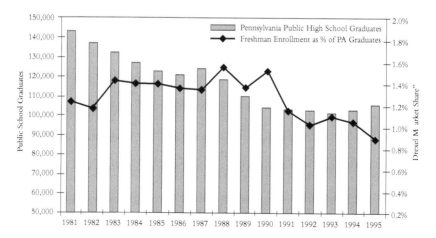

Figure 16. Drexel Fall Freshman Enrollment as Percentage of Pennsylvania Public School Graduates 1981–1995

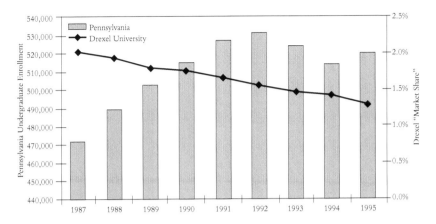

Figure 17. Drexel FTE Undergraduate Enrollment as Percentage of Pennsylvania Undergraduate Enrollment, 1987–1995

Figure 17,[12] finally, presents the Drexel "market share" as a percentage of the total undergraduate enrollment in the state. This graph factors in rising college participation rates, the percentage of high school graduates going on to college, that offset the decline in the number of high school graduates, and suggests a continuing decline in Drexel's market share during the period of Drexel's financial difficulties.

Within the competitive universe, as illustrated in Figure 18,[13] Drexel's decline was a contrast to two of its lower-cost, public school

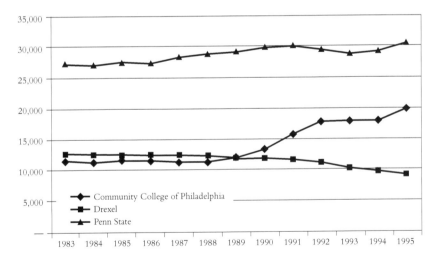

Figure 18. Drexel University, Penn State, and Philadelphia Community College Fall Enrollment, 1983–1995

competitors—Pennsylvania State University and Philadelphia Community College—which were experiencing rising enrollments during the early 1990s, notwithstanding the declines in graduating eighteen-year-olds. As in the case of New York University before it, Drexel, a school founded with a mission that fit the profile of a public institution, was facing competition from the emerging, lower-cost public school choices available to undergraduate students.

Faced with a competitive landscape that pitted Drexel increasingly against these public school competitors, Don Dickason argued for increases in the financial aid budget. Historically, financial aid was budgeted as an expenditure of funds not linked directly to tuition revenue, and not viewed as a tool for discounting tuition to enhance enrollment. Dickason introduced the notion of "net tuition revenue" into the dialogue at Drexel as a key tool for achieving enrollment goals.

The Drexel administration was focused on enrollment, but not on the net price it was receiving from the student. Decoupling tuition revenue and financial aid masked the true financial consequence of the enrollment decline, as budget projections failed to reflect the net price impact on revenues. In effect, the university was attracting new students by cutting its price, but without adjusting its revenue expectations accordingly. The net price, approximated here as undergraduate tuition revenue less financial aid, divided by full-time equivalent undergraduate enrollment, is presented in Figure 19[14] and compared to the net price growth implied by taking the net price in 1987 and escalating it at the rate of annual tuition increases. As illustrated here, by 1993 the net price growth was flat, and actually declined slightly in 1994.

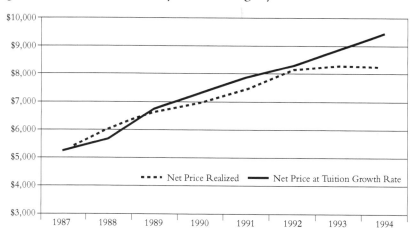

Figure 19. Net Realized Price of Tuition, 1987–1994

Breslin looked for the answer to the intractability of the enroll-ment decline in the structure of the academic program and promoted a change from the quarter system to the semester system that was prevalent among traditional colleges and universities. Tom Canavan reflected a widely held view within the institution that the continuing efforts to change the identity of the institution—the notion that Breslin aspired to create "Villanova-on-the-Schuylkill"—were ill-conceived and undermined Drexel's historical competitive niche as a co-op school, rather than seeking to build on that identity:

> One of the problems I always had with the various efforts to redefine mission, whether they were Bill Gaither's efforts, or Rick Breslin's efforts, was that the institution had an identity. It had a historical heritage. It was different from every other institution in the Delaware Valley. It had no like competitors. . . . It had had its own niche. And I kept saying, frankly, over the years, why are we behaving as if we need to reinvent ourselves? What we have is good. Let's figure out how we can make what we have better. . . . It gives us a market niche that nobody else in our competition area has.[15]

Gary Hamme saw the essence of the product that Drexel had to offer as technology, co-op education, and its urban location, the basic attributes of the university that he saw Breslin as trying to minimize. Hamme saw the failure of enrollment management under Breslin as rooted in Brelin's inclination to compete for the more traditional liberal arts student, and his lack of understanding of how essential co-op and the Philadephia location were to the core of Drexel's identity.[16]

For George Ross, marketing strategy was less of a concern than the evident decline in student quality that was growing out of the need to sustain enrollment in the face of declining applications. He viewed this as the greatest threat to halting what loomed as a death spiral for the institution. For Ross and other board members, who had found at Drexel a pathway to hard-fought success in their own lives, the decline in the quality of the students would ultimately destroy the institution:

> Drexel is a school where enrollment drives everything. We were getting to a point that we would practically admit every-body. What happens is—Drexel had a pretty good reputation in those days—and what happens is, if you admit Sammy, and

everyone knows Sammy's not too smart, why would the other kids in the class, who are fairly bright and ambitious, why would they want to go there, if Sammy's going to get in there. And that was what was happening. A lot of the schools, that were feeder schools to Drexel, were drying up.[17]

Seeking outside solutions to the problem, the newly formed board committee on enrollment management retained its own advisor on enrollment management, George Dehne. Dehne recommended the implementation of a "prospect management" strategy that would more closely target prospective students, but his recommendations were largely ignored by staff. One trustee, who was a corporate CEO with a background in operations, was perplexed by the enrollment management operation. He saw the continual failures of execution as a fundamental indictment of management:

> We had all sorts of different excuses every year. One year the computer broke and for two months we didn't get responses out to the prospects. Another year we were not making the pitch to the prospects in the right way. I mean there was excuse after excuse, and it was always a surprise. . . . I'm not sure that we knew how to measure what we were doing during the Breslin years. The metrics from a financial and an operational standpoint weren't really being shown to the board in a way that we could really understand what was happening. It was more a "gosh, what do we do now?"[18]

Enrollment for the fall of 1993 included a freshman class of 1,118, up from 1,050 the prior year. Enrollment was over budget, but 332 below the class size projected in the financial action plan just twenty-four months earlier. Four months after his May 12 letter expressing exasperation over the enrollment situation, Brelin expressed cause for optimism. In his September 15, 1993, letter to the Board, he began:

> What a difference a year makes! As our new academic year is about to begin, we find so many wonderful things on campus that are so positive. As of this writing, our freshman class is larger than expected and, for the fifth consecutive year, the quality of the inbound freshman class has improved. Preliminary figures place the average high school grade point average

for the incoming freshman at 3.13. . . . The audit performed
by KPMG Peat Marwick is once again "whistle clean," and the
University's financial reserves are greater than anticipated. It is
clear that the University has responded well to its enrollment
and financial challenges. Drexel is well-positioned to confront
the future by virtue of a Strategic Plan that is amongst the most
focused in the higher education community.[19]

Commenting specifically on the work of enrollment management,
Breslin noted:

> I have seen the work of Don Dickason and his staff literally
> transformed the manner in which we attract students to the
> University. As of this writing, the number of inquiries for the
> 1994 academic year has surpassed inquiries for the 1993 aca-
> demic year. The Board should have genuine confidence in Don
> Dickason and his staff as their expertise is remarkable and the
> results they are producing reflect their knowledge, expertise
> and dedication.[20]

The trustee quoted above would later comment that the pattern
of oscillation between positive and negative reports made concerted
board action on Breslin's presidency more difficult:

> That was why I think it took longer to make a change.
> Because there was a glimmer of hope coming out, and then
> boom, another million-dollar surprise. And whether that was
> delay via Enron-type accounting and we really didn't know
> that it was happening anyway, I don't know if we will ever
> understand that.[21]

In the fall of 1994, the decline in entering freshman would continue, as the university freshman enrollment fell to 949. Total full-time
university enrollment reached 7,288, a decline of 23 percent since the
beginning of the Breslin administration and 28 percent since the resignation of William Walsh Hagerty.

Financial Performance

While everyone agreed that Drexel faced enrollment problems that
were creating financial difficulties for the institution, there was dis-

agreement at the time and even in retrospect over whether by the fall of 1994 the situation was worsening, stabilizing, or improving. Breslin, Canavan, and others in the administration felt that the bottom had been reached and that the new enrollment management team was producing results,[22] while others looked at the continuing downward spiral in enrollment and saw no bottom in sight. While the differing interpretations of the data may have been due in part to the natural desire of the president to present a positive picture in order to rally the troops and sustain morale, by the fall of 1994 the fundamental factor was the board's loss of confidence in the ability of the administration to produce results in line with expectations.

As Breslin and the administration sought to find the light at the end of the tunnel, they viewed the problem as one of demographics and a mission that was outdated, and therefore looked to downsize the institution and broaden their marketing to target the more traditional market for undergraduate, liberal arts students. But as the administration sought to implement their chosen strategies, they ran up against severe obstacles. In the case of downsizing, Breslin found that it was difficult to restructure a high fixed-cost institution quickly enough to bring costs into line with revenues, while in the case of entering a new student market Don Dickason would quickly learn that Drexel simply lacked a competitive advantage to compete effectively in a broader market. As the board looked on, the confusion about what was happening and why, and what might be done to stem the cycle of decline, grew, and with it the frustration felt by the board of directors.

In his letter of September 15, Rick Breslin extolled the stabilization of the university's financial condition:

> When I met with our auditors, they told me they were extremely pleased with the quality of our staff and the manner in which we present our financial materials for audit. It is clear that if the University had not proactively made the wide range of adjustments and cuts of the last two years, we would today be an institution in serious financial difficulty. Fortunately, we have had the courage and conviction to do the right things, to make the appropriate cuts and, therefore, to place the institution in a reasonable strong financial position.[23]

What was not noted in the letter was that in the audit for the year ended June 30, 1993, the operating deficit for the university would exceed $4 million, as illustrated in Figure 20.[24] The fact that an audit

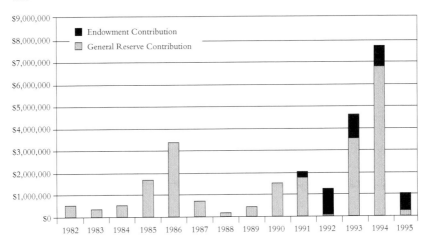

Figure 20. Annual Operating Deficit, 1982–1995

is "whistle clean," as Breslin indicated in his letter, does not speak to the quality of the outcome, only the quality of the data. The whistle clean audit showed the highest deficit in recent institutional history.

Two months later, in a November 30 letter in advance of the December board meeting, Breslin's tone had changed somewhat. The newly emerging problem was that financial aid expenditures were higher than anticipated, even given the lower enrollment.[25] As a result, Breslin informed the board that the current year shortfall was expected to approximate $3.4 million and the enrollment goals that had been the basis for the strategic plan approved less than one year earlier were no longer realistic.

> For numerous reasons, all within the community feel quite good about the full-time undergraduate enrollment, which has exceeded budget. For some, this connotes that our efforts have borne fruit, and such terms as "turned the corner" have been bandied about. . . .
>
> What concerns both the administration and Trustees is the rollover effect [of the $3.4 million deficit] on 1994–95 and the diminution of the University's reserves. Having fewer part-time and graduate students this year leads inexorably to the conclusion that the targeted goals in our Strategic Plan for enrollment for next fiscal year are now unrealistic and must be adjusted accordingly. Consequently, as we have seven months

left in this fiscal year, I have directed the senior management team of the University to effect all savings possible in order to lessen the impact on the next fiscal year. . . .

At the heart of the University's Strategic Plan, we stated categorically that we had to achieve the twin goals of fiscal stability and academic integrity. New data are now available, and we need to adjust to a new reality.[26]

In May 1994, Breslin argued for more dramatic steps in the "right sizing" of the institution, and to "set in motion a series of actions intended to transform the University." He indicated his intention to roll out an action plan with recommendations for a fundamental restructuring of the institution the following September. Breslin's clarion call reflected the need to reduce the cost of operations further, as aggregate university enrollment would continue to decline as the reduced level of freshman enrollment worked its way through the system.[27] Breslin's calls for further action, however, were falling on deaf ears, as one trustee noted:

> He presented those kinds of potential solutions because of the negative trend of bringing in students and having to borrow from the endowment, if we were smaller we could manage at this lower level. But it didn't look like there was an end to that and I don't think there was a perception at the board that we were going to stabilize. It was still going down, so it was hard to accept what is the right size here.[28]

One element of the new action plan that Breslin suggested he would roll out in September 1994 was the implementation of responsibility center budgeting (RCB). A budget and finance system developed for universities based on profit-center accounting, RCB looks at each academic unit as a revenue and expense center, and reallocates funds to support central operations and subsidize less profitable units using a process called "subvention," or more informally, taxes. A senior finance official described the effort later:

> [Provost] Denny Brown was really pushing this forward, basically to get money for the colleges, to get the deans involved in strategic planning and those kind of things. It didn't go through then because at that point we had reduced revenues and the deans couldn't really cut anything. So we spent a lot

of time arguing about how to allocate costs . . . we were trying
to do full allocated overhead, full subvention, the whole Penn
model actually, we got a bunch of stuff from Penn. The library
would be allocated based on what magazines they ordered for
what college. They had kept track of whose students used the
library more than other students, so that they could charge it
back to the colleges based on usage. In student life there was
a big discussion, how should you include graduate students, and
most of their stuff was geared toward undergrad, should it just
be allocated. So we went through that whole thing. . . . The
provost drove it.[29]

However, as this official described, the implementation of RCB
involved complicated debates over how to best allocate indirect costs,
without making a contribution to cost reduction itself:

I mean we're looking at five million dollar, eight million dollar
deficit and all anyone is doing is arguing about is how to
allocate costs and nobody. . . nobody was paying attention to
how to reduce costs.[30]

THE END OF THINGS

The end of the Breslin presidency finally came. Loss of faith in Breslin's
leadership, rumors that Drexel's goliath neighbor, the University of
Pennsylvania, was waiting in the wings to snap up the College of
Engineering, and the continuing sense on the part of the board that the
fiscal situation was continuing to deteriorate finally led to Breslin's
removal. When the end came, one long-time faculty member would
suggest later, Breslin was the only person who was surprised.[31]

In the November 30, 1993, board letter, Breslin commented on
his annual review with George Ross:

In mid-October, the Chairman of the Board sat with me to
review the past year and to discuss the major priorities for the
next year. We are in complete agreement that we must work
on enrollment management issues, the renaissance of the College of Business and Administration, student life, our campus
environment, and fund raising. These issues will prove to be
multi-year commitments, but there is a clear and certain urgency to them now.[32]

As noted in this letter, Breslin's formal annual reviews with the board continued to be positive. At the same time, the board's frustration with management issues and enrollment management grew to the point where members of the board began meeting privately, as one trustee recalled:

> It got to the point where he lost credibility with the board, to the extent that we were having meetings without him, in what I call kitchen cabinet meetings, five or six of us at a time, for dinner, trying to figure out what else we could do. . . . I think it just got so bad. You could only take so many million dollar negative surprises at board meetings. Finally, I think, that breaks the back. I don't remember a particular issue as much as almost every board meeting for two years was like that.[33]

Tom Canavan, who was at that point vice president for planning and implementation, recalled that by the end, whatever Breslin might have sought to do, the board was no longer listening:

> When he [Breslin] put together a group of people near the end of his career at the institution to rethink the institution's entire structure, some members of the board basically said, "Why the hell are you doing that?" . . . And ultimately, when a plan was developed for a very significant reorganization of the colleges, some members of the board just didn't see that as being necessary. . . . I even heard one member of the board characterize what was being done at the college at that point as the rearrangement of the chairs on the deck of the Titanic.[34]

Among the urban legends that surround the decline of the university is the suggestion that the University of Pennsylvania was considering the acquisition of the College of Engineering in the event that the university's financial plight led to the dissolution of the institution. While Steve Schutt, former chief of staff to Penn president Judith Rodin, recalled no such considerations at Penn,[35] one trustee recalled conversations among board members about exploring that possibility:

> We had strained so much in those days that we were having some sort of kitchen cabinet meetings that said that maybe we should think about doing something completely different with this university, like making it the engineering college of the

University of Pennsylvania, if we can't sustain our own financial position and foundation here, if we can't improve it.[36]

George Ross conveyed his own recollection related to Penn's potential interest in Drexel's facilities at the low point in the decline:

> A very, very close friend of mine was on the board of overseers of Wharton, may have been chairman, very involved with the Wharton School, there was a time I guess in the early nineties when they were planning what has become the new building, starting to plan. He called me one day from New York, "George, what the hell is going on at Drexel? I just came from this meeting of Wharton Overseers. Talking about our future and what to do, and someone said well let's wait and see what happens with Drexel."[37]

The greatest discrepancy in the perspectives on the financial decline and the end of the Breslin presidency rests with the question of whether the institution was already recovering from the problems that had plagued it. Breslin was of that view and believed that the enrollment management team under Don Dickason had put in place a program that was working, though the eighteen to twenty-four months that it would take to bear fruit ultimately extended beyond his tenure. Others, such as Tom Canavan, shared Breslin's perspective. Notwithstanding these views, the enrollment decline hit its low point in the fall of 1995, a year after Breslin's departure from the institution, as illustrated in Figure 21.[38]

In response to the question of why the board waited so long to remove a president that it saw as incapable of addressing the challenges facing the institution, Bruce Eisenstein suggested that board action was delayed by the board's determination not to acquiesce a second time to the faculty's desire to remove an unpopular president—at least until the financial problems became too acute to ignore:

> A lot of the board, fully a third if not half of the board, carried over from the Gaither days. And they harbored this lingering feeling that as I said was incorrect, that the faculty had engineered Gaither's demise. I don't think the board ever saw it the way . . . saw Gaither the way the faculty saw him. But there was absolutely no question in the faculty's mind that Breslin

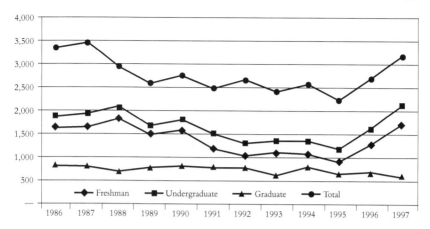

Figure 21. Enrollment 1986–1997

was a lot worse. Except Breslin . . . never lost support in the liberal arts areas. I think to the very end they still viewed him positively. And probably more than half the senate would have viewed him positively. He was never censured. Far from it. . . . The issue that finally got the board's attention and caused the board to put in Pennoni as CEO . . . what finally got their attention was the red ink. You know, we had just gotten to the point after we had exhausted the reserves. We were dipping into the endowment. The budgets were cut to the point where we couldn't cut them anymore . . . I think in particular Chuck Pennoni became aware that this was a business that was on the verge of bankruptcy. It was teetering.[39]

One day in September 1994, Breslin was called down to George Ross's office, where Ross, to Breslin's surprise, asked him to step aside as president. From Breslin's perspective, he had recently had his contract extended and there was little communication of board dissatisfaction. Despite the positive reviews he had received, along with substantial raises, a small group led by Ross had determined to terminate him with little discussion.

Bob Kirkwood, who had originally recommended Breslin to Drexel, ultimately resigned from the board in protest over the way in which Breslin's ultimate removal was handled. The executive committee had acted without broader board participation, in violation of the bylaws.

However, while Kirkwood objected to the way in which the decision was made and the attendant violation of the board process and bylaws, he did not disagree with the conclusion.[40] Another friend of Breslin's, a member of the faculty senate, concurred in the inevitability of the event:

> By the end of things, the only person who wanted Breslin to hang on any longer was Rick Breslin. But, as I see it, he was fighting for not much more than to hold his job for the five years he was here and that's a tough way to have to live. Okay, I'm still a little soft for the guy. He's a friend of mine. I don't think it was all his fault. I think he maybe wasn't tough enough or innovative enough or creative enough to quite do the job he was handed.[41]

SELLING THE FAMILY JEWELS

During a prior financial crisis at Drexel, during World War II when the war was rapidly draining the institute of students and tuition dollars, President George Peters Rea, in consultation with a board chaired at the time by A. J. Drexel Paul—father of "Drecky" Paul who served on the board during the 1980s and 1990s—determined to sell the Drexel collection of manuscripts and portions of the art collection and silver. These collections had been donated to the institute by Anthony Drexel and his friends and business partners, including George Childs and John Lankenau. In late 1943, the objects proposed for sale were taken from the bank vaults in which they were stored and shipped to the offices of the auction house Parke-Bernet in New York for evaluation and, ultimately, for sale.[42]

The rationale for the sale of the collections at that time was given in a board of trustees meeting on February 15, 1944, by trustee Charles Biddle, as recorded in the *Triangle* at the time:

> Mr. Biddle gave four specific reasons which were: a) increase in the cost of upkeep of the collection; b) need for money to further equip labs and classrooms; c) high market for art treasures; d) the fact that a good many pieces were stored and never seen by the public.[43]

While Biddle's rationale was unarguable, the prospective sale struck an emotional nerve across the community and caused an uproar among faculty and students alike. School lore has it that faculty and staff secreted away pieces of the art collection and the more valuable pieces of the silver, to keep them from the hands of the "men in light coats" from Parke-Bernet.[44] Faced with this unexpected response, the board—ironically, comprising men from the wealthiest families in the area—rescinded their action.

One-half century later, during the more recent period of crisis, rumors emerged that the once-saved collection was again being considered for sale as a means of providing liquidity for the struggling institution. Without question, the rationale offered fifty years earlier by Charles Biddle once again held true. The collection was costly to preserve, was largely hidden away in vaults, and provided little apparent benefit to the public. The emotional attachment to the art collection remained, however, and the collection was left intact.

For some members of the board during the Breslin presidency, the magnitude of the financial crisis never became that apparent. Many members were emeritus trustees not deeply involved in the day-to-day life of the school and were unaware of the severe financial impact of enrollment declines and the morale impact of the strike. The leadership of the board during the crisis came from the Drexel graduates, those for whom the school had special meaning in the contribution that it made to their own lives, including George Ross, Chuck Pennoni, and others, rather than the older ranks of leadership that came from the Drexel family and the Philadelphia aristocracy. For Paul Ingersoll, an emeritus trustee and member of the Drexel family who was in the art auction business, the prospective sale of pieces of the art collection struck home in a way that the strike itself and other indicators of decline had not:

> It made me very nervous, quite apart from the implications of it, because the founder and one of his business partners, his brother-in-law John Lankenau, put together that painting collection, along with George W. Childs. And working for an auction house, I felt a potential conflict. So it was all nervous-making, because of the loss to the university and because it was a very fine collection by any measure. For example the Rittenhouse clock at the end of the gallery is an extraordinarily rare clock. And that great wedding scene painting by Jules Stewart, which is a very rare, very fine work of art. So I think it would have been sad, a serious hallmark loss to the university if they sold it off.[45]

RUNNING IT LIKE A BUSINESS

Richard Breslin resigned his position as president of Drexel University on September 20, 1994, with an effective date of June 30, 1995. Officially, he resigned to "pursue unspecified 'opportunities,' " as suggested in the coverage of the story two days later by reporter Howard Goodman in the *Philadelphia Inquirer*.[46] He left the institution a changed place. The board was stronger and more engaged than it had been six years earlier. The faculty senate had been created and the faculty was fully involved in a wide range of planning activities. Internal communications among the faculty and administration, and particularly among the faculty leadership and the board, were substantially improved.

On November 2, the board of trustees approved the appointment of Chuck Pennoni as CEO of the university. Pennoni was a graduate of the Drexel Institute of Technology who had built his own successful engineering firm, Pennoni Associates. The designation of CEO was necessary rather than president as Breslin's attorney, noted Philadelphia litigator Richard Sprague, had retained Breslin's right to the title of president through the end of Breslin's term on June 30, 1995.

Pennoni, like Harold Myers before him, was an interim leader who enjoyed great support across the institution, and who saw his term as an opportunity to still the waters and assure a successful transition to a new, permanent leader for the institution. The swift acceptance of Pennoni across the institution as the interim leader reflected both the fact that people knew him and respected his commitment to the institution, and the respite that it offered during a period of continuing uncertainty.

Pennoni brought to the position the conviction that higher education, while a unique industry, demanded effective management in the same manner as any organization, or as he said to George Ross, "There's nothing wrong with Drexel University that good management won't correct."[47] He understood that in a turnaround situation the leader of the organization needed to roll up his sleeves and become directly engaged in the challenges of fixing what was not working. Pennoni described his view:

> Drexel's mission is higher education. However, it should be run in a businesslike manner, not run as a business where your focus is profit. Your focus is education, but it still should be run in a businesslike manner. The principles that you use in running a business are very similar to the principles you use in

running a university. And there's no reason why you can't do that. . . . The biggest thing that consumed my time when I first went to the university—and I could talk about morale; I could talk about finances; I could talk about physical plant; I could talk about seven union grievances that were filed when I went in that I had to deal with, there were a lot of things I was dealing with—but the thing that was central to the failure or success of Drexel University was enrollment. And I spent a lot of time with the people in the enrollment area.[48]

As he became engaged in the enrollment management efforts, Pennoni observed the dissonance that Don Dickason had described between the enrollment management staff and the external enrollment management consultant that had been hired by the Board, George Dehne and Associates:

The verbal reports I would get from George Dehne on the performance of the Drexel staff in the enrollment area and the actual performance and results were diametrically opposed. The people, in my opinion, on Drexel's staff in enrollment management either did not have the confidence in George Dehne or just did not want to do it his way.[49]

Pennoni had joined the Board in 1993, after the Teamsters strike, and noted that labor management was a defining weakness within the institution. Union relationships remained difficult following the strike, which he addressed by arranging a meeting with Teamsters leader Johnny Morris, where the two reached an accommodation to settle outstanding grievances.[50]

On March 6, 1995, Pennoni submitted an interim progress report to the board in advance of its March board of trustees meeting, the first meeting since his appointment as CEO the prior November. Commenting on the status of the implementation of the University Strategic Plan, Pennoni discussed the continuing implementation of RCB, responsibility center budgeting, the budget and finance system reform initiated by Provost Denny Brown:

Responsibility center budgeting seeks to better relate academic and administrative planning to financial planning. The basic thrust of the system is to place more responsibility for attaining good financial, as well as academic performance, with the colleges as responsibility centers. Colleges are responsible for maintaining and improving their instruction, research, and community service missions while earning sufficient income to cover the direct and indirect expenses of their programs. This distributed structure will provide better incentives to attain the financial performance that is a necessary condition for good instructional, research and service performance . . .[51]

Pennoni went on to comment on the prior failures to implement George Dehne's prospect management system in enrollment management due to ongoing across-the-board budget cuts and Pennoni's efforts to focus funding in that effort and coordinate the marketing efforts within institutional advancement and enrollment management, and the college level strategies. He closed his report with two observations that would inform his leadership as CEO and as board chair:

> At this point, I would like to add two overall observations; the first focuses on enrollment. . . . We know that we cannot compete on price with the public colleges and universities—their tuition is less than half of ours. Therefore, we must compete with the private institutions, and the only way to be successful in this arena is with quality programs. Quality as described in our adopted Strategic Plan. Therefore, we must define our strengths, or core business, and provide the resources necessary to support quality programs and a quality environment. We must invest in our institution if we are to be successful.
>
> My second observation deals with the culture at Drexel. I am told that ten or twelve years ago 70% of our students commuted to Drexel, and today 70% or more live on campus or within walking distance of their classes—obviously, a culture change. However, the same change has not occurred with faculty and administration; they are still commuters. It is evident when you attend any on-campus functions that there is a noticeable lack of faculty and administrators at these functions. I don't believe I need to go into detail to point out the benefit of faculty and administrators living in and around campus and participating in on-campus activities.[52]

That same month, vice president for planning and implementation Tom Canavan presented a report to the board of trustees recommending the reestablishment of the evening college as an independent academic unit with its own dean and business plan, a recommendation that had been formally presented to and approved by the faculty senate. The proposal, which was subsequently approved by the board in an amendment to the strategic plan, unwound the efforts undertaken since the Gaither administration to pull the academic programs of the evening college into the day colleges, and to rekindle the sense of independent identity that had previously characterized the evening college.

One month later, at the April 19 board of trustees meeting, chief financial officer Bert Landau reported that the annual deficit for the fiscal year ending the following June 30 was anticipated to be $600,000, rather than the previously estimated $400,000. Don Dickason reported "a small downward projection in engineering students entering in the fall term, 1995," and a 40 percent decline in graduate school applications, largely stemming from a downturn in applicants from Asian rim countries.[53]

As Pennoni continued his efforts to stabilize the financial situation, he sought and received the support of the city of Philadelphia in alleviating the university's fixed costs. David Cohen, chief of staff to Mayor Ed Rendell, who had previously assisted the university in the resolution of the Teamsters strike, agreed to a reduction in the university's planned $2.0 to 2.2 million payment in lieu of taxes to a payment of $200,000 over four years to help Drexel turn itself around.[54]

Based on the university's June 30, 1994, financial statements, as of that date the operating reserves of the university had declined to zero. During the prior twenty-four-month period, the university had used these reserves as well as unrestricted endowment dollars to fund $12 million in operating deficits. This represented the low point in the financial position of the institution. Chuck Pennoni had arrived as CEO as the decline of the university had reached its nadir. While his tenure as president was brief, he set a new tone for the management of the university. He provided a stabilizing influence during a period of uncertainty, and his administration marked the beginning of the turn-around of Drexel University.

THE NEXT SEARCH

For the third time in ten years, the board of trustees embarked on a national search for a new president. Board chair George Ross, who had chaired the advisory committee during the search that led to the hiring of Richard Breslin, led the search process, and was determined not to repeat the mistakes of the past. The problems that the university was facing lent greater clarity to the profile of a candidate. The board was seeking a manager, and an individual who would be deeply involved in the day-to-day work of turning the institution around.

Chuck Pennoni, who had viewed Breslin as a poor match for Drexel because of the mismatch between his prior experience and the needs of Drexel University, found the match that he was looking for in one of the three finalists who came to campus, Constantine "Taki" Papadakis, the dean of the College of Engineering at the University of Cincinatti. Papadakis had managed a budget almost the size of Drexel's, had improved enrollment, and had been an effective fundraiser. Pennoni reflected on the search:

> The board was looking for a good manager, somebody to come in and turn the university around. Somebody who could roll their sleeves up, because I was on the selection committee and that term was used, somebody who was going to roll their sleeves up and get the job done. I kept on using the phrase, demonstrated success, because I believe we had one hundred fifty applications. We had thirty-six we looked at seriously, fourteen we interviewed, and four we short-listed. But of the four we short-listed, three came to the campus for interviews, one refused. Of the three who came to the campus, there was no question. Papadakis was the best.[55]

As in the case with Breslin, a team from Drexel flew to Cincinnati to interview those who had worked with Papadakis to vet his candidacy. George Ross led this effort.

> When we thought Taki might be the guy, again, I have always felt that you just can't check enough, so I went out to Cincinnati with the senior faculty person on the committee. . . . We met with faculty, staff, the president. And we met separately, together, he went his way and did interviews, I went my way. Janitors, I mean we met everyone. By eight o'clock that night, we knew what made Taki tick. We knew his warts, and we knew who he was. And what we saw then is exactly who he is.[56]

Papadakis evaluated the Drexel situation in detail to come to his own understanding of the factors that had led to the financial problems and to develop an appropriate set of strategies for implementing a turnaround. His wife, Eliana, cautioned him against moving out of the good position that he had in Cincinatti and jumping into a situation that was fraught with uncertainty. Papadakis, however, thought he understood the problem and that he could turn it around. From his review of the financial statements he concluded that the problem was of high unit costs and that it needed to be addressed by increasing, not decreasing, the number of students:

> The university was not sized right. The former president— president and his team—had convinced themselves and the trustees that they needed to reduce the size more to become a liberal arts college. I don't know what they were trying to do. But they were actually trying to reduce the size to get better quality. So they were reducing the size, they were losing money and they were losing quality, every day, I mean continuously.
>
> So I had a fairly good feel of what needed to be done. When the CFO of the university came to give me a presentation for an hour during a whole day interview, I listened to what he was saying. He was the first one that I fired when I came in.[57]

Furthermore, Papdakis did not agree with the assessment that the demographics warranted or justified accepting a reduced enrollment goal. As he saw it, the board was looking at only half of the data. While nationally the number of eighteen-year-olds was declining, college participation rates—the percentage of graduating high school students who were going on to college—was rising. The net result was that the number of Pennsylvania eighteen-year-olds that were going to college—a proxy for the size of Drexel's core market—had been rising consistently. Papadakis saw the acceptance of the demographic rationale for declining enrollment as part of a larger problem of the board's lack of understanding of key information within the institution, including the board's inability to recognize the fiscal decline early on.

Papadakis liked his odds of succeeding at Drexel. He accepted the position of president of Drexel University, and he and his wife Eliana left Cincinnati and moved to Philadelphia.

CHAPTER EIGHT

Turnaround

The First Years of the Presidency of Constantine Papadakis 1995–1998

The choice of Constantine "Taki" Papadakis brought to Drexel a president with demonstrated capabilities in the areas now seen to be critical to the institution. He had proven capabilities as an administrator and as a fundraiser, or "demonstrated success" as Chuck Pennoni intoned. In addition, from his years at Cincinnati he understood and valued cooperative education. Understanding co-op was a critical element for Drexel University, because it dictated so many aspects of life, from pedagogy to course cycling to billing.

Leading any organization through a turnaround is a challenge that demands a specific set of skills. An effective manager must accurately diagnose the problem, design a plan, roll up his or her sleeves, pay attention to detail, and get to work. Papadakis would prove to fit that description to a tee. A turnaround in the academy, however, pitted the values of management and markets against the more timeless and inchoate values of academe. At Drexel, the prior president had been hired in large part to attend to the metaphysical, but that time was past. Papadakis would lead a swift and effective turnaround, but in so doing would set the faculty back to the days of William Hagerty and leave open the question of whether the values of the academy that are at the core of faculty culture could find a place within Anthony Drexel's institute.

THE HIRING OF TAKI PAPADAKIS

On May 17, 1995, the board of trustees hired Constantine Papadakis as the twelfth president of Drexel University, with a term to start the following November 1. At that same meeting, as the board adopted the operating budget for the coming year, Don Dickason noted that the budgeted goal of 1,050 entering freshman would not be realized and that the new operating budget goal was 1,029. As Bert Landau assured the board "that every effort will be made to ensure a balanced budget despite fall enrollment uncertaintics," the board passed a resolution requiring, as it had in prior years, that the university operate with a balanced budget, and that the administration provide the board with a recommendation for the "right-sizing" of the university.[1]

At the end of May, the Foundation for New Era Philanthropy declared bankruptcy. New Era, based in nearby Radnor, PA, had enticed many colleges and nonprofit organizations to deposit funds with the foundation with the promise of returning twice their investment in a six-month period through matching gifts from anonymous donors. Drexel had $5 million invested with New Era at the time, and George Ross had suggested to Papadakis before his arrival that the $10 million that New Era was to return to Drexel later that year would be a source of funding the deferred maintenance and other facilities needs of the university, as Papadakis recalled:

> The trustees had invested money of the university with New Era. They had given this guy a million; he returned them two million in six months. They said, that's pretty good. So they gave two million; he returned four back. And then they gave five million and he was to return ten. Right? So the chairman of the board said to me, we will have a gift for you of ten million dollars so you can start fixing places and do this and do that. I said, where is it coming from? He said, New Era. Then I come here. . . . The day of my appointment, New Era declares bankruptcy. So there goes the ten million, including the five million of the university.[2]

The Foundation for New Era Philanthropy, presented to colleges and charitable organizations as a means to dramatically increase endowments, turned out to be a Ponzi scheme that ultimately collapsed, affecting a number of organizations in the Philadelphia area. Paul Ingersoll recalled when he first heard about New Era as a potential source of funding for the University:

> Hell, I'll never forget walking down Chestnut Street with another trustee, and there was going to be a two million dollar deficit, whatever that year was, and he said, "We solved the problem." Well, how'd we do that? And it was New Era Foundation. And there are a lot of good citizens around here who had introduced New Era to whatever institutions they were interested in, and some of them really got hurt badly with the damn thing. Fortunately we got out of it in one piece.[3]

At the next board meeting, on June 7, fall freshman enrollments were once again projected to be "slightly less than anticipated" or below the budget projection of 1,029. Papadakis' starting date was moved up two months to August 1.

The second thing that happened when Papadakis arrived was that the new governor of Pennsylvania, Republican Tom Ridge, decided to continue efforts to cut state funding for state-aided private schools. The prior governor, Democrat Robert Casey, had finally succeeded in cutting the level of state funding by 50 percent in the fiscal year that ended on June 30, 1993, though half of the cut was restored in the subsequent fiscal year, as shown in Figure 22.[4] For the fiscal year set to begin on July 1, 1995, the new governor once again threatened a deep cut in public

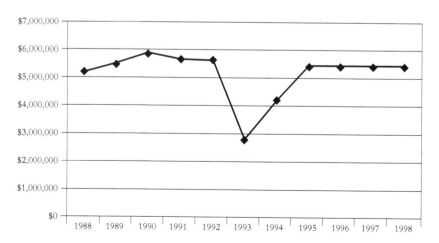

Figure 22. Drexel University State Appropriations, 1988–1998

support for the institution. The combined loss of the New Era funds and state support threatened to compound Drexel's financial difficulties.

TURNAROUND PLAN

Papadakis accepted the presidency understanding that the key issue was enrollment. While the cost structure was an issue, he saw the resolution of the university's fiscal difficulties in increasing revenues rather than further cost reduction efforts. He later suggested his conviction that in a turnaround situation one needed to come into the presidency with an advanced understanding of what the solutions would be:

> I didn't tell them what I'm going to do—I knew what to do before I came here— because these are precarious situations. You need to know what you want to do before you take the job because if you don't and then you cannot figure it out, then you are dead. So, I came in and I thought that the biggest issue was enrollment management.[5]

Perhaps a defining difference between Papadakis and Breslin was each of their reliance on outside experts and consultants for addressing critical problems. Rick Breslin brought to Drexel experts with national reputations, such as Richard Chait, Barbara Taylor, and Jim Fisher, and hired expert consultants such as Ron Ingersoll and Don Dickason into key staff positions. Papadakis did not look to external advisors, but rather relied heavily on his own instincts and direct involvement in addressing key problem areas. Credentials and past experience were less important than the proven ability to perform. This management philosophy was manifest in his swift removal of Don Dickason, a man with a deep history in the admissions arena, and replacing him with Gary Hamme, a Drexel employee with a proven record internally but no other industry experience, as Papadakis described later:

> The enrollment management director was from Cornell, high credentials and everything else. So I was one week on the job and he came in and he said, "I saved the university one and a half million dollars." I said, "Great. How did you do that?" He said. "We didn't give out the financial aid of sixteen and a half million we had. We gave fifteen million." I said, "You're fired." He said, "What?" I said, "You're fired." He said, "Why?" I said, "Because didn't you have two hundred other students that you

could give them a few thousand dollars each so that I can get the difference." I said, "What did you do? The airplane is empty. The seats are empty. Sell them for one dollar, whatever. Fill them up, as long as we don't get the quality down. As long as you have occupants who have a reasonable quality, give them, give them and bring them in." I said, "The plane is going and it's empty." It was the worst September in the history of Drexel in enrollments. Enrollment was nine hundred students, something like that. That was my first September. And this guy had kept one and a half million of financial aid. So I fired him and then I went home and I said, "Oh shit, what did I do?" I don't know how to run enrollment management.

And then the next day I was looking at the statistics, you know, enrollment management results. And there was a spike somewhere in the late eighties. So I said, "What happened here?" And they said, "We don't know." I said, "Well, any changes?" They said, "Yeah, this year was Gary Hamme was interim." I said, "Gary Hamme was interim and he got it up and then you guys got the other guy to take it down." Gary Hamme was the director of co-op. I said to him, "Do you want to do two jobs?"[6]

A Singular Strategy

On September 13, 1995, six weeks after assuming the presidency, Papadakis wrote a memo to the board in advance of the September 20 Board meeting, his first as president. In that memo, Papadakis informed the board that Don Dickason had decided to retire from Drexel University and his position would be assumed by Gary Hamme, who would retain his position as the head of co-op education as well as serving as head of enrollment management. Enrollment management would move forward with the implementation of the prospect management program set forth by George Dehne as "a full-blown enrollment strategy for the University,"[7] as Dehne and Hamme described later:

> [Papadakis] knew he had to increase full-time undergraduate enrollment, gain greater net revenue from the tuition, improve the recruitment of part-time and graduate students, reduce the number of students who voluntarily withdrew from the university, and bring back the luster on the Drexel reputation.[8]

Gary Hamme later commented on Dehne's 1994 enrollment management strategy:

> It's counterintuitive to most admissions people. It's very much like a development operation. You're constantly trying to identify those students who are most likely to apply. And you're working through your inquiry. So, you're not spinning your wheels on the twenty thousand people who inquire when you're really only going to get five thousand applications. So, the idea is move those ones and stay on those, and really make them apply. And hopefully get them to the point that they're accepted and admit . . . or enrolled.[9]

Papadakis described his own conversation with Dehne in light of the fact that Dehne had been the advisor to the prior administration during the period of declining enrollments, and the challenge that Papadakis presented to Dehne. Papadakis was willing to keep Dehne, but gave him one year to produce results for the university.

> Then we go and get George Dehne, the consultant that they had for years. So I said, "George, I want you to tell me, why should I not fire you since you have been here for so many years and the university has been going down the drain? You have failed as a consultant." He says, "Listen." He says, "Here are the reports that I gave them." And he gave me all the copies of the reports. "They never listened to me. They said, okay, that sounds good and they never implemented anything I told them." And then I told him, I said, "Okay, if I retain you, if I continue keeping you as my consultant . . . in one year I need to have a turnaround. If we fail, you are never going to work again as a consultant in the United States."[10]

George Dehne would later describe the essence of the enrollment management plan that he had developed for Drexel, and its focus on broadening Drexel's appeal from those students for whom a baccalaureate degree would be a terminal degree to the growing market for students that intend ultimately to pursue graduate work. Ironically, the essence of these recommendations mirrored Rick Breslin's own sense of direction for Drexel.

Our immediate concern was Drexel's reliance on a single message—preparation for a career immediately following college. Of course, the benefits of three six-month co-op experiences and Drexel's successful history of career placement made that choice obvious. Yet, we knew that more and more prospective students were interested in graduate and professional school. The university was missing opportunities on a variety of fronts. In our report, we made several suggestions:

1. Place more emphasis on graduate school preparation

2. Demonstrate that the co-op program is an excellent preparation for graduate and professional school.

3. Develop a program for undecided students. The emphasis on careers, we suspected, threatened the student who had not yet decided on a major.

4. Think about developing more four-year programs. Most of Drexel's programs were five-year with three six-month co-op experiences in an era where the expense has driven prospective students to find ways to cut the time to graduation.

5. Be aware that the traditional liberal arts fields are making a comeback. Show how co-op takes the risk out of a degree in the traditional liberal arts fields.[11]

The ensuing enrollment management strategy focused on increasing the number and quality of students concurrently. Papadakis did not accept the notion that a necessary price to pay for increasing enrollment would be a diminution of quality, and he and the board leadership shared the view that stemming the decline in the quality of the incoming students was critical to Drexel's recovery. They saw a critical linkage between enrollment stability, student quality, faculty quality, and the growth of externally funded research within the institution. This suggested that the long-term success of the turnaround would rest on the development of the university as a research institution.

Trustee Richard Greenawalt recalled the confidence that Papadakis conveyed to the board as he set forth this formulation and the execution of the plans for enrollment management:

[He] wanted to try to do both, which was to stabilize or even improve the quality of the students, at the same time getting more of them to apply and getting back to the point where we could get larger entry classes. And so I think he pretty much articulated that he felt that they could do both those things. And that would really be the financial driver, the engine that would drive the financials of the organization, basically to get a couple thousand more students, tuition-paying students. And he seemed to be pretty confident that this thing could be turned around. He didn't seem to have any expressed doubts that that was not doable.[12]

At the end of the day, Papadakis embraced a singular strategy as the cornerstone of the turnaround of Drexel University: rebuilding enrollment and enrollment management. He saw the demise of the institution as a function of a failure of management execution, and the willingness of both management and the board to explain away this failure as caused by demographic factors beyond their control. He saw the problem linked to board inattention to the signals of financial distress as they were emerging, and its failure to recognize and act on management's inability to accurately diagnose and remedy the enrollment problems. At the most basic level, the board had been beaten into inaction by years of financial decline, and the inability to make decisions and anticipate or rely upon predictable results.

They were completely beaten over the head. There was a bunch of people who were not participating. I would carry the meetings. I would make the presentations. The chairs of the various committees didn't have a clue what was going on. They couldn't give a report. And I didn't encourage it either because I needed to run the show. Without them necessarily being very much involved, I felt like I could get things turned around.

But they had the mentality as if they came out of the Big Depression. They were conservative; they didn't want to do anything. The first dormitory I proposed to open, to build, they basically said, "What happens if we don't get the students, then we'll have to board it up." I said, "When?" They said, "Twenty years from now." I said, "You guys are kidding me, right? Do you run your business like that? In that you don't build more capacity to produce products because you are afraid your customers will not come and buy them twenty years from now?"[13]

MATTERS OF EXECUTION

If the decade prior to Papadakis' arrival had proven anything, it was that strategy without execution was meaningless. Beginning with William Gaither's first strategic plan in 1985, the board of trustees of Drexel University had considered and approved a long-range strategic plan at least biennially. These plans, as a general matter, were thoughtful documents and several of them, particularly from the Gaither presidency, provide an articulate statement of principles, strategies, and action plans that even twenty years later were highly relevant to the challenges facing the university.

In the case of William Gaither, the strategic plans—forward-thinking and articulate documents—never gained credence across the institution. In the case of Rick Breslin, each strategic plan was quickly undermined by the rapidly deteriorating enrollment situation, even as his fundamental vision of the shift in the market toward the more traditional four-year student proved to be accurate over time.

The Credo

Papadakis arrived with a vision of the university that was arguably less bold or far-reaching than his predecessors, but that was tied to the realities of the moment. As a first order of business, the university had to pay attention to business. On September 13, 1995, Papadakis sent out a letter to the Drexel community in which he set forth his management credo:

> As our students and faculty return to campus for another rewarding academic year, I would like to share with you two fundamental premises that I hope will become the foundation of the University's renewal. First, we must universally recognize that Drexel is in the "business" of education. We must, therefore, deliver the highest quality service to our "customers," namely, Drexel's students and our graduates' employers, in a professional, efficient, and effective manner. . . . Second, Drexel's Administration must create the environment and the opportunities for our faculty to achieve their full potential. Let us set these two goals as the foundation of our new Strategic Plan.[14]

Papadakis arrived early and paid attention to the details of daily work life within the administration, including making sure people showed

up to work on time. To make good on his commitment to the customer, Papadakis made himself accessible. He gave out his e-mail address and invited people to write to him with problems or other
comments. He distributed the e-mails he received to his staff and gave
them twenty-four hours in which to respond.

Papakadis described meeting with the faculty and presenting the
same challenge to them, recalling James Carville's famous admonition
to the Bill Clinton presidential campaign in 1992, "It's the economy,
stupid." And he put on the table the key question facing the university,
given the dramatic changes in the competitive landscape: Why should
a student pay private school tuition to come to Drexel rather than
paying less than half the price to attend a state school?

> I told everybody, you pay attention to nothing else. It's the
> student, the student, the student, stupid. You don't pay attention
> to anything else. Service the students. Get them in. Create the
> environment where they want to come to us. Make it all
> professional. Go out and find the best practices. . . . The big-
> gest problem I had, I needed to have something to show. I had
> nothing to show. So I told the faculty in a big meeting when
> I came. I said when we come back in September, you need to
> tell me why a student should come to Drexel instead of going
> to another university. Why should the student come to Drexel
> and pay thirteen thousand dollars instead of going to Penn
> State and pay five thousand?[15]

Management Initiatives

In his board memo of September 13, Papadakis informed the board
that the responsibility center budgeting initiative that had begun under
provost Denny Brown would be modified to a "contribution margin"
model that would allocate direct revenues and direct costs to responsibility "centers"—principally the colleges and schools—but not focus
on the full-blown allocation of indirect costs as was the practice at
other institutions such as the University of Pennsylvania. RCB is
essentially a "profit center" type of financial reporting system that
provides incentives for operating managers—the deans primarily—to
develop new revenue sources and pay attention to cost and productivity. RCB is complicated for new practitioners, and Papadakis found
that the process of allocating indirect costs—costs that the operating

managers could do little to control— would not be a productive use of their time.

On November 7, 1995, Papadakis announced the revised responsibility center budgeting plans in a letter to the community, including an incentive program for undergraduate recruitment. The new incentive plan provided for 10 percent of new net tuition revenue generated by academic departments to flow back to the departments for faculty quality-of-life investments. In addition, the letter announced the creation of the Drexel Teaching-Learning Institute to provide support for faculty professional development, new methods of instruction, and new applications of technology and innovation in teaching.

One month later, on December 6, Papadakis informed the board that fall freshman enrollment was 949, and overall enrollment was 150 students short of the budgeted level, resulting in a $1.27 million decline in net tuition revenue and a revised deficit of $2 million. The board letter noted that the traditional practice of across-the-board budget cuts would reduce the enrollment management budget by $700,000, and Papadakis had submitted a proposal to the finance committee to remedy this cut. With respect to Fall 1996, the letter highlighted the initiatives that were underway in enrollment management and noted that two thousand applications had been received to date, compared to 740 at the same time the prior year.

In response to the final enrollment numbers, Papadakis implemented a plan to reduce costs at the middle management level, a strategy that he had anticipated before he arrived but that he had not discussed with the board, believing that they would not have hired him if they knew what he intended to do. He let go 150 managers, including all but one of the vice presidents under Breslin, and clamped down on spending.

> I stopped all spending. They were projecting a 2 million dollar loss and, with less students, I made two million profit. So it was a pretty good year after all. . . . It was to understand what was needed to be done and then to have the guts to do it. I didn't tell the university what I'm going to do because they wouldn't hire me. Then after I got a good opinion of what was needed, I told the chairman—the chairman was George Ross at the time—and he almost fainted. He almost fell to the floor.[16]

On January 16, 1996, Papadakis announced in letters to the staff and faculty a 3 percent raise, the first in several years.[17] On February

15, 1996, Papadakis' board letter provided an upbeat assessment of enrollment management, emphasizing the success to date in increasing applications while sustaining student quality, a core objective of the prospect management strategy. Applications were up 62 percent from the prior year.

> As of February 9, EM has received 4,112 applicants as com-pared to 2,537 at the same time last year, an increase of 62%. It is interesting to note that during the last part of January, our applications this year exceeded the whole number of applica-tions received in 1994–5, which totaled 3,513. . . . The quality of the applicants this year is equal to the last couple of years with SAT average scores around 1,100, and GPA of 3.3. There-fore, the efforts to attract more applicants has not resulted in any quality compromise.[18]

In that same letter, Papadakis completed his new management team as he introduced Frank Bachich as the new chief financial officer of the university. Bachich would quickly establish himself as a powerful presence in the institution. Bachich's arrival occurred at the same time as Papadakis had changed the form of financial reporting from the traditional fund accounting utilized by the university to an activity-based format that was more recognizable for board members with backgrounds in business. Papadakis also eliminated the use of the sus-pense fund that had been created to "hide" surpluses from the state—to buttress the case for state aid—but as he noted later, had also served to hide losses. One board member recalled Bachich's arrival and impact of the change in financial reporting on the ability of board members to understand the financial information:

> What a change that was . . . just a very disciplined CFO, in terms of presenting to the board metrics. . . . The first time Frank made a presentation to the board was probably the first time the board really saw a financial P and L for the university that could be understood and deciphered and that was mean-ingful. Prior to that we had so much of this funny-type ac-counting of funds here and funds there that we never really saw at one time a P and L that said this is what we have going on and here is where the institution needs to work.[19]

The responsibility center budgeting initiative was short-lived. Papadakis preferred to retain direct control over the allocation of budget dollars and saw little advantage in giving each dean a profit and loss statement, particularly as enrollment management was centralized. As he saw it, it added new complexities and the institution did not have deans with the necessary skill to make it work. Once enrollment management was centralized, there was little rationale for a profit and loss structure. After all, Papadakis concluded, if the deans didn't control revenues and were not aggressive enough to control cost, there was nothing left for them to do but argue about the indirect cost allocations, which were largely out of their control. From the faculty vantage point, the RCB initiative was a new source of anxiety, as Jacques Catudal would later recall, and Papadakis' decision not to proceed with it was well received.

> When RCB was introduced, the faculty did not know what to make of it. They were told that they now had to make money. They went nuts. One November it just disappeared. There was no decision, just one day it wasn't there.[20]

Enrollment Management

The enrollment management initiatives and university marketing strategy that evolved were built around the co-op program, the Philadelphia urban location, and technology. While Drexel was historically an engineering university with a reputation as a technology institution, the internal infrastructure was not strong. The microcomputer initiative of the early 1980s had not led to permanent leadership in this area, as Papadakis later recalled:

> So then we started formulating a marketing strategy. It was co-op, technology, and the urban location. Co-op, no problem. The technology we didn't have. It was mirrors and a lot of smoke. So I come here and all the professors have Apples and we have AppleTalk. Give me a break. What the hell kind of a technology university is this? AppleTalk? We didn't have a network. So I had to find the money to start immediately the construction of a fiber optic network.[21]

Papadakis introduced a coordinated marketing strategy to promote the "Drexel story" within the region, and to increase the name recognition and profile of the institution. The media campaign began with the local print media and was expanded to include underwriting support for the local public radio station programs that enjoyed high visibility among the parents of the targeted students. The enrollment management strategy included a number of core initiatives, including an emphasis on graduate acceptance rates into graduate and professional schools, an alumni campaign that provided a thousand dollar scholarship for students endorsed by an alumnus/a if the student enrolled, and the Anthony J. Drexel scholarship program to target high-achieving prospective applicants.

Gary Hamme later described the particular effectiveness of the A. J. Drexel scholarship program, which had the additional impact of motivating the faculty:

> We took the top forty percent of the admitted kids and required that they had to come to campus on a given day and interview with the faculty. Well, it was a big event for their parents and everything else. That put the best kids in front of the faculty. So, the faculty were instantaneously seeing kids who were looking at Penn, looking at Syracuse. They started to begin to feel good. They were saying, "Geez, we are competing for these kids." So, we were, frankly, . . . second and third choice. But by getting them to come to campus and meet the faculty by dangling the almighty dollar in front of them, all of a sudden we started to get these kids. And that was part of improving the quality and making the faculty say, "You know, we've got to teach to this level of kid." So, it all kind of works together.[22]

The determination to build programs around market demand resulted in the expansion of the number of four-year undergraduate programs. This raised a number of internal issues, particularly with the colleges that had built their undergraduate degree programs around the co-op experience. This led to the creation of four-year degree programs that required one six-month "internship" in the junior year, or what became know as the "four-year co-op." All other academic degree requirements were identical to the traditional five-year programs. The total price of the four-year program was equivalent to the five-year program, so annual tuition was approximately 25 percent higher.

In the mid-1990s, under Mayor Ed Rendell, the city of Philadelphia was itself enjoying a rebirth and financial turnaround. The changes

in the city, including efforts to clean up Center City and University
City, improvements in the University of Pennsylvania campus adjacent
to Drexel, and improved public safety, made Philadelphia a more desirable location for college students and contributed to Drexel's strategic
efforts. This was a significant change from the years of the 1980s and
early 1990s when the MOVE incidents, the burning of a city block by
the prior mayor, and other factors had made the city a less desirable
location. Papadakis commented on the overall change:

> In 1995 we were doing surveys with the students in the sum-
> mer, the students who were to come in, and so they didn't
> know the city much and the image of the city was negative, in
> the summer of 1995. They would say I'm coming because of
> co-op; I'm coming because of technology. . . . Then they were
> saying I don't like Philadelphia; it's dangerous; it's dirty. Three
> or four years later, Philadelphia has become the third reason
> they come to Drexel.[23]

Pricing the Product

While enrollment management was implementing a prospect management system that was successful in identifying likely prospects, strength-
ening enrollment, and engendering new program development tied to
areas of student demand, Papadakis moved forward with plans to increase the level of tuition and the average family income of incoming
Drexel students. He did not believe that low tuition was necessarily an
advantage, but rather that many students saw lower tuition as evidence
of an inferior product. At the same time, he limited large tuition increases to the incoming freshman class in order to avoid the student
backlash that had hurt Gaither a decade earlier.

> The tuition we're charging was thirteen thousand dollars, was
> below average for schools for of our style, technological, etc. So
> I thought, that's how the students perceive us—cheap, you pay
> for what you get; you get what you pay. So I told the board, we
> have to start charging more tuition. We have to start pushing the
> market and see how much can we push without a backlash. So
> I want to increase tuition faster but I don't want to report double
> digits and things of that sort. Because that's what killed the
> second year of Gaither, eighteen percent. So . . . every two years,
> we're going to have a step up in freshman tuition. That's the

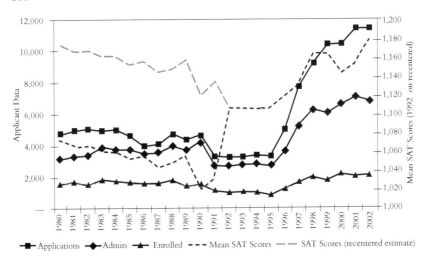

Figure 23. Applications, Admits, and Freshman Enrollment, 1980–2002

entering price. . . . You compare it with your other choices and you come or you don't come. It's not an increase; it's the entering price. That's how we price the freshman class. Then everybody else gets a four percent increase.[24]

Figure 23[25] presents the historic data on freshman applications, admissions and enrollments, as well as SAT scores, and illustrates the impact of the turnaround in enrollment management.

Figure 24[26] presents admit rate and yield data from the same enrollment management data. Of particular note in this graph is the continued downward trend in yields as Drexel University extended its reach beyond the regional market and co-op education niche and increasingly began to compete for the traditional four-year student.

Members of the Board, particularly those who were themselves from working-class backgrounds, were uncomfortable with the tuition increases, and the impact that it would have on affordability for the traditional Drexel student, but they did not push back or suggest that Papadakis curtail his pricing strategy. Papadakis enjoyed board support for both the personnel cuts and the pricing changes. The salary increase for faculty and staff was an important palliative that accompanied the other changes that were implemented.

Papadakis also made changes in other areas. Recognizing that student security was an issue, Papadakis contracted with a private secu-

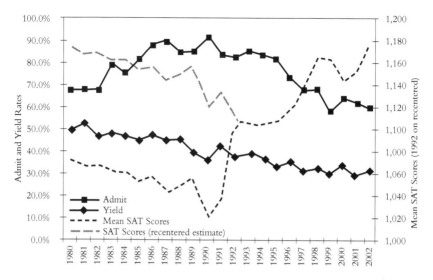

Figure 24. Admissions, Yields, and SAT Scores, 1980–2002

rity firm that worked with corporate clients and major professional
sporting events to augment the local police effort. To garner greater
support from the City of Philadelphia police department, he hired the
outgoing police commissioner to lead the campus security effort, and
invited the local police in for coffee during the week. As tuition revenue grew, he committed needed resources to student life and student
services, and overcame board resistance and used funds from the endowment to invest in the appearance of the campus.

Tony Glascock recalled the overriding change that Papadakis made
in management style and on the attitudes on campus.

> He did two things. . . . One was enrollment management. He
> made that number one and report directly to the president. He
> put Gary Hamme in there . . . and Taki had him report directly
> to the president, and he watched every day. I think he still
> watches it every day, maybe every other day, but at the begin-
> ning I think it was hourly. And the second thing he did was he
> merely started changing the whole attitude about Drexel, say-
> ing Drexel's a good place, should be better, and we will make
> it better. . . . That is one of the first things he did, was he
> started changing people's view about what Drexel was. And I
> think you can see the culmination of it. . . . Taki has managed

to change the perception and the attitude to make Drexel really an attractive place. . . . He could change the way people looked at Drexel. He just kept saying how great Drexel was. And he started doing something that I think was absolutely necessary and touting the fact that we were in Philadelphia.[27]

TURNAROUND RESULTS

The results of the turnaround effort, begun through the stabilizing influence of Chuck Pennoni and the leadership of Taki Papadakis, were swift and dramatic. The key to any turnaround at Drexel, as was well understood by all, was stabilizing enrollment, and freshman enrollment was the key revenue driver at the institution as it affected revenues for the subsequent five or six years. The most direct measure of the success of turnaround effort at Drexel, and its financial recovery, was freshman enrollment over the years following Papadakis arrival.

Figure 25[28] illustrates the pattern of freshman applications, admits, and enrollment from 1995 onward, as compared with the projected levels presented to the board in the fall of 1996. Beginning in 1995, the success in meeting multiyear projections stood in stark contrast to the chronic inability to meet enrollment projections that had plagued the institution during much of the prior eight years.

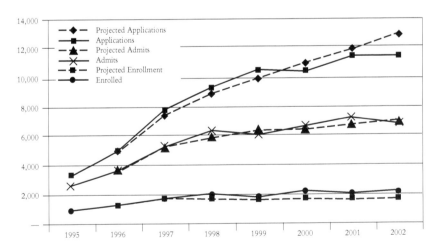

Figure 25. Applications, Admits, and Enrollment versus 1996 Projections, 1995–2002

The rebound in freshman enrollments was dramatic. Within two years, freshman enrollment almost doubled from the Fall 1995 enrollment of 949 to 1,742, a level not seen since 1988 during the enrollment upswing at the end of the Gaither presidency, and by 1998 aggregate enrollment levels had returned to the levels of a decade earlier, and overall enrollment growth significantly outstripped enrollment growth at peer institutions during the period.[29]

Over a five year period, applications rose threefold and the admit rate dropped from 82 percent to 60 percent, and continued to trend downward. While the tuition discount rate would rise for several years before beginning to fall again in the year 2000, net tuition revenue grew substantially and doubled by 2003. Figure 26 presents key data comparing the fiscal year ending June 30, 1996, and the fiscal year ending June 30, 2003.

In June 1999, Drexel University officials met with the national bond rating agencies to request a rating on the university's series of 1999 revenue bonds. The presentation was made principally by Papadakis and CFO Frank Bachich. The presentation is quite dramatic. In successive

	FY1996	FY2003
Freshman Applications	3,513	11,536
Freshman Admit Rate	80%	59%
Admissions Yield	34%	30%
Freshman Enrolled	949	2,012
Average SAT	1,117	1,182
Freshman Retention	78%	84%
Graduation Rate	56%	56%
FT Undergraduate Students	4,595	9,176
Total Student Enrollment	9,021	16,348
Net Tuition Revenue (000)	$82,000	$169,000
Operating Revenues (000)	$134,000	$280,000
Tenure/Tenure Track Faculty	295	391
Total Employees	1,450	5,300
Research Expenditures (000)	$15,000	$75,000
Endowment (000)	$90,000	$330,000

Source: Drexel University strategic planning documents.

Figure 26. Key University Data FY1996 and FY2003

pages, the presentation shows a growth in full-time undergraduate students from 4,665 to 7,181, growth in freshman applications from 3,398 to 9,287, freshman enrollment from 949 to 2,075 and a decline in the admit rate from 82 percent to 68 percent, in each case over a three-year period from 1995 to 1998. Over the course of the three-year period, the school had returned to and surpassed levels last seen in the 1980s. The presentation was a powerful illustration of an institution that had experienced a severe decline and rapidly reversed its fortunes.

MANAGEMENT STYLE AND VALUES

Papadakis' style was avowedly top-down, as a matter of personal management style, but also reflective of the exigencies of running an institution during a turnaround. While Papadakis largely left the academic side of the institution to the provost, he saw the development of the research enterprise as critical to increasing the prestige and visibility of the institution, and he sought to accelerate the growth in research expenditures. He achieved this through a focus on federal appropriations, in the same manner as had been pursued ten years earlier by William Gaither. Papadakis viewed the administration as able to achieve funding growth more effectively than the faculty or deans, and was particularly proud of his success in securing large increases in federal funds for research through Congressional earmarks. As he would note later, "It's the management team here that makes things happen. . . . We did it top down and it worked.[30]

Papadakis discussed his view of the critical factors in implementing a turnaround, beginning with the importance of the management team he assembled in the successful execution of the turnaround effort:

> The first one is the quality of people that work for you in critical positions. That is the most critical because if you don't have the right people then you are dead. It happened here. . . . If you take an organization that is in pretty bad shape, that's what you will find. You'll find that a lot of poor quality people have penetrated the organization through the years and you have to change them. And you have to figure out whom to bring in. You have to know whom you are going to bring in because you cannot be out there with a hundred openings and have nobody in your mind to fill them, other than getting a headhunter to find the people for you. . . .

Then the second step would be tackle the academics. And that's the more difficult one. We did it with the deans. I think if I had done it again, I would have penetrated it through the department chairs. In other words, I would have changed the heads, not waiting for the deans to do it. But again it's so important to have good management in the academic arena. And the provost's position is key, critical. . . .

Then, of course, the most important thing is how can you bring back financial stability because it all depends on that. If it takes you two, three years and you don't have enough cash and the endowment's suffering, you may be dead by that time or fired by that time.[31]

Papadakis' management and turnaround strategies built on an understanding of the economics of the university. He saw little flexibility to achieve a turnaround through cost cutting, but rather, as he had noted early on, believed that the institution must grow to a size that effectively leveraged its fixed cost structure. He articulated a concept of "pressurizing the system" that showed the application of his engineering background to his management philosophy. Under this strategy, costs were held down while more students were added and revenues grew, thereby increasing the load on the system. Just as in a pressurized system, the weakest parts of the system begin to fail. Papadakis would then watch to see how the system and the employees responded to the problems that ensue, giving him an ability to assess performance, commitment, and leadership.

Papadakis, a hands-on, top-down manager, saw strategic planning as an essential tool in university management. It served as the blueprint and guide for securing and allocating resources, and established clear goals and objectives. However, he used different plans for different purposes and audiences. Internally, he maintained a highly quantitative plan with clear metrics. This plan was only shared with trusted senior managers. At the same time, he tasked the provost to develop an institutional strategic plan for galvanizing community support toward agreed-upon objectives. Unlike his internal document, that document was intentionally vague and focused on general principals, in order to avoid internal conflicts over issues that could engender opposition and impede progress toward recovery.

Finally, one of Papadakis' most important roles at Drexel was as an external voice and cheerleader. The public relations role, important in the best of times, was of particular importance to the university at a time when its image in the marketplace, for students and faculty alike, needed to be resurrected.

George Ross reflected on the turnaround experience and the combined importance of market and management changes:

> Well, in all fairness, and I am not taking anything away from Taki, the demographics did change a bit. But I think one of the key things he did was really professionalize enrollment management. He made that really professional, organized—he took the guy who was the head of co-op education, who was a proven administrator, had been around a long time, made him the head of enrollment management, and gave him the resources to made that work, I think that was the first key thing. And he started, you know, becoming, like Ed Rendell became a great cheerleader for Philadelphia, he became a great cheerleader for the university. . . . I think everything helped, I think the economy, the city, the demographics, but Taki brought in good people, and really started to run the thing. Very aggressive. Hard-hitting. And really started making things happen. And enrollment started to turn around. And it started to feed on itself. And the rest is history.[32]

Shared Governance and Academic Values

The severity of the financial crisis at Drexel had the effect, for a time, of subordinating issues of shared governance and the broader values of the academic community that had been so central to the turmoil in the institution during the post-Hagerty years. Papadakis enjoyed a honeymoon with the faculty—largely built by eliminating the endless committee discussion of budgets, investing endowment money in improving the campus, and raising faculty salaries after years without increases—but his management style represented a throwback to the long history of centralized management at the institution. Except for a brief hiatus during the early Breslin years, Drexel had never been a faculty-centric community, and the notion of the university as a community of scholars, a notion that the humanists brought with them during the emergence of Drexel as a university, never permeated the core culture of the institution.

Over time, as the sense of crisis abated, the faculty senate became more vocal in its resistance to Papadakis' management style and pattern of ignoring the terms of shared governance that were set forth in the charter. In 2002, following a censure of actions of the president by the faculty senate, the faculty senate submitted to the board of trustees "A Statement on Shared Governance and Faculty Senate in Academia."[33] This document sought to elevate the discussion of the role of the faculty in the institution by tracing the history of share governance in academia and establishing the principal of the faculty as co-equal partners in the university enterprise. At the same time, the document opened by recognizing that while "*The Charter* clearly delineates the authority and responsibility of the Faculty on numerous issues related to the welfare of the University," the "strength and effectiveness of any such 'contract,' or 'covenant,' lies in the willingness and commitment of the partners to abide by the letter and spirit of its provisions." It was this willingness and commitment that was not operative at Drexel. The statement also laid claim to the credit for the survival and turnaround of the university:

> It is this unique commitment of Drexel's faculty that sustained the University during the difficult times of the first half of the 1990's, and it is the hard work of the faculty that carried the University during the rapid growth during the latter half of the 1990's. Throughout these two difficult periods Drexel faculty demonstrated a selfless attitude on behalf of the institution, continuous commitment and excellence in teaching and scholarship. It is the Faculty of Drexel that propelled the University to become the strong institution it is now. The high productivity level and success of the faculty were accomplished with limited infrastructure support and with little, if any, recognition.[34]

In its concluding remarks, the statement returned to the question of the core values of the institution: Was it the institute as it existed for its first three-quarters of a century or was it truly prepared to become, as a matter of form, substance, and core academic values, a university as defined in academe and as foreseen by the Drexel Planning Commission more than thirty years earlier?

> The Steering Committee of the Faculty Senate urges the Administration and the Board of Trustees to open a discussion with the faculty with the goal of re-instituting a *true* shared governance structure that establishes a mechanism for the Faculty

Senate to provide advice and recommendations on all issues related to the welfare of the institution . . .[35]

The irony of the concluding remarks, however, was in the use of the word *reinstituting* with respect to a true shared governance structure. A "true shared governance structure" had only been instituted during the early days of the Breslin administration, at a time when the board was weak and newly emerging as a true force in the institution, and the underlying principles that it represented were not ingrained in the community.

Papadakis himself was not imbued with the values of the academy, as he had become a dean after working in the private sector. He viewed the problem that the senate faced as one of becoming irrelevant to life within the now-thriving institution.

> They have the senate and the senate is a democratic instrument to take care of the academic affairs of the university. But what happens is there are no issues, no negative issues, for the faculty senate to rally behind; then the faculty senate is not needed. Nobody pays attention to them. So our faculty senate has been suffering from this for several years now. The faculty are getting good salaries. Our benefits are acceptable. We have been growing by leaps and bounds. Better environment; better this; better that. So they felt that they had to make issues out of nothing to prove to the rest of the faculty that they are aggressively pursuing their interests against the administration. That is unfortunate but it's always like that. It is against something.[36]

George Ross noted that the board had ceased the practice of having the faculty senate report directly to the board on a regular basis. His comments reflect the lack of centrality of the faculty in the eyes of the board.

> We used to have the president of the faculty . . . senate I guess it's called, the faculty senate, have a few minutes at the board meeting to address the board, bring them up to date on things that were of concern to the faculty. And we did the same thing with the president of the student body. That is not being done anymore. But I think that there is a recognition of the faculty. We all know they are very important.[37]

Chuck Pennoni recognized the importance of the faculty relationship to Papadakis and the institution as Drexel moves past the turnaround phase. However, Pennoni's view is rooted in a pragmatic view of what it takes to operate the institution effectively, rather than a view that embraces the values of the academy that are at the root of the faculty perspective:

> I would say that the one area that has been a challenge for Papadakis, is his dealing with faculty. And I think that he puts the business aspects, running Drexel like a business, not forsaking education, but realizes that it's very difficult to get anything accomplished if you're going to do it by committee to get total buy-in and to get consensus. In the beginning he had to go in there and make decisions and implement those decisions. And that style is still with him. Where today, he needs to make a transition toward working more with the faculty and being more collegial. That's a big challenge for Taki. Because for years he did what was right. Make your decisions; get it done. Now he's got to be a little more collegial.[38]

One longtime leader of the faculty council and faculty senate, who had seen the institution through the hiring and presidencies of William Gaither and Rick Breslin, the creation of the faculty senate under Breslin, the financial crisis, and the return to the strong presidency under Papadakis, reflected on the evolution of the role of the faculty relative to the president at Drexel. Papadakis, that observer noted, had been censored by the faculty senate for violating the charter, and failed to consult with the faculty on the hiring of administrators, and through it all had been able to use the crisis, or even manufacture the notion that there was a crisis, as a means to assume power within the institution.

> I think that is the most interesting question, whether there was a crisis. . . . I think he built on whatever was dismal in the financial area to say there was a crisis. . . . The other thing that happened that was in Taki's favor was the number of eighteen-year-olds going to college. At the same time he was creating a crisis and saying we had to increase enrollment, the people in the country were helping out by creating more eighteen-year-olds.[39]

CHANGING THE FACE OF THE INSTITUTION

In 1998, an opportunity presented itself that would further change the face and fortunes of Drexel University. Recently emerging from its own brush with financial collapse, Drexel was offered the opportunity to assume the management of the Allegheny University of the Health Sciences. Allegheny University was part of the Allegheny Health System, a regional network of hospitals that was facing bankruptcy. Allegheny University comprised the former Medical College of Pennsylvania and Hahnemann Medical College, and three other professional schools. The medical school was the largest private medical school in the United States.

The opportunity came to Drexel in the wake of the impending bankruptcy of Allegheny Health System. Tenet Healthcare Corp. and Vanguard Health Systems, each seeking to acquire the Allegheny hospitals in Philadelphia sought to interest Drexel in assuming the management, and potentially ownership, of the medical and professional schools. The relationship with Drexel began with individual department chairs approaching Drexel in search of new homes for their individual units, and evolved into something bigger.

For Papadakis, the potential to acquire a medical school offered Drexel a means to enter the growing health care market, as well as access to the research funding streams of the National Institutes of Health and the pharmaceutical companies. The potential for linking an engineering university with a health care complex could further differentiate Drexel University in the higher education market.

Papadakis' management team launched into the analysis of the new opportunity and determined that they would need $150 million and two to three years to complete a turnaround of the medical school. In addition, the university demanded and received a $50 million contribution from the Allegheny creditors' committee to the university endowment. The bankruptcy court, Tenet, and the Allegheny creditors agreed to Drexel's terms, and the university entered into a five-year agreement to manage the medical school.

On July 1, 2003, the university agreed to acquire the medical and professional schools, creating the Drexel University College of Medicine, the College of Nursing and Health Professions, and the School of Public Health. The College of Medicine was created as a separate corporate entity to provide some protection from financial risk or other liabilities that could have an adverse impact on the university.

The acquisition of the medical school was controversial. For some, the financial risks to the institution were seen as too great and the potential benefits uncertain. For others, absorbing a medical school would take time, attention, and resources away from the important and unfinished work of improving the quality and physical condition of the core colleges and schools. And as Chuck Pennoni noted, some of the resistance to change reflected parochial self-interest.

> They resist change. . . . The people in some of the colleges, like the engineering college, were very concerned because they always considered themselves the flagship college of the university, and they said once we get a medical school that's going to overshadow the College of Engineering, we're no longer going to be the flagship college of the university. And when I would ask about that in what's better for the university, they weren't thinking about what's better for the university; they were thinking about what's better for their college and for themselves.[40]

Reflecting on the Changes

Jacques Catudal, vice provost during the development of the new strategic plan, commented on the speed with which Papadakis was moving to change the face of the university.

> I think what's happening, however, is that, particularly in the last two years, Taki is so far ahead of everybody, and the deals are—not the deals because that has a bad connotation to it and I don't mean it that way—the business end of it is so far ahead of the faculty. . . . I don't think there is the least bit conception of what's going on, with Taki and the moves that he is making now to develop the school, in the faculty senate. I mean, they haven't got a clue about the law school. I mean, they haven't got a clue about the corporations, and how the corporations work. They haven't got a clue, and I don't think they have time to deal with it all.[41]

Bruce Eisenstein saw in the creation of the new Drexel a consistency with the founder's vision for the Drexel Institute. The integration of medical sciences with Drexel's traditional schools offered the opportunity to integrate diverse fields of inquiry and give new opportunities, new skills, and new core disciplines for students to take into the world, just as Anthony Drexel would have wanted it. Like Catudal, Eisenstein had no illusion that the faculty could be brought along through the process or keep up with the speed with which changes took place. To expect that was to not understand the ways of the Academy.

> Someone told me a story a long time ago about a department that was reforming its curriculum. I don't know if you ever heard this story. There are two ways that you could have curriculum reform in a department. There's the natural process, and then there's a miracle. If an angel came down from heaven and presented the new curriculum on gold tablets, that's the natural process. And if the faculty ever agreed on the new curriculum, that's the miracle. The faculty would never get . . . you'll never get bottom up consensus on radical change. You know, phrased a different way, Louis Gerstner said when he took over IBM, he said that a corporation must first face death before it will reinvent itself.[42]

For Chuck Pennoni, Drexel alumnus, board member, former board chair and former CEO of the university, the acquisition of MCP/Hahnemann was a perfect complement to Drexel University's mission, and ultimately essential to its ability to survive in a competitive marketplace.

> Drexel cannot compete with the community colleges because of cost; can't compete with the state systems because of cost. So you have to offer something. The one thing you're going to offer is quality. . . . Quality, urban, private, technology-based, cooperative education, residence university. Quality is first, deliberately. Quality, quality, quality. And it's not just quality in physical plant, it's not just quality with your faculty. It's quality in that you're offering new knowledge. What are the best universities? It's the ones that are out there exploring new knowledge and creating knowledge. They're your best universities, the think tank at Princeton. It's the creation of knowledge. That's what puts you above everybody else. Everyone can teach conventional calculus.[43]

Papadakis' View

Papadakis once articulated his management philosophy as three simple rules: move fast, keep people busy so they can't get in your way, and don't tell people where you are going. He is quite sure that if he had told the trustees of Drexel University about the plans he had for their university, they never would have hired him. Meeting in the fall of 2003 after reviewing the financial statements for the fiscal year ended June 30, 2003, Papadakis seemed slightly amazed at his own creation.

> I was just looking at numbers. You know that we got ranked in the top one hundred twenty-six [*USNews and World Report*] but in addition they reported seventy-four million, three hundred thousand dollars in government contracts and grants. That puts us eighty-third among all universities in the U.S. Our endowment right now is three hundred sixty-two million. . . . When I came here the question, somebody wanted to be funny, and asked me, "Do you know how much our endowment is?"—when I was interviewing—in the big auditorium, in the theatre. I said, "Yes." He said, "How much is it?" I said, "Ninety million." He said, "How do you know?" I said, "I read the financial statements." So, everybody was laughing because everybody thought a different number. So, ninety million and we are at three hundred sixty-two million, and that puts us one hundred twelve out of all universities in the U.S.[44]

Papadakis views the outcome of his tenure at Drexel and the acquisition of MCP/Hahnemann as far beyond what he envisioned when he arrived at Drexel. As he reflected on the outcome, he thought back to his early assurances to his wife, Eliana, that if they left Cincinatti, he would succeed at Drexel:

> So the position that we have presently, it's incredible what's happening here. Beyond my wildest dreams, by the way, because I thought that I would be successful. I said to Eliana, "Don't worry." She said, "You have a great job, a great lifestyle and what are you doing? How are you going to do this?" I said, "Look, don't worry. There's no way that we can do worse than the previous team."[45]

Remembrance of Things Past

A senior university official who had arrived at Drexel late in the Gaither presidency recalled how the community pulled together during all of the long years of ARFs, RIFs, and cutbacks at Drexel during the Breslin years. She viewed the mantra of "running it like a business" as reflective of an institution that had lost its sense of intimacy and community. She observed a loss of the sense of community that enabled people to pull together when times got tough, and doubts whether in a future period of difficulty people would pull together the way that they once did.

A senior member of the faculty expressed a similar sentiment, though from a faculty rather than staff perspective:

> Taki did very nice things for the university. . . . He introduced many good changes. . . . The endowment improved tremendously, right? This was the strength of Taki. Taki takes all the credit for himself. This is a mistake. . . . If he were only to expose himself, and the faculty really believed him, I am going to help him. That is our interest. Our interest is to build the institution, because the reputation of the institution is our reputation. . . . And Taki does not understand this, that he can win us to help him, but beside also, this thinking that my ideas are the only good ideas, it is somewhat provincial and unintellectual. If he would listen a little bit, he can buy so many ideas from other people, and reformat it to other much better ideas that he may have. . . . I don't think he has had this experience of listening. It is sad for the university. . . . And the attitude also, the issue of human engineering is neglected here, understanding of human engineering. Trust, loyalty. . . . The community is lacking here, the sense of community at Drexel. We had it once, it doesn't exist any more.[46]

RETURN OF THE FAMILY JEWELS

In 2003, Drexel University opened the Antoinette and Ray Westphall Picture Gallery on the third floor of the Main Building. The Westphall Gallery was created as a permanent, climate controlled, gallery for the display of pieces of the art collection held by the university and originally contributed by the founder, George Childs, John Lankenau, and other associates of Anthony Drexel. None of the art collection has been sold.

CHAPTER NINE

The End of the Story

During the last quarter of the twentieth century, the Drexel Institute of Technology evolved into Drexel University and during that period was transformed. In the forty years from when William Walsh Hagerty arrived in 1963, it evolved from a "pipe-rack" school of technology into a research university with a full cadre of professional schools. From a school whose faculty included a small minority with terminal degrees, it evolved into a doctoral institution with a chartered faculty senate. From a largely commuter school serving the working-class and first-generation college students of Philadelphia, it became a nationally recognized residential university. In short, by the close of the century, while not yet MIT-on-the-Delaware, Drexel University had nonetheless become the university of Hagerty's imagination.

But along the way, Drexel University suffered through a dramatic decline, the cause of which is still a matter of disagreement to observers and participants alike. There are, roughly speaking, six reasons that people cite when seeking to assign blame for Drexel's decline. The first and most common argument is that Drexel was victimized by adverse economic and demographic trends. This argument suggests that Drexel's enrollment decline paralleled the decline in Drexel's primary student market—as illustrated by the declining number of high school graduates within the state and from Philadelphia Catholic schools—and was exacerbated by the national recession of the early 1980s and its long, lingering affect on the Philadelphia economy into the 1990s. The corollary to this argument suggests that just as Drexel's enrollment decline and financial difficulties derived from the decline in the number of high school graduates in the region, the turnaround of Drexel University was largely a function of the improvement in the regional student market and the recovery of the Philadelphia economy.

While this argument has merit, it is more persuasive as an explanation of the enrollment decline that Drexel experienced than of the subsequent turnaround. The simple demographic argument masks the fact that the student market that began its decline in the 1980s never came back. The sector of the student market that began to disappear in the 1980s was the market that Drexel had relied upon since its founding—comprising regional commuter and evening school students—while throughout that same period Drexel's residential student population shrank only slightly. What ultimately afflicted Drexel was less a decline in the student market than a shift in the nature of student demand, and as such a reversal of the declining demographics alone would not have solved Drexel's problem. The school that Hagerty left in 1984 could not have survived as it was—a bare-bones, old world, private institution—in the face of growing public competitors and changing student preferences, and Hagerty, more than any other person at the institution, recognized the changes that were taking place in the competitive market and understood the threat that those changes posed for Drexel.

The second explanation offered for Drexel's decline is one of pricing and competition. This argument suggests that the dramatic price increases implemented during the mid-1980s, when coupled with the growth in low-cost public school competition, placed Drexel at a competitive disadvantage as it became incrementally less competitive within its traditional target student market. This argument has merit, as it suggests a parallel with other private institutions—most notably New York University—that faced the struggle of competing for market share in the face of the growth of public higher educational alternatives.[1] However, the corollary of this argument—that if Gaither had not raised the price the institution would have been fine—is not compelling. The decline of commuter applicants that began in the early 1980s, and the subsequent but related decline in the evening college, was a clear market indicator of the growing competitive threat of the low-cost public alternatives. Gaither understood that Drexel could not hope to succeed by competing with public schools on price, but rather that its survival required that it differentiate itself from its competitors and identify market segments in which it could compete effectively. Gaither's strategic plan, albeit not embraced by the faculty at the time, reflected this understanding and mirrored the plans that were subsequently implemented a decade later. Gaither's plan emphasized the importance of marketing Drexel based upon the same core attributes—co-op, technology, and its urban environment—that would become the focus of the revenue-driven turnaround of the institution under Papadakis. Faced with an evolving student market, and low-cost competitors, both Gaither and Papadakis sought to build a market niche based around a unique and differentiating set of attributes where they could compete on value rather than price.

The third explanation blames the enrollment declines and the ensuing financial problems at Drexel on the staffing of enrollment management. This argument has the strongest following among long-time administrators at Drexel, who never understood why Gary Hamme was removed from his position in enrollment management and Breslin's contemporaneous efforts to move Drexel away from its roots as an urban, cooperative educational institution. This argument is compelling, for while Rick Breslin accurately recognized that the traditional Drexel market was in a state of decline, the direction that he chose for Drexel was at odds with the historical culture of the institution and left it competing in the highly competitive liberal arts marketplace without any definable competitive advantages.

The fourth argument, one that several participants allude to, is that Drexel's difficulties were exacerbated by the poor quality and lack of transparency of internal information, particularly financial information. The lack of coherent information impaired decision making and made it difficult for the leadership to assess the nature of the problems that Drexel was facing at any given point in time. One only has to spend time trying to analyze the historical financial information at Drexel to understand—as Tom Hindelang and others observed—that the form of financial presentation and the nature of the information provided changed from period to period, making it very difficult to track financial trends. Papadakis, however, appropriately gives this argument little credence as an excuse for either Breslin's or the board's not understanding that a crisis was approaching due to the absolute magnitude of the downturn. "When you see that you are losing money and you are using the endowment—when you see your enrollment's going from eight thousand five hundred to four thousand five hundred—what the hell is going on? You lost half the university, for God's sake."[2]

The fifth argument, one that points away from external and market forces and looks instead at cultural issues that emerged during a period of change, is the one offered by David Brooks Arnold—the United

Nations mediator brought in during the tail end of the Gaither presidency. Arnold argued that the drama that unfolded at Drexel began with Hagerty's determination to turn the Drexel Institute into a university and build a traditional humanities faculty. This decision brought into Hagerty's quiet and controlled Institute a faculty imbued with the values of the academy and determined to assert their rights and privileges on an unsuspecting community. This change presaged the removal of Gaither, the hiring of Breslin, the mistaken foray away from Drexel's core values and co-op traditions into the liberal arts market, and the alienation of the traditional engineering faculty. Some find this argument too soft—the kind a humanist might make to an engineer—but Arnold's summation upon his departure was both accurate and prescient, and he alone in 1987 predicted that even as the wrenching events of the Gaither period appeared to have run their course, the worst days for the university lay ahead.

This then leads to the sixth argument. The decline of Drexel University is fundamentally a story about the failure of corporate governance, albeit in the nonprofit sector. While this may seem a harsh judgment to some, as each of the above-mentioned arguments hold elements of truth, the board in any corporation must be accountable for the direction and ultimate success of the institution. In the case of Drexel University, the natural inclination of most directors to trust the leadership of the chief executive was exacerbated by the long history of one-man rule at the institution. As such, this conclusion is not an indictment of the Drexel board per se, but rather an indictment of the form and structure of corporate governance as it has evolved in higher education.

The board of trustees at Drexel existed in a state of somnolence under Hagerty, as the long-tenured president was the unquestioned leader of the institution. Hagerty encouraged that condition as a means of assuring his control of the institution. The board began to awaken during the Gaither crisis, as it found itself faced with an organizational and public relations disaster of frightening proportions. The Drexel board finally found its own voice under the leadership of Rick Breslin, who understood and believed in the importance of board leadership at academic institutions, and who embraced board development as a key area of responsibility of the president.

Through it all, the Drexel board, like most others, was dependent on the president for information on the conditions of the organization. However, as Papadakis suggests, the annual financial reports and monthly enrollment data provided sufficient indicators that the institution was in a downward spiral. In addition, it is clear from the historical record that the board received financial information that suggested that the university was in a fiscally precarious state for years. Yet despite all of this information, even a businessman with significant board experience such as Drexel trustee Paul Ingersoll had only a vague understanding that the university was in a period of fiscal distress.

The decline of Drexel University raises the question as to whether the nature of nonprofit organizations, and the lack of shareholders with a financial interest in corporate performance, mitigates against effective board governance within that sector. However, Ingersoll resists this suggestion, as he takes the view that weakness in board governance is not inherently related to whether the organization is for-profit or nonprofit. He suggests instead that as a general matter board members are less likely to give the same attention to an organization where they are on the board as they would to their own company, and they are more likely to defer to management.

Bob Kirkwood, a man with years of experience leading a university accrediting agency who served as a member of the Drexel board with Ingersoll during Breslin's tenure, concurred in the view that board governance is a weak institution across sectors.

> Whether they be corporations or academic institutions or nonprofit, charitable organizations or whatever, the boards invariably are the weakest link largely because there are too many people who like to have their names as members of boards but who do so more because it will look good in their obituary than because of any contribution they can make.[3]

Ingersoll and Kirkwood suggest that the problems of board leadership, governance, and oversight are not accentuated in the nonprofit sector, where shareholder financial losses are not at issue, but rather are inherent to the board model of organizational governance. The issue of the failure of this model of corporate governance has been engaged at many levels of public debate, as Congress passed the Sarbanes-Oxley Act, intended to strengthen the quality and integrity of financial disclosure, and the Justice Department continues to pursue the issue of director accountability to shareholders.

These public actions to strengthen corporate governance have grown out of abuses in the for-profit sector, and address issues of fiduciary accountability to shareholders. In the university sector, the

Drexel experience suggests that different accountability measures are warranted. While Drexel University has made a public statement by embracing Sarbanes-Oxley, improved financial disclosure would not have solved the problem of board passivity and the lack of appreciation of issues of organizational culture that were at the root of the Drexel crisis.

Drexel University suffered from not having individuals on its board who brought a combined understanding of the university culture and competitive markets, and who could open up the discussion, challenge the president when necessary, and enable the broader board community to consider the impact of decisions that were theirs to make. The board of trustees never embraced the traditional values of the academy with respect to the role and rights of the faculty, nor did they appreciate the depth of the faculty views on this subject. While George Ross suggested that the board knows that the faculty "are very important," the board view of faculty participation in shared governance certainly falls short of reflecting the faculty's view of the university as "a democratic community of scholars" in which "shared governance is the fundamental ingredient of a healthy academic institution."[4]

The fundamental tension between the values of the board and those of the faculty remains a central challenge for Drexel University and has led to an attitude of resignation and alienation among some faculty. This tension has real consequences for the university as it moves forward on a strategic plan that is predicated on building a combined academic and research enterprise that integrates the medical school and biosciences with the traditional schools and faculties. That integration demands commitment and engagement on the part of the faculty, qualities that have been undermined by the tensions over shared governance.

The Drexel story highlights the ineffectiveness of shared governance structures in advancing the interests of the organization when faced with external challenges. The three-party relationship—among the board, the president, and the faculty—lacked structures for real participation, notwithstanding an array of committees created to oversee the budget reductions during the Breslin years. While in the corporate sector a wide variety of structures have been created to provide for worker ownership and participation in management in order to create organizational alignment, these models are less apparent in the university sector, despite that sector having the most well-educated "workforce."

The Drexel story also suggests that as in the corporate world, a turnaround strategy must address the causes of decline. Downsizing has become a buzzword of U.S. economic discourse. However, it may lack salience as a core strategy for many university turnarounds. The case of Drexel University suggests that an understanding of the cost structure of the institution is critical to the development of a management plan in response to decline. Drexel University under Breslin was a typical higher educational institution, with high fixed operating costs. Accordingly, as Papadakis observed, even as management adopted a downsizing strategy in response to enrollment declines, the cost per student rose due to the high fixed cost structure. As enrollment declined, the costs of facilities remained, the faculty-student ratio rose, and debt service per FTE rose. All of these were measures of productivity that were going in the wrong direction.

The premise of institutional downsizing is that there is a new viable equilibrium of demand and supply. This presumes that from an enrollment standpoint there is stable demand in the marketplace, albeit at a lower level, based on the value proposition presented by the institution. During the Drexel decline, the Breslin administration and its external consultants clung to the notion that regional demographics were the root of the problem, and that a new equilibrium would be found at lower levels of enrollment. The frustration faced by the board of trustees during the Breslin era was that the board members could not see a bottom based on the trajectory of the data presented to them. Therefore, the premise of downsizing that there was a new viable equilibrium point was not evident.

While the early mission of Drexel was forced to evolve in the face of market changes, a central failing of the Breslin administration was its inability to recognize that its surviving mission of cooperative education tied to the workplace had created a niche market that proved to be enormously resilient in the face of other market changes during the 1980s and '90s. The enrollment decline during the Breslin years derived not simply from pure demographic changes, but rather from the abandonment—intentional or not—of the historical market niche that the institution had enjoyed and the preference to focus on the more traditional college student market, a market in which the university lacked competitive advantage.

As Don Dickason suggested, Drexel proved unable to compete as just another liberal arts college for students from suburban high schools. It lacked both the reputation and the facilities to do that, and ultimately saw its net price flatten and fall as evidence of its lack of competitive advantage. The loss of Drexel's sense of identity in the market reflected the president's own disregard for the value of co-op as a central feature of the Drexel education, and ultimately the lack of understanding of the brand value that Drexel had in a niche market that it had created over the years. Ironically, as Breslin developed the board, the ascendant voices became those of the Drexel alumni who understood and valued co-op and increasingly saw the president as out of step with the history and core values of the institution.

Taki Papadakis brought to Drexel several essential attributes that enabled him to succeed. First and foremost he was a strong leader, much in the model of Hagerty himself, and brought back a strong central presence that resonated with the culture of the institution. Like Hagerty, he had a clear understanding of where he was going and what he had to do to get there, and also like Hagerty he kept his own counsel and would tell only his closest associates where he was heading, in order to minimize conflict and opposition. Second, Papadakis came to Drexel from Cincinnati, well versed in the unique attributes of cooperative education and its impact on both internal operations and market position. Finally, Papadakis was a civil engineer who brought to Drexel a familiar style that was comforting to the old-school faculty.

Papadakis' immediate conclusion that the turnaround solution must be revenue-driven was a significant one for the institution and for others experiencing declining enrollment. He did not believe that the demographics were the problem, but rather that they had become the excuse for management failure. Similarly, he saw that downsizing could not be effective due to the high fixed cost structure of the institution. The problem faced by Drexel during the period of decline was not the availability of students, but rather the effectiveness of management and the quality of the presentation of the value proposition to the segment of the market for which that proposition had salience. The solution was to fill the seats.

The Drexel experience suggests that, as in the corporate arena, an essential first step in the planning of a turnaround in higher education is an effective diagnosis of the problem. In the Drexel case, two conclusions are evident with the benefit of hindsight. The first is that cutting costs for the sake of cutting costs was not going to solve the problem, even if it was essential in a given budget year. Papadakis understood this as he saw that the high fixed cost base of the institution made further cost cutting impractical. The second is that enrollment declines need to be addressed by clarifying the value proposition of the institution with an understanding of the markets within which the institution is competing. Papadakis emphasized this upon his arrival as a central issue for the entire community, as he challenged the faculty to tell him why a parent should spend the money to send a child there. Papadakis' hiring of Gary Hamme to run enrollment management based upon Hamme's success in that position years earlier brought back into the marketing role an individual with a clear understanding of Drexel's value proposition, and the ability to answer the question Papadakis put to the faculty.

The impact of markets on higher education is not that they turn academic institutions into businesses, but rather that they challenge the primacy of each institution's own mission in the face of a competitive universe. The essence of higher education as a collective industry remains its essential and unique role in the preservation and continuation of a common culture, the accumulation and transmission of knowledge, the engagement and preparation of the citizenry to participate in democratic society, and the success and vibrancy of a nation's economy. Yet even as the industry as a whole is essential, the survival of any individual institution is far from assured. For each individual college or university, understanding its own unique attributes and finding and sustaining its own niche in the competitive marketplace are critical to its long-term survival.

Over the course of the past half-century, the higher education industry has seen the professionalization of its administrative staff. With the professionalization of management and the encroachment of business and the language of markets, the root tension between the faculty and the administration has increased. The greatest threat to higher educational institutions, ironically, is their failure to evolve into learning organizations where market feedback is embraced as an opportunity for growth and evolution in ways that enable each institution and all of the participants therein—beginning with the faculty—to recommit themselves to the vision and ideals that are the heart of the institution. Only by embracing the opportunity for continued transformation and growth can each institution hope to fulfill its mission and at the same time succeed in the new market realities.

Postscript

Dr. Victor H. Hutchinson, Professor Emeritus of Zoology, University of Oklahoma, suggests that the metaphor of the frog in boiling water is not born out by scientific evidence.

> The legend is entirely incorrect! The *critical thermal maxima* of many species of frogs have been determined by several investigators. In this procedure, the water in which a frog is submerged is heated gradually at about two degrees Fahrenheit per minute. As the temperature of the water is gradually increased, the frog will eventually become more and more active in attempts to escape the heated water. If the container size and opening allow the frog to jump out, it will do so.
>
> So where does that leave us with the metaphor for the human response to environmental degradation? Well, the idea that you can induce a frog to remain in boiling water if you start it off in cold water is not true biologically.[5]

Survival, it seems, for frogs as well as for organizations, is an instinctive response, once the water gets hot enough.

Note on Research Methods

The research that produced this book included five sequential phases of data development and analysis. The first phase involved the compilation and analysis of financial and admissions-related data during the period 1980 to 1998, and included financial analysis, trend analysis, and tracking of the key performance indicators of fiscal distress. The second phase included an assessment of similar trends in financial performance and enrollment information with respect to a cohort of similar institutions during the same time period based on information available from the IPEDS database. The purpose of this analysis was to determine the extent to which trends identified in the analysis of the Drexel data reflected or deviated from those experienced by peer institutions, and to provide a deeper understanding of the market in which Drexel was competing. The third phase entailed document analysis of historical materials from the period of decline through the turnaround phase in order to establish a chronological record of the events, discussions, and decision making, to juxtapose the timing and trends in the data analysis developed during the earlier phases against this time line, to seek to understand the linkage between the phase one data and the chronological record, and to understand the extent to which that data appeared to have been available and to have influenced decision making over the course of the events as they unfolded. The fourth phase comprised oral interviews with members of the university community during the period 1980–1998, through which I sought to identify themes and patterns related to the events as they transpired, and ultimately to understand the nature of the decision-making process and the relationships across groups as they actually existed at the time of the decline and turnaround. The final phase included a process of triangulation to link the analysis from the earlier stages into an internally consistent understanding of what the key factors and decisions were that contributed to the decline and turnaround as it unfolded.

Notes

CHAPTER ONE. INTRODUCTION

1. Schumpeter, 1975.
2. Carnegie Foundation for the Advancement of Teaching, 1975.
3. Keller, 1983.
4. Zemsky, 2002.
5. Commission on the Future of Higher Education, 2006.
6. Seibel, 1999.
7. Enrollment information from monthly enrollment reports to the board of trustees and executive committee of the board as well as from university bond official statements. It was notable that while the trustees received regular and comprehensive information on enrollment, the data generally provided a snapshot of the institution rather than year over year comparisons, and did not therefore highlight salient trends that arguably would have facilitated trustee understanding of the direction of the institution.
8. Bibeault, 1982; Chakraborty & Dixit, 1992; and Harker, 1996.
9. Hardy, 1989; and Paul, 2005.
10. The stories of NYU and Northeastern, similar "schools of immigrants" tightly woven into the fabric of the cities whose population they served, can be found in Frusciano, & Pettit, 1997; Chernow, 1979; and Nicklin, 1994.
11. Bok, 2003.

CHAPTER TWO. ANTHONY DREXEL'S LEGACY

1. Kotzin, 1983.
2. Ibid.
3. Rottenberg, 2001.
4. Kotzin, op. cit.
5. Ibid.
6. Ibid.

7. Ibid.

8. Ibid.

9. Kotzin, op. cit.

10. Drexel, who died two years after the opening of his institute, recognized that as markets changed, the institute would need to adapt. As such, his vision was in direct contrast to the academic notion of a core curriculum that is timeless in nature. Of course, the institute was not created as a traditional academic institution, a central issue that would emerge as it sought to build an academic identity. The imperative of change, however, is vastly different for a well-endowed institution than for one that is largely tuition dependent. When A. J. Drexel admonished the institute to change as the markets changed, it was to assure that it continued to be of value to its students. In today's market environment, the imperative of change for Drexel University is driven by the need to remain competitive and fiscally sound. There are, therefore, three perspectives on change between the founder, the institution today, and the faculty. For the founder, as evidenced by his and Child's writing, change was an issue of value creation for the students to be served by the institute. For the institution today it is an issue of market viability, growth, and status, which are seen as interconnected. For the faculty, as articulated in the statements of the faculty senate, it is a matter of guiding the institution toward the core and less temporal values of the pursuit of knowledge.

CHAPTER THREE. THE PAST AS PROLOGUE

1. Drexel University, 1970. The emergence of the faculty council was contemporaneous with the application for university status. The Report of the Drexel Planning Commission, *Emergence of a University,* published in Spring 1970, articulated the rationale for a representative faculty assembly as a participant in the governance of the institution:

> The governance of a modern university must be predicated upon constant and intense interaction among the various components of the university community. . . without interaction in governance, rational administration is impossible.

The commission called for the establishment of two committees, the Composite Committee and the University Committee, to oversee the university governance process, with faculty council representation on both. Finally, the report recognized that university status brought with it the endorsement of a faculty role consistent with AAUP publications:

> We recognize that university faculties traditionally have had a major influence in the development and implementation of university policies. We reassert the faculty's rights and responsibilities in these areas.

2. Ibid. The Report of the Drexel Planning Commission makes clear that the competition for a doctoral faculty was a prime consideration in the urgency of migration to university status. The report cited Drexel's application to the Commonwealth of Pennsylvania for university status:

> Only those universities that are able to provide the challenge of teaching graduate students—and opportunities for scholars to pursue their scholarship through research—only these can attract the most competent teachers.

3. Interview with Bruce Eisenstein, 9/29/03.

4. While this may be true of many universities, at Drexel the ceremony when the new president is formally installed continues to be referred to as a coronation, and Hagerty himself was referred to as "King Hagerty."

5. Interview with Thomas Canavan, 10/8/03.

6. Interview, 10/27/03.

7. Provost Harvill Eaton described "Eaton's Laws" of life at Drexel, wherein the institution was defined by co-op, the quarter system, and the train schedules. Co-op, with the resulting impact of having large portions of the student body away from campus on six-month co-ops at any given point of time, places far greater demands on course cycling, academic programming, and other matters. That, in combination with the quarter system, requires a full schedule of summer courses, something that most faculty are loath to embrace. The train schedules reflect the fact of a commuter faculty that prefer, even more than most, to teach midday courses.

8. The Soffa story, as related by William Gaither, is highly instructive about the direction of the Drexel mission over the course of the years. Notwithstanding the oft-cited role of Drexel as graduating 50 percent of the black engineers in Pennsylvania over a period of years, the African American population at the university has historically been and continues to be very low, a notable fact for an urban university, much less one created with a mission of service to the urban working class. The Soffa story suggests that the impact of co-op placement considerations in the admissions process effectively resulted in the migration of religious and racial biases in the workplace to university admissions, as a matter of outcome if not intent. The irony of this evolution is the contrast that it presents with the founding mission and philosophy of the institution and the commitment of service to the African American community of Katherine Drexel, Anthony Drexel's niece and collaborator.

9. Hagerty's views were conveyed most vividly by those faculty who were hired during his presidency, including Tom Canavan (10/8/03), Jacques Catudal (9/22/03 and 10/28/03), Bruce Eisenstein (9/29/03), and Andy Verzilli (10/7/03). A clear motivation for the drive for doctoral program development was the market for faculty, as articulated in the 1970 Drexel Planning Commission report. The drive for status and prestige has been an ongoing aspect

of institutional management over the past half-century. As a new, endowed institution, the founding mission was anti-status, as its focus was one of paternalistic social welfare rather than academic pursuit. Needing paying customers has a way of changing things—an emerging and central fact of life in the academy these days—and so it did at Drexel. Hagerty witnessed the emergence of the competitive marketplace in what had been a cloistered niche market. Drexel through most of his tenure had strong brand loyalty within its core market, but Hagerty saw that whither during his tenure.

10. Interview, 10/8/03.

11. Ibid.

12. Reflected in interviews with Jonathan Awerbuck, Jacques Catudal, and Anthony Glascock.

13. Interview with university trustee, 10/28/03.

14. Interview, 9/29/03.

15. Rick Breslin and William Gaither may not have agreed on much, but they agreed in their summation of the lack of financial support provided to the institution. Paul Ingersoll, who worked with Breslin on the centennial events and the celebration of the beatification of Katherine Drexel, lamented the lack of family commitment to the institution.

16. Interview, 10/8/03.

17. Interview with Tom Hindelang, 9/27/03.

18. Ibid.

19. *Philadelphia Inquirer*, 4/25/84.

20. The board meeting minutes beginning in 1982 repeatedly reflect the urgency of building residential capacity and expanding the enrollment market, in response to the enrollment trends in the northeast and the decline in the commuter student market. The comments were not restricted to Hagerty, but came from Barbara Fritze (dean of admissions), John Neal (registrar), and Art Joblin (a physicist who served in a range of administrative capacities over the years, and at the time was vice president for student affairs).

21. Data from enrollment management reports included in Drexel bond official statements and Board materials.

22. Tuition data from board reports. Consumer price information from U.S. Bureau of Labor Statistics.

23. Interview, 10/27/03.

24. Bruce Eisenstein related this from a conversation with Hagerty. "Hagerty told me this story. . . . Bernie Sagik had suggested to him that we require every engineering student to have a personal computer, buy it and have access to it. Hagerty thought that that was the stupidest thing he had ever heard. . . . He thought computers were a passing fad. It was going to be like a lot of other things. He said it would just disappear and it would not be something that would be around in ten years or fifteen years, and it was also really dumb. So, Hagerty went out to his country club . . . Hagerty prided himself on having two presidencies. He was president of Aronimink Country

Club in addition to being president of Drexel. And he used to laugh and laugh and laugh and say the most important to him is Aronimink. . . . In any case, he was out at the country club one day, and he was sitting around with a bunch of his cronies. And he said to them, 'Do you know what these fuzzy-headed people at Drexel are proposing? They're proposing that every engineering student have their own computer. Can you imagine anything so dumb?' And colleagues said, 'We think this is a great idea. But it would be an even better idea if you did it for every student at the school.' So, Hagerty stopped. He paused. He said, 'What do you mean?' They said, 'Imagine how much PR you'd get if you had the fashion design people and the English majors and everyone else with their own computer.' So next day, Hagerty went back and called up Sagik and said, 'You've got permission to do your computer thing, but only if you require it of every student in the school, every single student.' And that's how we got started in this. He never actually believed in it." Interview, 9/29/03.

25. Thomas Canavan recalled the public attention that the initiative brought to Drexel through David Jones's documentary on the Drexel microcomputer initiative entitled "Going National: The Drexel Microcomputer Project." "When it was shown for the first time with great fanfare in the Mandell Theatre, Steve Jobs was present to congratulate the university on its 'cutting edge' decision." E-mail, 3/5/06.

26. This story illuminates an important aspect of the Drexel culture. The tension within the institution between the pedagogical value of initiatives versus the public relations value is one that continues today and is linked to the underlying theme of the relationship between the institutional mission and market forces. Sagik was presenting an initiative that he proposed to be gradually introduced into the classroom as a tool for teaching and learning. Hagerty's cronies suggested a more immediate value to the initiative, and one that turned out to be of enduring importance in the public eye. Hagerty understood that Drexel was a creature of the market from its inception, and that to value what was appealing in the marketplace was not a compromise for Drexel, but rather a premise on which it was founded. Most academic institutions— and their faculty—find their presence in markets confusing and disorienting, and view market forces as ones that inherently distort or threaten their core mission and values. In that regard Drexel is fundamentally different, as it was not created as an "academic" institution. For Anthony Drexel, the ultimate validation of his institute was the value perceived by the student in the world of work, and he explicitly stated that it must change as markets dictated.

27. Pothier, September 18, 1983.

CHAPTER FOUR. THE DISPOSABLE PRESIDENT

1. See Gerstner, 2002. Lou Gerstner writes that the essential step in turnaround leadership is the creation of a sense of urgency:

The *sine qua non* of any successful corporate transformation is public acknowledgement of the existence of a crisis. If employees do not believe a crisis exists, they will not make the sacrifices that are necessary to change. Nobody likes change . . . change represents uncertainty and, potentially, pain. So there must be a crisis, and it is the job of the CEO to define and communicate that crisis, its magnitude, its severity, and its impact. Just as important, the CEO must be able to communicate how to end the crisis—the strategy, the new company model, the new culture. All of this takes enormous commitment from the CEO to communicate, communicate, and communicate some more.

2. Interview, 10/27/03.

3. Walton, August 9, 1987.

4. Both board and faculty members interviewed confirmed the lack of contact between the board and the faculty through the end of the Gaither presidency.

5. It is unclear what happened to Hagerty's support of Sagik, as Hagerty's support would no doubt have swayed Everett and Rauth. One faculty member from the time presumed that Sagik proved himself to be too close to the faculty and not directive enough as a matter of management style to suit either Hagerty or the board leadership.

6. Drexel University, 1987.

7. Walton, op. cit.

8. Ibid.

9. This was the view of several board members, though it was one of the few comments in the interviews of board members that was requested to be used without attribution.

10. Gaither, 2002.

11. Gaither's relationship with the community was related in interviews with William Gaither, 10/27/03, Richard Schneider, 10/27/03, and community member John Claypool, 11/3/03.

12. Interview, 10/27/03.

13. Ibid.

14. Interview with William Gaither, 10/27/03.

15. Interview, 10/27/03.

16. Stapleton, April 11, 1986.

17. Odom, August 31, 1984.

18. Sutton & Odom, September 8, 1984.

19. Board meeting minutes, 12/19/84.

20. Interview with William Gaither, 10/27/03.

21. Ibid.

22. Drexel University, 1984.

23. Interview, 10/27/03.

24. Ibid.

25. Interview, 10/8/03.

26. Board minutes, 9/18/85.

27. The quotations from the strategic plan on the following pages are from the *Drexel University Long-range Plan 1985–1995* dated September 18, 1985. The detail from that plan is important in the insight that it offers on the challenges facing the institution, the similarity with the circumstances of the institution some twenty years later, and in the juxtaposition between the insights it contained and the absolute hostility that it engendered as a document that emerged lacking the community support that would enable it to become a galvanizing plan for the future. Of course, it was, as a matter of process, totally in character with the history of the institution.

28. Interview, 10/27/03.

29. Drexel University, 1985.

30. Faculty Council. 1985.

31. Auerbach, 1985.

32. Gaither, December 11, 1985.

33. Pothier, February 13, 1986.

34. Pothier, February 19, 1986,

35. Saunders, March 14, 1986.

36. Interview with Bruce Eisenstein, 9/29/03.

37. Interview with Tom Canavan, 10/8/03.

38. Saunders, April 18, 1986.

39. Interview, 10/27/03.

40. Giraffe, 1986.

41. Buchman, 1986.

42. Klivington, May 2, 1986.

43. Interview, 10/27/03.

44. Ibid.

45. One of the enduring conflicts within the institution related to the pursuit of university status is that it was perceived internally as a strategy of winners and losers. The College of Engineering has historically been the "flagship" school within the institution, and has seen reform efforts that build new areas of strength as undermining its primacy, to say nothing of taking its money. This tension emerged with the efforts to build a stronger arts and sciences faculty under Hagerty and continues to this day with a merger with the medical school that offers a world of new opportunities (and risks) but threatens the centrality of the College of Engineering.

46. Blackney, October 17, 1986.

47. Ibid.

48. Ibid.

49. Blank, October 17, 1986.

50. Ibid.

51. Interview, 10/27/03.

52. Blackney, January 9, 1987.

53. Ibid.

54. Ibid.

55. Saunders, May 8, 1987.

56. Collins, May 7, 1987.

57. Collins, May 9, 1987.

58. Collins, May 12, 1987.

59. Saunders, May 15, 1987.

60. Ibid.

61. Drexel University, May 21, 1987.

62. Grace & Konolige, May 22, 1987.

63. Morschek, 1987.

64. Several faculty interviewed described this scene, offering a sense of wonder, more than a decade later, at the "surreal" image of a President Gaither presiding at his own censure motion.

65. Interview, 1/30/04.

66. Daughen, June 12, 1987.

67. Walton, op. cit.

68. Ibid.

69. Quoted in Walton, op. cit.

70. Drexel University, 1987.

71. Ibid.

72. Interview with William Gaither, 10/27/03.

73. Interview with George Ross, 10/9/03.

74. Interview with Anthony Glascock, 7/28/03.

75. Arnold, October 21, 1987.

76. Ibid.

77. Myers, October 24, 1987.

CHAPTER FIVE. TAKING STOCK

1. Woodall & Collins, October 21, 1987.

2. Interview, 10/27/03.

3. Gaither shared this correspondence, but asked that the recipient and details remain confidential.

4. Interview with George Ross, 10/9/03.

5. Data from U.S. Dept. Education, National Center for Education Statistics, and board reports.

6. Interview, 9/29/03.

7. Data from board reports. Consumer price information from the U.S. Bureau of Labor Statistics.

8. Data from Drexel bond official statements and board reports.

9. Similar to Drexel, NYU was an urban private university with a history of serving the particular needs of first-generation and immigrant students. In the late 1960s and early 1970s, faced with competition from lower

cost, public schools, NYU went through a dramatic fiscal crisis. It successfully emerged from that challenge and has repositioned itself as a premier national university. See Frusciano & Pettit, op. cit.

10. Data from board reports. Income data from the U.S. Bureau of Economic Analysis.

11. Data from Drexel bond official statements and board reports.

12. Board meeting minutes, June 1988.

13. Still, 1988.

14. Interview with Bob Kirkwood, 10/20/03.

15. Interview, 9/30/03.

16. Interview, 10/9/03.

CHAPTER SIX. REDEMPTION

1. Board report, 9/21/88.

2. Board Report, 10/88.

3. Board Report, 12/88.

4. Interview, 9/8/03.

5. Faculty Council, 1988.

6. Collins, March 16, 1989.

7. Ingersoll, January 10, 1989.

8. Board Report, 5/89.

9. Breslin engaged advisors with considerable reputations as he sought to address the issues as he saw them at Drexel. It is nonetheless unclear what Breslin's diagnosis of the problem was in enrollment management that led him to invest considerable effort in making changes there. Enrollment had rebounded from its slide in the mid-1980s and applications were rising. Breslin's actions did suggest that he saw the institution as troubled across the board, and he sought out the best advisors in the field to help him in his work. The outcome of all of that advice was mixed at best, as both Breslin and his advisors presumed that Drexel was similar to other institutions. Don Dickason, who headed enrollment management under Breslin, noted how different Drexel was in the area of enrollment and that what worked other places was not relevant to Drexel. Hamme, as a Drexel graduate and director of co-op, understood what Drexel was about and could sell it, notwithstanding his lack of credentials. Breslin either could not see past the credentialing issue or simply wanted his own people leading critical areas of the institution, not an uncommon leadership preference.

10. Interview with Gary Hamme, 9/24/03. An interesting aspect of higher education culture is that on the one hand institutional history is of great importance and institutions are often defined by certain seminal leaders, while on the other hand, time begins anew with the arrival of a new president. The presumption on Breslin's part that the former team had little value to add reflected not just his own style, and reliance on industry experts, but this

phenomenon of a new president preferring to move forward with a new team. Succession planning, a key responsibility of a corporate chief executive, is not historically practiced in higher education, and senior leaders are rarely seen as future presidents. This predisposition can mitigate against organizational learning and management strategies that build upon knowledge resident within the institution. In the Drexel case in particular this attitude had unfortunate consequences, as Drexel is truly distinct in mission, values, and market position from other institutions. Leaders and senior administrators—and experts, for that matter—brought in from outside generally had a steep learning curve to understand co-op and the peculiarities of higher education at Drexel.

11. Interview, 9/24/03.
12. Interview with Vincent Stach, 10/28/03.
13. Board minutes, 2/8/89.
14. Board meeting minutes, 3/15/89.
15. Board meeting minutes, 3/15/89.
16. Board meeting minutes, 3/15/89.
17. Board Report, 5/89.
18. Breslin, 1989.
19. Ibid.
20. Ibid.
21. Zemsky & Massy, 1989.
22. Board meeting minutes, 10/11/89.
23. Gallot, 1989.
24. Collins, February 7, 1990.
25. Interview, 9/28/03.
26. Interview with Tom Canavan, 10/8/03.
27. Interview, 9/30/03.
28. Breslin, 1990.
29. Ibid.
30. Interview with Jacques Catudal, 9/22/03.
31. This comment was made with the request of anonymity.
32. Board meeting minutes, 3/21/90.
33. Investment Committee minutes, 5/1/90.
34. Investment Committee minutes, 5/23/90.
35. Investment Committee minutes, 5/23/90.
36. Finance Committee meeting minutes, 6/90.
37. Executive Committee meeting minutes, 6/90.
38. Language itself is an obstacle in discussions at the interstices between the academy and corporate universes. Words such as *markets, product,* and *customer* elicit immediate and negative reactions when brought into the academic world. On the other hand, *committee* has the same impact on senior executives, in the manner that it is used here by Breslin. For bankers serving on a university board to be told that urgent fiscal matters will be assigned to a "very important Blue Ribbon Commission" to be addressed would be a sure

sign that little would be done. Such a view is validated by the notion that academic committees are often designed to promote inaction rather than action, as suggested by Cohen & March, 1986, and as such are an inappropriate tool to use in a crisis situation.

39 Executive Committee meeting minutes, 6/90.

40. Board meeting minutes, 9/90.

41. Board meeting minutes, 12/90.

42. Finance Committee minutes, 2/91.

43. Interview, 10/28/03.

44. Collison, 1991.

45. Collins, March 19, 1991.

46. Collins, March 28, 1991.

47. Finance Committee meeting minutes, 2/91.

48. Collins, June 6, 1991.

49. Interview with Richard Schneider, 10/27/03.

50. Data from board reports.

51. Interview, 9/24/03.

52. Data from Philadelphia Community College and board reports.

53. Breslin, 1991.

54. Board minutes, May 1991.

55. Interview, 10/28/03.

56. Breslin, 1991.

57. Interview with Anthony Glascock, 7/28/03.

58. Data from Drexel bond official statements and board reports.

59. Interview with Bruce Eisenstein, 9/29/03.

60. *Philadelphia Inquirer*, 10/23/91.

61. Data from Drexel Annual Reports and board reports. CPI from U.S. Bureau of Labor Statistics.

62. Interview with trustee, 10/28/03.

63. Interview, 9/24/03.

64. Interview with Andy Verzilli, 10/7/03.

65. Interview with Don Dickason, 11/3/03.

66. Ibid.

67. Breslin, 1992.

68. Interview, 10/8/03.

69. Interview with Tom Hindelang, 9/27/03.

70. Interview, 2/29/03.

71. Interview, 10/8/03.

72. Interview, 9/29/03.

73. Breslin, 1992.

74. Faculty Senate, 1992.

75. Ibid.

76. Interview, 9/22/03.

77. Interview, 10/8/03.

78. Interview, 10/28/03.
79. Ibid.
80. Interview with Anthony Glascock, 7/28/03.
81. Interview, 10/20/03.
82. Interview, 10/8/03.
83. Ibid.
84. Interview, 10/28/03.
85. Interview, 7/28/03.
86. Interview, 9/29/03.
87. Interview, 10/9/03.
88. As recalled by Anthony Glascock from his negotiations with the Teamsters. Interview, 7/28/03.
89. Interview, 10/20/03.
90. The depth of Verzilli's anger at Breslin, so evident a decade after he resigned his tenure, is mirrored by his own love for Drexel. Verzilli saw by the end that Breslin had little regard for Drexel's core virtues: co-operative education, applied learning, and a commitment to a student population not embraced by the most elite higher educational institutions. By turning his back on the core Drexel audience and market, Breslin was abandoning both the mission and the community, and Verzilli could not abide being part of it and complicit in bringing him into the institution. Verzilli gave voice to the core dilemma that emerged around Breslin: that the flaw in the trustees' selection of Breslin was that they had selected a leader who failed to take the core mission and values of the community seriously, and to listen to and understand the essential nature of the community and the institution.
91. Paolantonio, December 10, 1992.
92. Breslin, 1992.
93. Paolantonio, op. cit.
94. Ibid.
95. Interview, 9/24/03.
96. Argenti, 1976.
97. Data from Drexel bond official statements and board reports.
98. Faculty member requested anonymity.
99. Interview, 10/28/03.

CHAPTER SEVEN. HITTING BOTTOM

1. Board minutes, March 1993.
2. Breslin,1993.
3. Hardy, 1993.
4. Breslin, op. cit.
5. Interview, 10/9/03.
6. Interview, 10/22/03.
7. Interview, 10/28/03.

8. Data from Drexel University DUIMS database.

9. Data from Drexel bond official statements and board reports.

10. Data from the Philadelphia Archdiocese and Drexel bond official statements.

11. Data from the U.S. Department of Education, National Center for Education Statistics, and Drexel bond official statements.

12. Data from the NSF WebCASPAR Database and Drexel bond official statements.

13. Data from NSF WebCASPAR Database, Philadelphia Community College, and Drexel bond official statements.

14. Net price calculated from data in Drexel Annual Reports, board reports, and Drexel bond official statements.

15. Interview, 10/8/03.

16. Interview with Gary Hamme, 9/24/03.

17. Interview, 10/9/03.

18. Interview, 10/28/03.

19. Breslin, 1993.

20. Ibid.

21. Interview, 10/28/03.

22. This view was conveyed directly in interviews, though it does not appear to be supported by the enrollment data. The low point for enrollment, whether one looks at freshman, full-time undergraduate, or total, was not reached until the fall, and net tuition revenue per FTE appeared to be flat at best.

23. Breslin, op. cit.

24. Data from Drexel annual financial reports.

25. The fact of increasing financial aid expenditures in the face of declining enrollments was evidence that the school was unable to sustain its price in the marketplace, as discussed earlier. This likely mirrored the rising admit rate and declining yields, signaling the need to discount tuition to attract students, but also likely reflected the move out of Drexel's traditional market niche and away from a focus on students whose interest in co-op made them predisposed to consider Drexel. In past years, Drexel had enjoyed very high yields, paid close attention to the level of tuition, and had a very small financial aid budget.

26. Breslin, 1993.

27. Breslin, 1994.

28. Interview, 10/28/03.

29. Responsibility center budgeting, or management, is a tool for the management of complex institutions, and provides a means of incentivizing behavior and achieving other management goals. However, it is not a turn-around strategy. In fact, RCB implementation can take years, as it requires new types of behavior and new skills among participants. Even in the best of circumstances, effective implementation requires skillful senior management to

navigate the fears and competitive behaviors that are unleashed. To implement RCB in a situation that is already dire only exacerbates these challenges.

30. Anonymity requested.

31. Anonymity requested.

32. Breslin, op. cit.

33. Interview, 10/28/03.

34. Interview, 10/8/03.

35. Interview with Steve Schutt, 10/15/03.

36. Interview, 10/28/03.

37. Interview, 10/9/03.

38. Data from board reports.

39. Interview, 9/29/03.

40. Interview with Robert Kirkwood, 10/20/03.

41. Anonymity requested.

42. Kotzin, op. cit.

43. Ibid. p. 58.

44. Ibid.

45. Interview with Paul Ingersoll, 10/22/03.

46. Goodman, September 22, 1994.

47. Interview with Chuck Pennoni, 10/16/03.

48. Ibid.

49. Ibid.

50. Ibid.

51. Pennoni, 1995.

52. Ibid.

53. Board minutes, April 1995.

54. Interview, 10/16/03.

55. Ibid.

56. Interview, 10/9/03.

57. Interview with Taki Papadakis, 10/19/03.

CHAPTER EIGHT. TURNAROUND

1. Board minutes, 5/95.

2. Interview with Taki Papadakis, 9/19/03.

3. Interview with Paul Ingersoll, 10/22/03.

4. Data from Drexel financial reports.

5. Interview, 9/19/03.

6. Ibid.

7. Hamme, Dehne, & Terranova, 1997.

8. Ibid.

9. Interview, 9/24/03.

10. Interview, 9/19/03.

11. Hamme, Dehne, & Terranova, op. cit.

12. Interview with Richard Greenawalt, 10/20/03.

13. Interview, 9/19/03.

14. Papadakis, 1995.

15. Interview, 9/19/03.

16. Ibid.

17. Papadakis, 1996.

18. Papadakis, 1996.

19. Interview with trustee, 10/28/03.

20. Interview with Jacques Catudal, 10/28/03.

21. Interview, 9/19/03.

22. Interview, 9/24/03.

23. Interview, 9/19/03.

24. Ibid.

25. Data from Drexel bond official statements and board reports.

26. Data from Drexel bond official statements and board reports.

27. Interview with Anthony Glascock, 7/28/03.

28. Data from Drexel bond official statements and board reports.

29. Data from the National Science Foundation IPEDS database on a cohort of technology institutes and co-op schools used for planning and peer analysis purposes by the Drexel University Faculty Senate.

30. Interview, 9/19/03

31. Interview, 10/3/03.

32. Interview, 10/9/03.

33. Faculty Senate, 2002.

34. Ibid.

35. Ibid.

36. Interview, 10/3/03.

37. Interview, 10/9/03.

38. Interview, 10/16/03.

39. Anonymity requested.

40. Interview, 10/16/03.

41. Interview, 10/28/03.

42. Interview, 9/29/03.

43. Interview, 10/16/03.

44. Interview, 9/29/03.

45. Ibid.

46. Anonymity requested.

CHAPTER NINE. THE END OF THE STORY

1. For information on the New York University story see Frusciano & Pettit, op. cit.

2. Interview with Taki Papadakis, 9/29/03.

3. Interview with Bob Kirkwood, 10/20/03.

4. Faculty Senate, op. cit.

5. Gibbons, 2002.

References

Argenti, J. (1976). *Corporate collapse*. New York: John Wiley and Sons.

Arnold, D. B. (October 21, 1987). Drexel's identity problem. *Philadelphia Inquirer*.

Astro, R. (1997). *Drexel academic vision—2010. Memorandum to the university community*. Philadelphia: Drexel University.

Auerbach, I. (1985). Comments on long-range plan.

Baer, J. (July 3, 1987). Senate kills Drexel U. money bill. *Philadelphia Daily News*, p. 5.

Bibeault, D. B. (1982). *Management turnaround*. New York: McGraw-Hill.

Blackney, K. (January 9, 1987). Academic review panel submits findings. *The Triangle*.

———. (October 17, 1986). Faculty council and Gaither disagree on long range plan and bylaws. *The Triangle*.

Blagbrough, N. (April 6, 1987). Letter to William S. Gaither.

Blank, R. (October 17, 1986). Faculty meet in Mandell Theater. *The Triangle*.

Bok, D. (2003). *Universities in the marketplace*. Princeton: Princeton University Press.

Breslin, R. (1988). Letter to Robert McClements, chairman, search committee. April 11.

———. (1988). *The president's report. September 21, 1988*. Philadelphia: Drexel University.

———. (1988). *The president's report. October 12, 1988*. Philadelphia: Drexel University.

———. (1988). *The president's report. December 14, 1988*. Philadelphia: Drexel University.

———. (1989). *The president's report. October 3, 1989*. Philadelphia: Drexel University.

———. (1989). *The president's report for the board's quarterly meeting. March 2, 1989*. Philadelphia: Drexel University.

———. (1989). *The president's report for the board's quarterly meeting. May 9, 1989*. Philadelphia: Drexel University.

————. (1989). *State of the university address. September 19, 1989.* Philadelphia: Drexel University.

————. (1990). *The blue ribbon commission on the quality and scope of academic life. Draft report.* Philadelphia: Drexel University.

————. (1990). *Finance committee meeting. January 17, 1990.* Philadelphia: Drexel University.

————. (1990). *Memorandum to the members of the board of trustees.* December 13, 1990.

————. (1990). *Review of December 20, 1989 meeting.* Philadelphia: Drexel University.

————. (1991). *Memorandum to the members of the board of trustees.* March 7, 1991.

————. (1991). *President's report. December 4, 1991.* Philadelphia: Drexel University.

————. (1992). *Building a bridge to our future: Drexel's strategic plan through 1996.* Philadelphia: Drexel University.

————. (1992). *Memorandum regarding the board meeting of December 9, 1992.*

————. (1992). *The president's letter. September 8, 1992.* Philadelphia: Drexel University.

————. (1992). *The president's report. March 11, 1992.* Philadelphia: Drexel University.

————. (1992). *The president's report. May 11, 1992.* Philadelphia: Drexel University.

————. (1993). *Board of trustees report, December 8, 1993.* Philadelphia: Drexel University.

————. (1993). *Memorandum to members of the board of trustees.* September 15, 1993.

————. (1993). *Memorandum to the board of trustees.* March 10, 1993.

————. (1993). *Memorandum to the members of the board of trustees.* May 12, 1993.

————. (1994). *The future of the university. Memorandum to board of trustees.* May 10, 1994.

————. (1994). *Memorandum regarding the November 2, 1994 board meeting.*

————. (1994). *Memorandum to the members of the board of trustees.* March 8, 1994.

————. (2000). Lessons from the presidential trenches. *Chronicle of Higher Education, 47*(11).

Brewer, D. J., Gates, S. M., & Goldman, C. A. (2002). *In pursuit of prestige: Strategy and competition in U.S. higher education.* New Brunswick, NJ: Transaction Publishers.

Brown, D. (1995). Memorandum regarding contingency budgets for 1995–96.

Bruch, L. (May 18, 1995). New Drexel president called 'a doer.' *Philadelphia Inquirer,* p. B1.

Buchman, L. (1986). Letter to the editor, The Triangle. April 25, 1986.

Cage, M. C. (1995). Re-engineering. *The Chronicle of Higher Education, 41*(30), A16, A19–20.

Campisi, G. (October 5, 1987). Ex-U.N. peacekeeper called to Drexel war. *Philadelphia Daily News,* p. 14.

Canavan, T. (1989). *Academic affairs report. October 2, 1989.* Philadelphia: Drexel University.

———. (2006). E-mail to David Paul. March 5, 2006.

Carnegie Foundation for the Advancement of Teaching. (1975). *More than survival: Prospects for higher education in a period of uncertainty.* San Francisco.

Chakraborty, S., & Dixit, S. (1992). Developing a turnaround strategy: A case study approach. *OMEGA International Journal of Management Science, 20*(3), 345–352.

Chernow, R. (1979). John Sawhill: Academe's crisis manager. *Change, 11*(4).

Cohen, M. D., & March, J. G. (1986). *Leadership and ambiguity* (2nd ed.). Boston: Harvard Business School Press.

Collins, H. (March 15, 1988). Applications on the rise at Drexel. *Philadelphia Inquirer,* p. B2.

———. (March 19, 1991). Applications plunge at city's biggest colleges. *Philadelphia Inquirer,* p. B1.

———. (May 7, 1987). At Drexel, more calls for ouster. *Philadelphia Inquirer,* p. B1.

———. (September 28, 1988). A bustling beginning for Drexel chief. *Philadelphia Inquirer,* p. B1.

———. (October 30, 1988). Colleges see rise in rolls despite decline in student pool. *Philadelphia Inquirer,* p. B1.

———. (April 17, 1987). Colleges take offensive to defend higher tuition. *Philadelphia Inquirer,* p. A1.

———. (May 12, 1987). Discord marks Drexel chief's tenure. *Philadelphia Inquirer,* p. A1.

———. (June 18, 1987). Drexel board backs Gaither. *Philadelphia Inquirer,* p. B1.

———. (March 16, 1989). Drexel board creates faculty senate. *Philadelphia Inquirer,* p. B8.

———. (May 14, 1987). Drexel chief is criticized at a forum. *Philadelphia Inquirer,* p. B7.

———. (May 9, 1987). Drexel chief warns deans on call for ouster. *Philadelphia Inquirer,* p. B3.

———. (March 28, 1991). Drexel eliminates 94 jobs to slow growth of tuition. *Philadelphia Inquirer,* p. B3.

———. (December 17, 1987). Drexel sets criteria for search panels. *Philadelphia Inquirer,* p. B5.

———. (June 6, 1991). Drexel U. head plans austerity moves. *Philadelphia Inquirer,* p. B5.

———. (February 7, 1990). Drexel U. to overhaul operations. *Philadelphia Inquirer,* p. B1.

———. (July 4, 1987). Drexel wins budget battle. *Philadelphia Inquirer,* p. B3.

————. (May 6, 1987). Faculty asks Drexel chief to resign. *Philadelphia Inquirer,* p. A1.

————. (June 3, 1987). Faculty: No confidence in Gaither. *Philadelphia Inquirer,* p. A1.

————. (June 30, 1988). Former priest named Drexel University chief. *Philadelphia Inquirer,* p. B1.

————. (July 17, 1987). Frequent opponent of Gaither resigns. *Philadelphia Inquirer,* p. B1.

————. (July 25, 1990). Making its presence svelte Drexel president prepares for leaner future. *Philadelphia Inquirer,* p. B1.

————. (August 13, 1987). Outside committee begins review of Drexel president's leadership. *Philadelphia Inquirer,* p. B6.

————. (February 11, 1992). Private colleges prepare to fight for public aid. *Philadelphia Inquirer,* p. B1.

————. (June 7, 1987). Recent cases ignite protests of sexual harassment on campus. *Philadelphia Inquirer,* p. E1.

————. (August 27, 1990). Student shortage felt by colleges across U.S. *Philadelphia Inquirer,* p. A1.

————. (February 1, 1989). Top colleges seeing a decline in applicants. *Philadelphia Inquirer,* p. B1.

————. (February 17, 1989). Wider faculty role urged at Drexel. *Philadelphia Inquirer,* p. B5.

————, & Woodall, M. (October 18, 1987). Gaither's future hinges on board vote this week. *Philadelphia Inquirer,* p. B1.

Collison, M. N.-K. (1991). Acceptance rate up for this semester at many colleges. *Chronicle of Higher Education, 38*(14).

————. (1991). Applications down at private campuses and up at public colleges. *Chronicle of Higher Education, 37*(25).

Commission on the Academic Presidency. (1996). *Renewing the academic presidency: Stronger leadership for tougher times.* Washington, DC: Association of Governing Boards of Universities and Colleges.

Commission on the Future of Higher Education. (2006). *A test of leadership: Charting the future of U.S. higher education.* Washington, DC: U.S. Department of Education.

Competition in U.S. higher education. New Brunswick: Transaction Publishers.

Coopers & Lybrand. (1993). *Analysis of projected tuition revenue for the current and proposed undergraduate degree programs.* Philadelphia: Drexel University.

Copeland, L. (December 21, 1992). Workers at Drexel approve contract. *Philadelphia Inquirer,* p. B1.

Council, I. Open letter to the Drexel University board of trustees. June 9, 1987.

Coyne, M. (October 30, 1987). Chairman defends board actions. *The Triangle,* p. 1.

————. (February 14, 1986). U. investigating possible faculty cuts. *The Triangle.*

Crown, S. (March 11, 1988). Drexel posts 17% rise in applicants. *The Triangle,* p. 1.

Czerwinski, R. (May 9, 1986). Students protest question session. *The Triangle.*

Daughen, J. (June 12, 1987). Did prexy's sex hints make 3 quit. *Philadelphia Daily News,* p. 3.

———. (September 28, 1987). Drexel faculty raises Gaither-must-go legal fund. *Philadelphia Daily News,* p. 9.

———. (June 5, 1987). Drexel furor: Can prez have the rite idea? *Philadelphia Daily News,* p. 4.

———. (October 21, 1987). Drexel prez drops effort to keep job. *Philadelphia Daily News,* p. 3.

———. (October 6, 1987). Drexel prez foes conspicuous by absence. *Philadelphia Daily News,* p. 3.

———. (May 5, 1989). Ex-priest at helm of Drexel. *Philadelphia Daily News,* p. 15.

Davies, P. (October 27, 1997). Not dragon his feet businesslike Drexel prez making swift changes. *Philadelphia Daily News,* p. 26.

DeWolf, R. (March 11, 1993). Executive compensation 101 pay and perks for college presidents are an increasingly controversial subject. *Philadelphia Daily News,* p. 22.

Drexel Institute. (1896). Service in memory of Anthony J. Drexel founder of the Drexel Institute of Art, Science and Industry. Philadelphia.

Drexel University. Annual financial reports 1987–2002.

———. Board of trustees discussion, educational issues at Drexel University. May 2, 1996.

———. FY2004–2009 Strategic plan. President's cabinet. June 2, 2003.

———. Minutes of the board of trustees meetings 1981–1997.

———. Minutes of the executive committee of the board of trustees 1987–1997.

———. Minutes of the finance committee of the board of trustees 1987–1997.

———. Minutes of the investment committee of the board of trustees 1981–1995.

———. Statement of attendance and admissions data. Monthly. 1981–1997. Report of the president.

———. Statement of the trustees of Drexel University. May 21, 1987.

———. (1970). *Emergence of a university: Recommendations of the Drexel planning commission.* Philadelphia: Drexel University.

———. (1984). *Long-range plan 1985–1995. Report of research consulting team.* Philadelphia.

———. (1985). *Long-range plan 1985–1995.* Philadelphia.

———. (1985). *Official statement. Revenue bonds, first series of 1985.* Philadelphia.

———. (1986). *Long-range plan 1986–1996.* Philadelphia.

———. (1986). *A total admissions plan for Drexel University.* Philadelphia.

———. (1987). *Long-range plan 1987–1997. Draft.* Philadelphia.

———. (1987). *The stewardship of President William S. Gaither for the three-year period September 1, 1984–August 31, 1987.* Philadelphia.

———. (1988). Board of trustees, finance workshop material. June 7, 1988.

———. (1988). *Charge to the presidential search committee.* Philadelphia.

———. (1988). *Official statement. Revenue bonds, first series of 1988.* Philadelphia.

———. (1988). *Presidential search committee and advisory board. Report of January 21, 1988 meeting.* Philadelphia.

———. (1988). Search committee minutes and materials.

———. (1989). Board of trustees. Financial presentation. April 4, 1989.

———. (1989). Board of trustees. Meeting book. December 20, 1989.

———. (1989). Charge to the administration. March 15, 1989. Philadelphia.

———. (1989). Ethics/convocation day agenda. October 17, 1989.

———. (1989). Executive committee resolution. June 21, 1989.

———. (1990). Board of trustees report. Review of strategic plan draft #1. September 26, 1990. Philadelphia.

———. (1990). *Official statement. Revenue bonds, first series of 1990.* Philadelphia.

———. (1990). Presentation of strategic long-range plan. December 19, 1990.

———. (1991). *Drexel 1991 senior-freshman student study.* Philadelphia.

———. (1991). Finance committee meeting agenda and material. April 8, 1991.

———. (1991). *Into the second century: An action plan for Drexel University.* Philadelphia.

———. (1992). Finance committee meeting agenda and material.

———. (1993). *College of Business and Administration. Strategic plan 1994–1997: Managing the future.* Philadelphia.

———. (1993). *Official statement. Revenue bonds, series of 1993.* Philadelphia.

———. (1995). *"Building a bridge to our future" updated. Drexel University's strategic plan.* Philadelphia: Drexel University.

———. (1996). *Official statement. Revenue bonds, series of 1996.* Philadelphia.

———. (1996). *Rating agency presentation.*

———. (1997). *1996–1998 tactical plan (updated February 1997).* Philadelphia.

———. (1999). *Official statement. Revenue bonds, series of 1999.* Philadelphia.

———. (1999). Standard & Poor's presentation, revenue bonds, series of 1999.

———. (2000). *Official statement. Revenue bonds, series of 2000.* Philadelphia.

———. (2001). *Enriching the Drexel difference: Drexel University president's report 1995–2000.* Philadelphia.

———. (2002). Official statement. *Revenue bonds, series A of 2002.*

———. (2002). *A statement on shared governance and faculty senate in academia submitted to the chairman of Drexel's board of trustees by the steering committee of the faculty senate of Drexel University.* Philadelphia.

Ellis, L. (December 20, 1992). Drexel, Teamsters reach tentative pact. *Philadelphia Inquirer,* p. B1.

Evangelauf, J. (1990). Tuition may outpace the rate of inflation for 10th year in row. *Chronicle of Higher Education, 36*(22).

Faculty Council. (1985). *Faculty council critique of the long-range plan.* Philadelphia: Drexel University.

———. (1988). *Report of the chair. December 21, 1988.* Philadelphia: Drexel University.

———. (1988). *Report of the chair. December 21, 1988.*

Faculty Senate. (1992). *Resolution on President Breslin's recommended strategic planning process. June 24, 1992.* Philadelphia: Drexel University.

———. (1992). *Review of the proposed university 1992–93 operating budget. May 11, 1992.* Philadelphia: Drexel University.

———. (2002). *A Statement on shared governance and faculty senate in academia.* Philadelphia: Drexel University.

Faggins, B. (May 12, 1987). Rep. "not surprised" by Drexel scandal. *Philadelphia Tribune.*

Fancher, C. (May 14, 1981). Students flock to cooperative education at Drexel. *Philadelphia Inquirer,* p. B5.

Flander, S. (May 21, 1987). Drexel weighs fate of president. *Philadelphia Daily News,* p. 8.

Frusciano, T. J., & Pettit, M. H. (1997). *New York University and the city.* New Brunswick: Rutgers University Press.

Gaither, W. *Gaither response to points raised by Auerbach letter of August 9, 1985.* September 5, 1985.

———. *Letter to board of trustees.* September 11, 1987.

———. *Letter to David Wilmerding, chairman, finance committee.* February 25, 1986.

———. *Letter to members of interfaith council.* June 12, 1987.

———. *Letter to Robert McClements, chairman, board of trustees.* October 21, 1987.

———. *Major accomplishments and crises averted during the William S. Gaither presidency.* 16 April 2002.

———. *Memorandum regarding enrollment task force.* November 26, 1985.

———. *Memorandum regarding financial management task force.* November 22, 1985.

———. *Memorandum regarding task force on program quality and student retention.* December 11, 1985.

———. *Report of the president to the board of trustees, October 16, 1985.* Philadelphia: Drexel University.

———. *Report of the president: Becoming oriented to the university and plans for the future.* September 19, 1984.

———. *Statement from Drexel University president William S. Gaither.* June 3, 1987.

———. (2002). *Major accomplishments and crises averted during the William S. Gaither presidency.*

Gallot, F. (1989). Finance committee meeting package. December 11, 1989.

———. (1989). *Financial report for the fiscal year ending June 30, 1989.* Philadelphia: Drexel University.

Geraghty, M. (1996). Private colleges in the Northeast see a surge in enroll-
    ment. *Chronicle of Higher Education, 43*(4).

Gerstner Jr., L.V. (2002). *Who says elephants can't dance.* New York: HarperBusiness.

Gibbons, W. (2002). Legend of the boiling frog is just a legend. *Ecoviews.*
    November 18, 2002.

Giraffe, F. (1986). Letter to the editor, *The Triangle.* April 25, 1986.

Glascock, A. (1990). Report by the chair. *Faculty Senate Update, 1*(3).

Goodman, H. (May 4, 1996). Drexel anoints 11th president. *Philadelphia In-
    quirer,* p. B2.

———. (September 22, 1994). Drexel U. president resigning. *Philadelphia In-
    quirer,* p. A1.

———. (October 4, 1995). New Drexel head comes roaring out of the gate.
    Philadelphia Inquirer, p. B2.

———. (November 4, 1994). Trustee will be Drexel's interim chief. *Philadel-
    phia Inquirer,* p. B1.

———. (March 25, 1996). With competition stiff, colleges try hard sell. *Phila-
    delphia Inquirer,* p. A1.

Grace, J. (June 15, 1987). Drexel commences with applause. *Philadelphia Daily
    News,* p. 3.

———, & Konolige, K. (May 22, 1987). Drexel dismisses findings, keeps prez.
    Philadelphia Daily News, p. 5.

Grassmuck, K. (1990). Increases in academic-support staffs prompt growing
    concerns. *Chronicle of Higher Education, 36*(28).

Hamme, G., Dehne, G., & Terranova, P. (1997). An anatomy of an educational
    turnaround, *Symposium for the Marketing of Higher Education.* Boston:
    American Marketing Association.

Hardy, C. (1989). Turnaround strategies in universities. *Planning for Higher
    Education, 16*(1), 9–23.

Hardy, R. (1993). *1994 operating and capital budget and long range financial plan
    memorandum.* Philadelphia: Drexel University.

Harker, M. (1996). Managing company turnarounds: How to develop destiny.
    Marketing Intelligence & Planning, 14(3), 5–10.

Harris, L. (March 12, 2000). On the mend, two schools celebrate. *Philadelphia
    Inquirer,* p. B1.

Harrison, C. (1989). Humanist restores hope to once-troubled Drexel U. with
    a "magic wand"—and successful fundraising. *Chronicle of Higher Educa-
    tion, 36*(7), A3.

Hartnett, E. (August 21, 1987). Powelton responds to the Inquirer. *The Triangle,*
    p. 1.

Heinemann, H. N., Wilson, J. W., Heller, B. R., & Craft, M. (1982). Cooperative
    education in the United States. *Journal of Cooperative Education, 19*(1), 1–14.

Ingersoll, R. (1989) *Memorandum regarding enrollment management.* January 10,
    1989.

Kane Parson & Associates. (1992). Sections of study on admissions and development at Drexel University.

Keller, G. (1983). *Academic strategy.* Baltimore: Johns Hopkins University Press.

——. (1990). *Remarks to Drexel University board of trustees.* May 16, 1990.

Klivington, D. (May 2, 1986). Presidential forum. *The Triangle.*

Konolige, K. (July 3, 1987). In victory, Drexel gets $5.2 million. *Philadelphia Daily News,* p. 3.

Kotzin, M. N. (1983). *A history of Drexel University 1941–1963.* Philadelphia: Drexel University.

LaBorie, E. (August 7, 1987). Inquirer focuses on DU. *The Triangle.*

Landau, B. (1993). Finance committee meeting agenda and material. October 25, 1993.

Lewis, C. (May 16, 1987). Gaither deserves to stay on the job. *Philadelphia Inquirer,* p. A9.

Mangan, K. (1987). President, accused of harrassment, vows to heal campus wounds. *Chronicle of Higher Education, 33*(38), 11.

——. (1999). A university tries to revive an ailing medical school. *Chronicle of Higher Education, 46*(9).

Mathieson, A. C. (1997). *Historical comparison fiscal years 1984 to 1987.* Philadelphia: Drexel University.

Mercer, J. (1992). Pennsylvania private colleges fight governor's plan. *Chronicle of Higher Education, 38*(38).

——. (1992). Philadelphia-area colleges lose millions in state funds as Pennsylvania cuts direct aid to private institutions. *Chronicle of Higher Education, 38*(45).

——. (1995). Claims against "New Era." *Chronicle of Higher Education, 42*(6).

——. (1996). Colleges told to return millions they received from "New Era." *Chronicle of Higher Education, 42*(18).

Mezzacappa, D. (December 7, 1987). At Drexel, the president is receiving. *Philadelphia Inquirer,* p. B1.

Moody's Investors Service. Bond rating reports. 1988–2002.

Morschek, C. (1987). Letter to the editor, *The Triangle.* May 29, 1987.

Myers, H. (October 24, 1987). Drexel has stayed on course. *Philadelphia Inquirer.*

Nicklin, J. L. (1990). Citing high costs, Drexel will close its health center. *Chronicle of Higher Education, 36*(35), A32.

——. (1994). 2 roads to restructuring: Northeastern U. cuts itself down to size. *Chronicle of Higher Education, 41*(9), A39–40.

O'Neill, J. (March 13, 1999). City colleges enjoying boom in applications. *Philadelphia Inquirer,* p. A1.

——. (April 21, 1998). Drexel draws fire on plan for additional housing. *Philadelphia Inquirer,* p. B2.

——. (September 30, 1998). Med school could boost Drexel image\It also could pose risks. *Philadelphia Inquirer,* p. A16.

O'Reilly, D. (June 3, 1993). Out to win Richard Breslin is paid very well to make tough decisions. *Philadelphia Inquirer,* p. G1.

Obituary. (June 19, 2003). Antelo Devereux. *Philadelphia Inquirer*, p. B9.

Obituary. (January 15, 1986). William W. Hagerty, 69. *Philadelphia Inquirer*, p. B7.

Odom, M. (August 31, 1984). Drexel fraternity to reopen, despite warnings. *Philadelphia Inquirer*, p. B1.

Paolantonio, S. A. (December 10, 1992). Drexel plans deep changes to cut losses. *Philadelphia Inquirer*, p. B1.

Papadakis, C. (1995). *Board letter*. December 6, 1995.

————. (1995). *Letter to the board of trustees*. September 13, 1995.

————. (1995). *Letter to the Drexel community*. November 7, 1995.

————. (1995). *Letter to the Drexel University community*. September 13, 1995.

————. (1995). *Memorandum to Drexel University community regarding responsibility center budgeting*.

————. (1996). *Board letter*. February 15, 1996.

————. (1996). Board material for May 2, 1996 board meeting.

————. (1996). *Memo to Drexel University faculty*. January 16, 1996.

————. (1996). *Memo to professional and administrative staff*. January 16, 1996.

————. (2001, December 6, 2001). *Drexel University: A university with a difference*.

Pappas Consulting Group. (1993). *Financial analysis. Drexel strategic plan.* Philadelphia: Drexel University.

Paul, D. (2005). Higher education in competitive markets: Literature on organizational decline and turnaround. *The Journal of General Education. 54*(2), 106–138.

Pennoni, C. (1995). *Interim progress report to the board of trustees*. March 6, 1995.

————. (1995). May 17, 1995 board meeting report.

————. (1995). *Memorandum to Constantine Papadakis regarding ongoing initiatives*.

Pothier, D. (November 18, 1986). College rolls growing despite predictions. *Philadelphia Inquirer*, p. B1.

————. (February 19, 1986). Constraints won't mean faculty layoffs, Drexel official says. *Philadelphia Inquirer*, p. B4.

————. (May 6, 1986). Drexel chief defends 19% tuition increase. *Philadelphia Inquirer*, p. B7.

————. (January 22, 1986). Drexel lays off 24 employees, cites finances. *Philadelphia Inquirer*, p. B4.

————. (February 13, 1986). Drexel may cut faculty by 10%. *Philadelphia Inquirer*, p. B5.

————. (April 27, 1985). Drexel to install a president with undersea vision. *Philadelphia Inquirer*, p. B1.

————. (April 25, 1984). Fraternity investigated by Drexel. *Philadelphia Inquirer*, p. B6.

————. (May 18, 1984). Hagerty retiring after 21 years as Drexel President. *Philadelphia Inquirer*, p. B3.

————. (September 18, 1983). Lower tuition keeps enrollment at community colleges growing. *Philadelphia Inquirer*, p. F3.

————. (May 4, 1982). More area colleges increase their tuitions. *Philadelphia*

Inquirer, p. B1.

Presidential Search Committee. (1988). *Desired presidential qualifications. Draft. February 2, 1988.* Philadelphia: Drexel University.

———. (1988). *Guidelines for checking references. April 18, 1988.* Philadelphia: Drexel University.

———. (1988). *Things to talk about and probe. March 8, 1988.* Philadelphia: Drexel University.

PSCS. (1987). *Report from the presidential search consultation service to the board of trustees.* Philadelphia: Drexel University.

Rottenberg, D. (2001). *The man who made Wall Street: Anthony J. Drexel and the rise of modern finance.* Philadelphia: University of Pennsylvania Press.

Santiago, D.-M. (November 15, 1987). Drexel veteran works to steady the helm. *Philadelphia Inquirer,* p. H22.

Saunders, J. (April 18, 1986). Board votes 19% tuition increase. *The Triangle.*

——— (March 14, 1986). Faculty and Gaiter debate. *The Triangle.*

———. (May 15, 1987). Faculty, staff, students "speak out." *The Triangle.*

Schneider, R. (May 1, 1992). Memorandum. Items of importance for the board of trustees.

———. (1992). Memorandum to members of the finance committee. Ideal instructional budget. January 16, 1992.

Schumpeter, J. A. (1975). *Capitalism, socialism, and democracy.* New York: Harper.

Scism, L. (June 18, 1987). Gaither 10, foes 9 as Drexel president stays on trustee vote. *Philadelphia Daily News,* p. 4.

Seibel, W. (1999). Successful failure. In H. K. Anheier (Ed.), *When things go wrong.* Thousand Oaks: Sage.

Senate Budget, Planning and Development C. (1992). *Report on proposed operating budget 1992–93. April 21, 1992.* Philadelphia: Drexel University.

Seymour, G. (April 25, 1986). Drexel students face a 19% tuition boost. *Philadelphia Daily News,* p. 11.

Standard & Poor's Corp. Bond Rating Reports. 1990–2002.

Standard & Poor's Corp. (1998). *Private colleges and university ratio analysis.* New York.

Stapleton, J. D. (April 11, 1986). $7 million lost to Martin Marietta. *The Triangle.*

Stecklow, S. (September 15, 1997). New Era Foundation founder Bennet is scheduled for sentencing this week. *Wall Street Journal,* p. B10.

Still, H. (1988). Remarks delivered to combined meeting of search committee and advisory panel. January 21, 1988.

Sutton, W., & Odom, M. (September 8, 1984). Drexel fraternity's reopening assailed. *Philadelphia Inquirer,* p. B2.

U.S. Census Bureau. (2000). *Statistical abstract of the United States.* Washington, DC.

Versilli, A. (1993). *Resolution to university faculty.* April 29, 1993.

Walton, M. (August 9, 1987). Inside the Drexel scandal: The rocky rule of Bill Gaither. *Philadelphia Inquirer.*

Wieckowski, T. (1989). *Progress report on enrollment management. September 1989.*

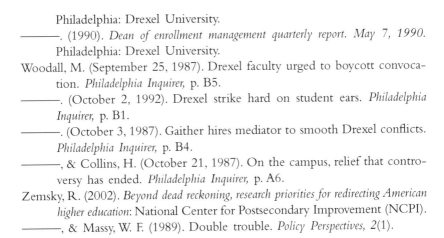

Philadelphia: Drexel University.

———. (1990). *Dean of enrollment management quarterly report. May 7, 1990.* Philadelphia: Drexel University.

Woodall, M. (September 25, 1987). Drexel faculty urged to boycott convocation. *Philadelphia Inquirer,* p. B5.

———. (October 2, 1992). Drexel strike hard on student ears. *Philadelphia Inquirer,* p. B1.

———. (October 3, 1987). Gaither hires mediator to smooth Drexel conflicts. *Philadelphia Inquirer,* p. B4.

———, & Collins, H. (October 21, 1987). On the campus, relief that controversy has ended. *Philadelphia Inquirer,* p. A6.

Zemsky, R. (2002). *Beyond dead reckoning, research priorities for redirecting American higher education*: National Center for Postsecondary Improvement (NCPI).

———, & Massy, W. F. (1989). Double trouble. *Policy Perspectives, 2*(1).

Index

35210504R00139

Made in the USA
Lexington, KY
03 September 2014